Animal Production Systems in Neolithic Central Europe

Margaret Glass

BAR International Series 572

1991

Published in 2019 by
BAR Publishing, Oxford

BAR International Series 572

Animal Production Systems in Neolithic Central Europe

ISBN 9780860547228 paperback
ISBN 9781407348711 e-book

DOI https://doi.org/10.30861/9780860547228

A catalogue record for this book is available from the British Library

This book is available at www.barpublishing.com

BAR Publishing is the trading name of British Archaeological Reports (Oxford) Ltd.
British Archaeological Reports was first incorporated in 1974 to publish the BAR
Series, International and British. In 1992 Hadrian Books Ltd became part of the BAR
group. This volume was originally published by Tempvs Reparatvm in conjunction
with British Archaeological Reports (Oxford) Ltd / Hadrian Books Ltd, the Series
principal publisher, in 1991. This present volume is published by BAR Publishing,
2019.

BAR
PUBLISHING

BAR titles are available from:

BAR Publishing
122 Banbury Rd, Oxford, OX2 7BP, UK
EMAIL   info@barpublishing.com
PHONE   +44 (0)1865 310431
FAX   +44 (0)1865 316916
www.barpublishing.com

Contents

List of Tables v

List of Figures vii

Acknowledgments ix

INTRODUCTION 1

HISTORICAL PERSPECTIVES ON NEOLITHIC ECONOMY 3
    Interpretive Frameworks in European Prehistory 3
    Syntheses of Neolithic Subsistence 5
        The Impact of Radiocarbon Dating 6
        A Current View of the Neolithic 6

RECONSTRUCTIONS OF NEOLITHIC FARMING SYSTEMS 9
    The Early Neolithic Expansion 10
    The Nature of the Late Neolithic Transition 14
        Cultural Classification in the Fourth and Third Millennia BC 14
        Environmental Change in the Fourth and Third Millennia BC 15
    Economic Evidence in the Late Neolithic 15
        Early Fourth Millennium Groups 15
        Late Fourth/Early Third Millennium Groups 19
        The End of the Neolithic in Central Europe 21
    Reconstructing Diet at Neolithic Sites 21
    Evaluating Evidence for Animal Management in the Neolithic 22

PARAMETERS OF ANIMAL PRODUCTION IN NEOLITHIC EUROPE 25
    Systems of Animal Production 26
        Land Use 26
        Labor 26
        The Animals 28
    Increasing Animal Production 31
        Energy 31
        Herd Security 31
        Scheduling of Labor 32
        Specialization 32
        Diversification 32

NEOLITHIC FAUNAL ASSEMBLAGES 35
    Interpreting Economic Strategies From Faunal Remains 36

TAXONOMIC DIVERSITY IN NEOLITHIC FAUNAL ASSEMBLAGES 39
    Measuring Diversity 39
        Richness 40
        Evenness 40
        Heterogeneity 40
    Analysis of Neolithic Faunal Diversity 40
        The Problem of Sample Size 41
        Simulations of Neolithic Faunal Richness and Heterogeneity 41
    The Meaning of Taxonomic Diversity 45
        Sample Size Differences 46
        Sources of Variability in Diversity 46
    Summary 47

TAXONOMIC ABUNDANCE IN NEOLITHIC FAUNAL ASSEMBLAGES 49
    Units Of Analysis 49
        NISP 49
        MNI 50
        Bone Weight 51
    Dominance of Taxa/Evenness 52
    Species Abundance 52
    Variance and Covariance Among Taxa 53
        Early Neolithic 55
        Late Neolithic 56
    Variance and Covariance of Assemblages 58
        Early Neolithic 60
        Late Neolithic 62
    Summary 63

CATTLE EXPLOITATION IN THE LATE NEOLITHIC 65
    Cattle Domestication in Neolithic Europe 65
        Co-occurrence of Aurochs and Cattle 66
        Ratios of Sex and Age of Aurochs 66
        Presence of Transitional Forms 66
        Cattle and Aurochs in Neolithic Sites 68
    Economic Functions of Cattle in the Neolithic 69
        Age Data 69
        Sex Data 69
        Assumptions About Representation of Age and Sex Classes 70
        Cattle and Assemblage Diversity 72
        Comparison with Early Neolithic Data 73
    Cattle Management in Neolithic Central Europe 74

ANIMAL USE AND ECONOMIC CHANGE IN THE NEOLITHIC 75
    Problems in Faunal Interpretation 75
    Early Neolithic Animal Production 75
    Late Neolithic Animal Production 76
        Assemblage Diversity and Taxonomic Dominance in the Late Neolithic 76
        Cattle Management in the Late Neolithic 76
    Comparison of Early and Late Neolithic Production Strategies 76
    Animals and Economic Intensification 77

References Cited 79

Appendix 1 93

List of Tables

Table 1. Major domestic animals in descending rank order according to different types of energy yields. 32

Table 2. List of assemblages used in analyses with cultural affiliation and major bibliographic references.............36

Table 3. Sample size, richness and heterogeneity values for Neolithic faunal assemblages...............................42

Table 4. NISP for nine taxa in Neolithic assemblages. 50

Table 5. Loadings of major taxa on first three components for early Neolithic assemblages. 53

Table 6. Loadings of major taxa on first three components for late Neolithic assemblages...............................54

Table 7. Three-cluster solution for early Neolithic assemblages. 59

Table 8. Four-cluster solution for late Neolithic assemblages. 61

Table 9. Distribution of cluster assignments among late Neolithic archaeological cultures..............................63

Table 10. Numbers of age determinations made on mandibles from late Neolithic assemblages.........................70

Table 11. Numbers of bones identified to sex in late Neolithic assemblages...71

Table 12. Average values of cattle age and sex characteristics in late Neolithic clusters...................................73

Table 13. Cattle abundance, age and sex data for early Neolithic assemblages. 74

List of Figures

Figure 1. Map showing modern political borders and general region of central Europe. 9

Figure 2. Chronological chart of major Neolithic cultures in western central Europe. 10

Figure 3. Estimates of seasonal labor and food requirements associated with domestic animal production. 33

Figure 4. Map of west-central Europe showing distribution of Neolithic sites. 35

Figure 5. Results of richness simulation. 43

Figure 6. Histogram of deviations of richness scores for early Neolithic faunal assemblages. 44

Figure 7. Histogram of deviations of richness scores for late Neolithic faunal assemblages. 44

Figure 8. Results of heterogeneity simulation. 44

Figure 9. Histogram of heterogeneity values for early and late Neolithic faunal assemblages. 45

Figure 10. Histogram of taxonomic evenness. 52

Figure 11. Histogram of cattle frequencies in Neolithic assemblages. 52

Figure 12. Histogram of ovicaprine frequencies in Neolithic assemblages. 52

Figure 13. Histogram of pig frequencies in Neolithic assemblages. 53

Figure 14. Histogram of red deer frequencies in Neolithic assemblages. 53

Figure 15. Plot of percent cattle and percent ovicaprines for early Neolithic assemblages. 54

Figure 16. Plot of percent cattle and heterogeneity for early Neolithic. 55

Figure 17. Representation of major taxa at sites 3, 19, 20 and 5. 55

Figure 18. Plot of percent cattle and percent ovicaprines in late Neolithic assemblages. 56

Figure 19. Plot of percent cattle and heterogeneity for 21 late Neolithic assemblages. 56

Figure 20. Plot of percent red deer and heterogeneity for 14 late Neolithic assemblages. 57

Figure 21. Representation of major taxa in assemblages 29, 38, 40, and 44. 57

Figure 22. Representation of major taxa in assemblages 26, 33, and 35. 57

Figure 23. Triangle graph of percent cattle, percent red deer and percent pig for late Neolithic assemblages. 58

Figure 24. Plot of SSE at different cluster solutions for early and late Neolithic assemblages. 59

Figure 25. Geographical distribution of assemblages in each cluster for the early Neolithic. 60

Figure 26. Geographical distribution of assemblages in each cluster for the late Neolithic. 62

Figure 27. Histogram of percent aurochs in early and late Neolithic assemblages. 66

Figure 28. Comparison of withers heights of Neolithic female cattle and aurochs. 67

Figure 29. Comparison of withers heights for female cattle from nine late Neolithic assemblages. 68

Figure 30. Triangle graph of cattle age categories. 72

Figure 31. Triangle graph of cattle sex categories for late Neolithic assemblages. 72

Figure 32. Plot of percent juvenile cattle and heterogeneity for late Neolithic assemblages. 72

Figure 33. Plot of percent juveniles and percent females for cattle in cluster 1 sites. 73

Acknowledgments

This is a revised version of a doctoral dissertation submitted to the Department of Archaeology, University of Calgary, Calgary, Alberta, Canada. Funding for the original research came from Izaak Walton Killam Memorial scholarships, a University of Calgary Thesis Research Grant, and a Fulbright doctoral fellowship. I would like to thank a number of people at Calgary for contributions to this work at different stages, especially J. Scott Raymond, Jane Kelley, Vladimir Markotic and Valerius Geist. In Germany, my thanks go to H. Müller-Beck, Susanne Münzel and Hans-Peter Uerpmann at the Institut für Urgeschichte, Tübingen. Peter McCartney donated both his time and considerable expertise toward the final production of this volume. Any errors or inconsistencies, however, are solely my responsibility. Revisions of the original work were carried out in Tübingen with the support of a postdoctoral Fulbright research grant.

Chapter 1

INTRODUCTION

Models of social change in Neolithic Europe have frequently been related to changes in the subsistence economy inferred for this period. In particular, a dramatic change in the role of animals has traditionally been associated with the later phases of the Neolithic, related either to changing ecological conditions or the development of new economic strategies. In either case, this hypothesized change in the subsistence economy has been ultimately linked to evolving systems of social differentiation in the Neolithic and later periods of prehistory. However, there are still problems with understanding the kinds of variability in faunal assemblages from Neolithic contexts and comparing these types of data over large areas. This is necessary before changes in subsistence economy can be successfully integrated into models of prehistoric social systems.

A major goal of this book is to investigate the kinds of variability in Neolithic faunal assemblages from a large region within central Europe. The spread of farming economies within central Europe has long been recognized as having two major stages. Initial colonization of the loess covered zones by Bandkeramik groups in the sixth millennium BC was followed by a relatively stable period of localized settlement development lasting a millennium or more. This was followed by an expansion of farming settlements into new environmental zones with different ecological characteristics beginning in the fourth millennium BC. Assemblages associated with both of these stages of Neolithic occupation are analyzed in order to identify points of similarity and difference between patterns of animal exploitation. Although this does not provide a true diachronic perspective, it does allow the discrimination of major patterns in faunal use for both periods, which may then be related to models of social and economic complexity traditionally based on other types of archaeological data.

This book is structured in two main parts. The following three chapters address the basic problems involved in understanding and interpreting variability in Neolithic economy. In Chapter 2, an initial discussion surrounds the relative importance attributed to economic factors under the various interpretive frameworks adopted in European archaeology in recent decades. This is followed by a discussion of major syntheses of Neolithic economy. Chapter 3 provides a more detailed review of the evidence which has contributed to our present knowledge of subsistence economy in the early and late Neolithic. Chapter 4 presents a series of generalizations derived from economic theory which are useful in interpreting the role of animals in subsistence agricultural economies. Parameters which may have been most important in maintaining or increasing production levels in the Neolithic are identified.

The second set of chapters presents analyses of faunal assemblages from early and late Neolithic sites throughout western central Europe. The individual assemblages are introduced in Chapter 5. Chapter 6 addresses the differences in structure between assemblages from these two time periods through an analysis of taxonomic diversity. Patterns of species dominance and covariance among particular taxa are investigated in Chapter 7. Specific hypothesis related to domestic animal production in the late Neolithic are approached in Chapter 8 through the analysis of selected osteometric and demographic observations made on cattle remains. Finally, Chapter 9 reviews the results of the individual analyses, presents characterizations of animal production in the early and late Neolithic, and relates these to some general models of economic change for this period.

1

Chapter 2

HISTORICAL PERSPECTIVES ON NEOLITHIC ECONOMY

Changing perceptions of Neolithic economy must be understood within the context of general theoretical trends in European prehistory. Within the past few generations, there have been major shifts in the importance which has been accorded economic factors both as a subject for study and as a causal force in prehistoric change. Some of these can be attributed to shifting interpretive frameworks, while others relate to more substantive methodological advances, for instance, the development of radiometric dating. General syntheses of Neolithic subsistence economy and current models relating increases in social complexity to economic change have been based within this changing theoretical framework.

Interpretive Frameworks in European Prehistory

Certain themes and individuals in European archaeology have contributed significantly to the development of current ideas about economic change in the Neolithic. The dominant interpretive paradigms of the last century, on the one hand, a concern with identifying the relative roles of diffusion versus migration, on the other hand, an attempt to incorporate evolutionary processes into culture history, were both reflected in the synthesis of European prehistory formulated by Childe. The past few decades have been dominated by a concern with understanding the relationships between environmental and cultural processes, and, in recent years, by an attempt to recognize social hierarchies and ideological systems using archaeological data. Each of these stages of research reflects a set of distinct theoretical orientations that have affected specific questions and interpretations pertaining to the study of Neolithic economy.

The movement of people and the transmission of ideas were considered the dominant forces behind cultural development in Europe throughout the early nineteenth century. Even until the second half of this century, most researchers attempted to derive virtually all major cultural innovations, like farming and metallurgy, from the areas of ancient civilization in the Near East or Mediterranean. Initially, emphasis was put on successive population movements to explain change; later versions put priority on trade, or nebulous processes of cultural influence (Renfrew 1979a:6; Sklenar 1983:128). Toward the late 1800s, diffusionism was developed to an extreme form in both England and Austria, and became an object of study in its own right (Daniel 1971:147). Under the Kulturkreislehre tradition, variability in the subsistence practices of prehistoric cultures was recognized, and at-

tributed to geographic differences augmented by differential diffusion of other traits among adjacent cultures.

The gradual infilling of spatial and temporal gaps in the archaeological record during the late nineteenth and early twentieth centuries has confirmed occupational (though not necessarily cultural) continuity for most areas of continental Europe, eliminating the need to explain discontinuities by large-scale migrations or invasions. In addition, the development of radiocarbon dating undermined the chronological priority of the Near East and eastern Mediterranean, destroying the evidential basis of the diffusionist argument (Renfrew 1979b:105). In recent years, causes of social and economic change have been sought within continental, if not local, contexts. However, the relative importance of population movement versus the transmission of ideas remains a topic of debate for two major episodes associated with the Neolithic: the initial spread of farming economies, and the appearance of widespread cultural networks in the third millennium BC.

Long before the elaboration of the theory of biological evolution, there was a growing awareness among European scholars that economic conditions had passed through a developmental process. The technological model of the Three-Age System is the best known result of this awareness: museum collections were arranged in order of stone, bronze and iron by Thomsen sometime before 1820; his sequence would be validated by the stratigraphic observations of Worsaae a few decades later (Sklenar 1983:88-89). A parallel trend involved the abstraction and ordering of more general stages of subsistence. By 1817, Ziegler had proposed the sequence: food gathering, hunting and fishing; nomadic pastoral life; settled farming (Sklenar 1983:97). Originally based primarily on ethnographic comparisons, this model had slowly developed since the end of the eighteenth century, and was finally integrated into prehistory in the 1830s. The Swedish zoologist Nilsson has been credited as the first to associate specific archaeological data with this scheme, leading to a progressive subsistence model firmly rooted in the past (Daniel 1971:142).

The latter half of the nineteenth century witnessed a flourish of evolutionary syntheses across Europe, as ethnographic and archaeological data were assimilated into universal schemes. Tripartite sequences of economic development (hunting to pastoral life to settled farming) were ubiquitous (Barker 1985; Sklenar 1983). Morgan's elaboration of seven "ethnical periods" took Nilsson's subsistence model one step further by applying ethnographic parallels literally to the archaeological record (Daniel 1971:147). Morgan's stages, combined with Darwin's theory of natural selection, were incorporated into Marx's and Engels's materialist conception of history, in which conflict arising from economic conditions assumed a primary role in the social evolution of mankind. The subsistence economy in particular played a central part in the traditional Marxist scheme; as part of the infrastructural relations of production, it is the ultimate source of the surpluses which lead to the differential accumulation of wealth at the heart of the dialectic process.

Childe has been seen as most responsible for integrating these two approaches characteristic of the early twentieth century. Throughout his career, a belief in the complete derivation of European culture from the east gradually gave way to a "modified diffusionism" (Daniel 1971:148; Renfrew 1979a:8) in which a certain degree of cultural autonomy was granted central Europe from at least the Bronze Age. Childe turned to Marxism because it allowed the development of prehistoric cultures to be explained without relying on unseen external factors (Childe 1958:72). He adopted the idea of economy as the integrating force in society, and correlated points of major economic divisions with changes in the archaeological record. Childe was the first to adopt an economic complex rather than a typological trait as the distinguishing character of the Neolithic (Childe 1958): the tripartite subsistence scheme was simplified into food-gathering versus food-production, and the latter identified with the Neolithic (Childe 1942). Within the era of food-production, Childe further distinguished a series of archaeological cultures with differing economic strategies. This approach presented a stark contrast to the monolithic reconstruction of this period by many other prehistorians (Piggott 1958:76).

It is difficult to generalize about current theoretical approaches to the study of prehistory over so wide a geographical and cultural area as Europe. At first glance, there seem to be no general tendencies to follow and no unified consensus among practitioners of European archaeology about how specific problems in prehistory can or should be investigated. On a concrete level, this results from the practical need of archaeologists to develop regional interests, which, until the last generation, were closely tied to questions of national and ethnic identity. This has led to a strong tradition emphasizing fine-scaled, culture-historical studies. On a more abstract level, theoretical developments in European archaeology are harder to trace, especially from an Americanist perspective, because the way in which this branch of science proceeds is so different from the programmatic statements of the American New Archaeology about how archaeology as a science should proceed. Most European archaeologists tend to argue rather directly from a particular set of empirical data, and explanations often consist of inductive generalizations that best fit that data set (Bogucki 1985). The debate surrounding the use of induction versus de-

duction in generating inferences can now be seen to have arisen largely from a misunderstanding of philosophical concepts among some American archaeologists in the early 1970s. There is no reason not to accept inductive generalizations as valid inferences and, in actual practice, attempts at explanation by American and European archaeologists often do not differ that much. What does differ significantly between the two traditions is the degree of generality considered necessary or appropriate for explanations (ie. how far an inference can be removed from the empirical data upon which it is based) and an overwhelming concern on the part of American archaeologists for building a body of general theory which can be used to understand human behavior in a variety of spatiotemporal contexts.

Recent approaches to the study of prehistory among British and Scandinavian archaeologists closely parallel the trend observed for American archaeology of an increased attention to general theory building (Shennan 1987). This is not to say that theoretical concerns are totally absent from the rest of the continent, but it is difficult to identify any other unified treatment of European archaeological data which goes beyond a specific temporal or geographical focus.

The development of an economic approach to prehistory as initiated by Childe was further stimulated by the writings of J.G.D. Clark beginning in the 1940s and 1950s. Clark's primary interest in technology and subsistence practices was combined with detailed investigation of paleoenvironmental conditions to explain major economic changes in prehistory throughout Europe. This detailed attention to local ecological relationships became the hallmark of the British Academy Major Research Project in Early Agriculture, directed by Higgs, and later Jarman, in the 1970s and early 1980s. In its later stages, the site-catchment program developed by Higgs and his students was characterized by the reconstruction of microregional, often site-specific, subsistence strategies by a standardized methodology (eg. Jarman, Bailey and Jarman 1982). This project made the important contribution of directing attention to the analysis of ecological systems for understanding the development of agriculture in Europe (Shennan 1987).

The British Academy Early Agriculture Project represents only one example of a widespread trend of integration of paleoenvironmental or geographical observations with archaeological data characteristic of many countries. This is evident from a number of regional projects carried out in the 1970s in central Europe which investigated changes in site location throughout the Neolithic, and associated these changes with particular economic strategies. Some of the more important of these include Gallay's (Gallay 1970) and Sielmann's (Sielmann 1971a) work in the Rhine Valley, Linke's study in Westphalia and north Hessen (Linke 1976), and Kruk's investigation of southern Poland (Kruk 1980). This concern with detailed settlement pattern analysis as a tool for investigating prehistoric economy has continued in a number of long-term studies, including the joint British-Hungarian project (Sherratt 1982, 1983a), investigations on the Aldenhovener Platte west of Köln (eg. Boelicke et al. 1977; Boelicke et al. 1980; Kuper et al. 1974), and the Bodensee Project (Landesdenkmalamt Baden-Württemberg 1984, 1985, 1990).

In the 1980s, there was a shift in the goals of archaeological investigations in Europe best characterized as a new optimism about the ability to address questions of social organization and relations (Bogucki 1985:785). The program of social archaeology most often associated with Renfrew can be seen as the source of this new optimism. Attention turned to more social anthropological concerns, such as the analysis of exchange and burial systems to infer aspects of social structure (eg. Kristiansen 1982; Renfrew and Shennan 1982). These studies show less of an emphasis on the subsistence economy, and more on other aspects of the general economy, in particular, trade.

This trend toward interpretations of social organization is accentuated even more in the current post-processualists. This term lumps together a variety of very diverse approaches - structuralism, neo-Marxism, and world systems theory - which are all now being applied to analyses of later European prehistory. Again, emphasis is aimed at the investigation of social relations with, for instance, identification of ideological systems a focal theme (eg. Hodder 1982, 1984; Shanks and Tilley 1982).

There seems to have been a definite shift away from direct investigation of subsistence economy associated with many of these contemporary interpretive frameworks. To be sure, reconstruction of local or regional settlement and subsistence strategies is still a common goal of many (perhaps most) field projects, but at first glance it would appear that such studies have little to contribute to general theoretical concerns. However, characteristics of the subsistence base form an integral, if implicit, part of these frameworks just mentioned. For instance, neo-Marxism, with its emphasis on social production and reproduction (Shennan 1987), would seem to depend rather fundamentally on assumptions about the nature of the subsistence economy and management of the resource base. Although relatively rare, there are some examples showing how elements of the subsistence economy can be examined in the context of the social relations surrounding their exploitation (Ingold 1980 is probably the clearest example). The importance of the transition to food production in terms of a surplus economy and consequent social differentiation has been acknowledged since the time of Childe. Yet many assumptions about the subsistence base in the Neolithic, and changes from early to late Neolithic, remain largely untested. It is the goal of this book to contribute to a better understanding of economic and social change in the Neolithic by addressing some of these assumptions about subsistence practices.

Syntheses of Neolithic Subsistence

Interpretations of Neolithic subsistence have undergone dramatic revision in the past century of research. Major points of change include perceptions about the importance of particular resources and new ideas of the pace of cultural development necessitated by chronological revisions. A short review of major models of Neolithic development helps provide a background for understanding current ideas about subsistence economy in this period.

Following the progressive subsistence schemes described above, early twentieth century reconstructions of the development of agricultural systems in Europe put initial priority on the animal component of the economy (eg. Menghin 1931). Neolithic economy was thought to have been based at first upon the use of forest-adapted stock with some limited grain cultivation in small adjacent clearings, perhaps accomplished through simple hoe cultivation. Relatively open areas in the dense, temperate forests were supposedly chosen for settlement in order to minimize problems of land clearance. Through time, continued forest grazing eventually opened up more areas for cultivation. The Germanic form of agriculture as observed by Romans was suggested as an analogy: heavy reliance upon domestic animals and their products, combined with an extensive form of agriculture characterized by short periods of crop cultivation and long fallow intervals (eg. Firbas 1952:354-355).

The most extensive and influential synthesis of European economic prehistory is that of Childe, first published in the 1920s, and repeated with minor modifications into the late 1950s. As mentioned above, Childe was the first to break down the Neolithic into a series of economic stages, and associate specific cultures, or material culture complexes, with these stages. Three of Childe's economic periods were originally devoted to the Neolithic, and each was characterized by multiple cultural complexes with different economic emphases. Although the period construct was later abandoned, the sequence of changes embedded in this scheme remained the dominant model of Neolithic development for a number of generations. For this reason, it is worth summarizing the major traits of these periods as originally described by Childe.

Period I began with the relatively uniform Linearbandkeramik (LBK) culture, which appeared on the loess lands from Slovakia in the east to Holland and Belgium in the northwest. The type of agriculture practiced by this culture was presumed to be a form of *Hackbau*, or garden cultivation without crop rotation or systematic manuring. The paucity of animal bones from such sites suggested that agricultural crops formed the basis of the diet, and that stock keeping and hunting were of little or no importance. Reliance on this primitive form of agriculture and the lack of any tell-like accumulations of settlement debris implied a short-term occupation of sites, with frequent moves to new areas for cultivation. Later cultural variants in Period I showed slight economic differences, such as a greater emphasis on hunting and new elements in the technological inventory, which were attributed to the assimilation of Mesolithic ethnic elements (Childe 1929:45-51).

Period II was originally described rather simply as an outgrowth from a Danubian 1 substratum, perhaps somewhat more enriched by cultural borrowings from adjacent, non-agricultural groups (Childe 1929:95-96). Over the years, however, Childe's description of this second period changed significantly. By 1946, the end of Period I was identified as a time of increased pressure on the land due to population growth and the eastward spread of western Neolithic tribes practicing a pastoral economy. In Period II itself, a rural economy with more permanent settlements emerged in which crop cultivation was better balanced by cattle-breeding, hunting and fishing. Cattle represented an easily portable form of wealth, and supplied a motive for conflict (Childe 1950:96-98). In his final edition of *The Dawn of European Civilisation*, Childe emphasized even more the divergence of cultures in Period II. The uniformity of the First Danubian peasantry dissolved into a multiplicity of distinct regional cultures, and competition among the descendants of the early farmers, Mesolithic survivors, and new groups from the southeast and west was seen as a major theme (Childe 1957:161).

Interpretations of Period III also shifted somewhat throughout the time of Childe's writing. Originally, it was depicted simply as a departure from the Danubian continuum, with counter-currents set up by complex interactions among Mesolithic, and southern, eastern and western Neolithic groups. Pastoralism and trade increased in economic importance, with industrial specialization emerging in association with early metallurgy. A martial character was inferred for much of the interaction during this period, especially toward the end (Childe 1929:112, 129). In later versions, this basic description was elaborated into the late Neolithic crisis, precipitated by a deterioration of the landscape from combined cultural and climatic factors (Childe 1950:106). Hunting and pastoralism, especially sheep herding, took predominance over agriculture. Natural population growth continued, with the surplus population becoming involved in trade. The bewildering variety of small conflicting groups identified for early Period III were overrun in the end by several warlike and pastoral groups (Childe 1957:162).

The Impact of Radiocarbon Dating

The introduction of radiocarbon dating has been the single most important force behind re-evaluations of cultural and economic change in Neolithic Europe. Traditional chronological schemes had allowed only a little over a millennium for the development of Neolithic cultures throughout Europe. Childe had suggested a date of approximately 2700 BC for the beginning of the Balkan Neolithic, with farming reaching Britain and Scandinavia by about 2400 BC (Burkitt and Childe

1932). Milojcic (1949) had supported a slightly earlier beginning date of 3400 or 3300 BC for the earliest Neolithic cultures both in southeast and central Europe. The end of the Neolithic was put sometime between 2100 and 1600 BC, with the Bronze Age arising out of trade relations between the Minoans and Mycenaeans and their northern neighbors (Childe 1957:163; Renfrew 1979b:99).

For most regions, early radiocarbon dates for the Neolithic were a millennium or more earlier than those of the conventional chronology (Clark 1965), implying a drastically different pace of cultural development than previously accepted. A detailed comparison of the new absolute chronology and the traditional one based on historical relationships (Neustupny 1968) showed that the relative chronologies for most regions remained unchanged, but have been pushed en bloc further back in time. With the most recent calibrations of the radiocarbon curve (Stuiver and Kra 1986), supported by a longer European tree-ring chronology, the total amount of time allotted to the Neolithic has doubled and even tripled in some regions. In central Europe, dates from the earliest Linearbandkeramik sites extend back to the mid-sixth millennium BC. Latest dates for the end of the Neolithic in southern Germany and Switzerland cluster around 2550 to 2450 BC, with the earliest Bronze Age following shortly after, by about 2300 BC (Becker, Krause and Kromer 1989).

A Current View of the Neolithic

The most recent synthesis of Neolithic economy has emerged from attempts to incorporate new observations on archaeological data into a modified evolutionary framework of the development of social complexity in prehistoric Europe (eg. Shennan 1986). The initial spread of agricultural systems across Europe continues to be a major research focus. There is general agreement regarding the origin of the Linearbandkeramik on or around the Great Hungarian plain in the sixth millennium BC, but the relative importance of migration and diffusion in the early Neolithic expansion is still under debate (eg. Renfrew 1987, 1988). The role of assimilation of indigenous Mesolithic groups into a food-producing economy has been increasingly recognized around the margins of central Europe - the best examples are to north (Rowley-Conwy 1984) and east (Dolukhanov 1979; Tringham 1971). Although some period of coexistence of hunter-gatherers with early food producers is generally assumed for central Europe, the archaeological evidence of this co-occupation is virtually nonexistent. Consequently, the nature of interaction between these groups or mechanisms for the adoption of food production have rarely been elaborated (but see Bogucki 1987; Gregg 1988).

Current ideas of early Neolithic farming systems show some contrasts with the model proposed by Childe, which had served as a standard reconstruction for some time. In particular, LBK agriculture is no longer pictured as a predatory, expansive system. Rather, the predominant model is one of intensive land use with a very marked preference for specific environmental zones best suited for a kind of temperate garden horticulture for which there is no modern analog. Based on the limited faunal data available, the animal component is still hypothesized to have played a restricted role. Sherratt has suggested that hunting was of little importance, and that probably only small numbers of domestic stock, primarily cattle, were kept (Sherratt 1981). Some environmental reconstructions may indicate incipient transhumance to ease problems of stock feeding (Bakels 1982).

The later Neolithic remains a relatively poorly understood period for most of central Europe, with the exception of the lake regions of southwestern Germany and Switzerland. A series of widespread changes in settlement pattern in the fourth millennium BC has long been noted for almost all of Europe. Increased settlement nucleation and the more frequent establishment of sites in defensible positions have been related to increased conflict over access to resources, especially land. The entire period has been characterized as one of endemic conflict and localized warfare (eg. Shennan 1986:131), in a manner reminiscent of Childe's Period II described above.

Based on a number of lines of evidence, Sherratt has inferred a major transformation in the nature of European agriculture coincident with the settlement shifts noted for the later Neolithic. His secondary products revolution presents the hypothesis that there was a shift through time in the use of domestic animals from a primary importance for meat to their use for purposes such as traction, transport, milk, and wool production (Sherratt 1981). He attributes these shifts in animal use to the introduction of plow agriculture, the spread of horse and wool sheep and a selective pressure favoring milk-drinking among agricultural populations expanding northwards into temperate Europe. The earliest evidence for the scratch plow north of the Alps dates to the mid-fourth millennium BC, which can be considered an approximate starting point for this series of innovations (Sherratt 1983b:92). These changes in domestic animal use are thought to have contributed to the formation of a radically new agricultural strategy, characterized by the ability to exploit a greater variety of soil types and ecological zones and allowing

the expansion or intensification of farming systems throughout Europe (Sherratt 1981).

Sherratt himself has stated that these widescale changes inferred for domestic animal use have not yet been fully tested (1981:285). The problem in this regard is not so much a lack of faunal data as it is a paucity of analyses which attempt to address these types of changes. There are a number of researchers who have investigated shifts in domestic animal function in Neolithic Europe (Bökönyi 1974; Greenfield 1988; Higham 1966; Sakellaridis 1979, to name only a few). However, many works deal either with very localized geographical areas or with relatively late temporal periods, leaving the question of general change from the early to the late Neolithic largely untouched. This study represents an effort to bridge this analytical gap through the investigation of a large sample of Neolithic faunal remains for evidence which may be directly related to some of the changes inferred above for the animal economy in this period.

In conclusion, it is clear that the social and economic changes inferred for the Neolithic have traditionally been related rather directly to changes in the subsistence base. Childe and his contemporaries traced a transition from shifting plant cultivation to a mixed farming village economy, followed by mobile pastoralism. The current scenario replaces an initial land-intensive horticultural system with an extensive agricultural strategy incorporating new technology with different uses of the animal segment of the economy.

The past few decades have shown a growing recognition that the conditions which have contributed to the uniqueness of the European cultural situation probably arose in the millennia preceding the Bronze Age (Champion, Gamble, Shennan and Whittle 1985:154; Cunliffe 1973 in introduction to reprinted edition of Childe 1957). Recent attempts to explain the emerging social differentiation in the Bronze Age rely rather strongly on inferences about economic changes in the late Neolithic (eg. Shennan 1986). The fourth and third millennia BC have emerged as a crucial period in the evolution of social complexity in the general sequence of European prehistory. Specifically, changes in the animal economy in the late Neolithic have been implicated as an important foundation for subsequent increases in social differentiation (Sherratt 1981, 1983b).

Chapter 3

RECONSTRUCTIONS OF NEOLITHIC FARMING SYSTEMS

This chapter provides a review of cultural groups from western central Europe which yield data that may be used to test ideas about changes in the animal segment of the subsistence economy within the Neolithic. Figure 1 provides a map of modern political borders and outlines the general area of central Europe. Within central Europe, the region included in this study is bordered on the west by the Rhine, extends to mid-Austria and Czechoslovakia in the east, and runs from the Alps northward to the margins of the northern European lowland plain (central Poland and central Germany). The investigation of such a broad geographical area was dictated by the research question I wished to address. An important consistency to be noted in the syntheses of Neolithic economy presented in Chapter 2 is the repeated differentiation between the initial expansion of farming groups across the loess belt

of central Europe and the subsequent spread into new environmental zones a millennium or so later. The current view of the Neolithic advocated by Sherratt explicitly associates this secondary expansion with a series of agricultural innovations, including shifts in the use of domestic animals. The geographical scope of this study was specifically chosen to include a large region of initial Neolithic occupation and a large region first inhabited by farmers beginning in about 4000 BC (the Alpine foreland).

In a corresponding fashion, the chronological scale of this study has been organized to allow the comparison of these two stages of Neolithic expansion. Two periods of roughly equal duration are considered. The early Neolithic in central Europe is represented by sites of the

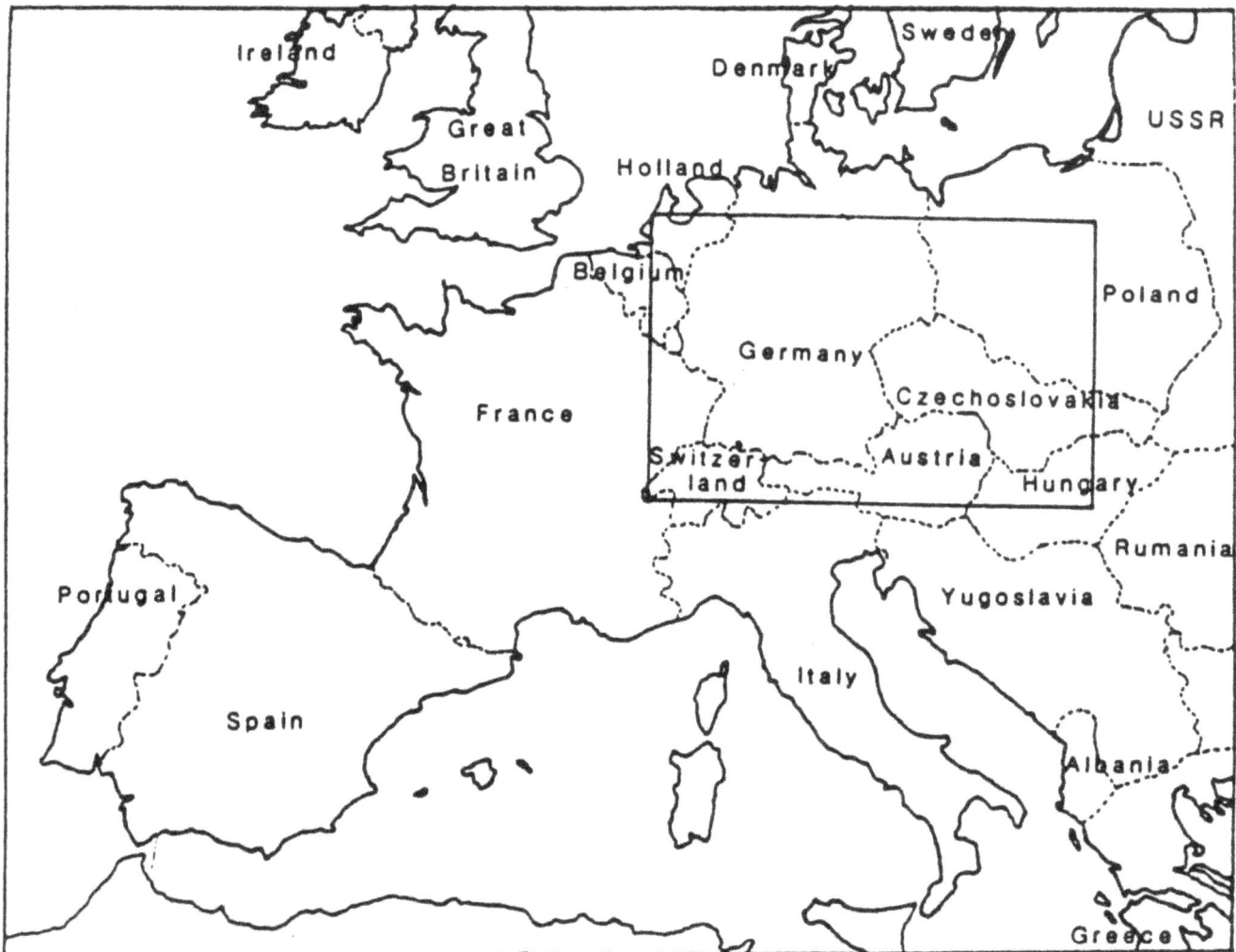

Figure 1. Map showing modern political borders and general region of central Europe.

9

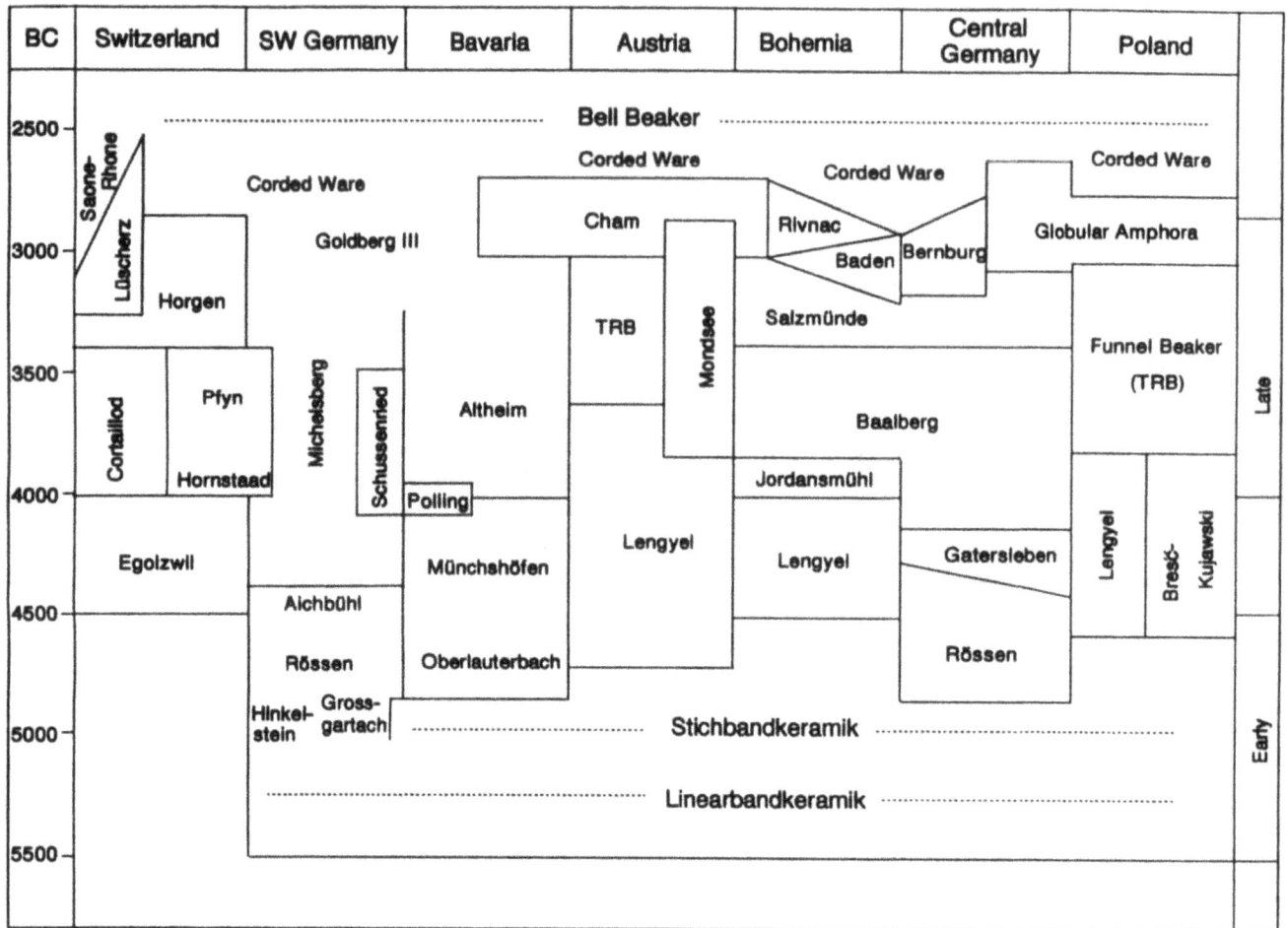

Figure 2. Chronological chart of major Neolithic cultures in western central Europe.

Linearbandkeramik culture, and some localized groups derived from the general Bandkeramik tradition (throughout this discussion, "Linearbandkeramik" refers specifically to the earliest manifestation of farming cultures, "Bandkeramik" is used more generically to include both LBK and somewhat later regional material culture complexes like Stichbandkeramik). Temporally, these sites range from about the mid-sixth to the mid-fifth millennium BC. A second group of sites derives from the various regional cultures which have been identified for the period from the fourth to the early third millennium BC. Within their specific regions, these cultures may be labelled as middle, late, young or end Neolithic, according to the local occupational sequence and terminological conventions. They are here lumped together under the term "late" because of their general association with the wave of Neolithic expansion beginning in the fourth millennium BC. Figure 2 presents a simplified chronological chart of the cultural groups discussed in this chapter. Dates are in calibrated calendar years BC and have been based on a number of sources including Breunig (1987), Raetzel-Fabian (1986) and Whittle (1985). All dates in this book are cited in calibrated years BC. Some discrepancies may exist between the dates used here and those presented in other sources, due to the acceptance or rejection of specific radiocarbon determinations and to the use

of different calibration curves. Despite these inconsistencies, it is still important to attempt to work within a calibrated time frame in order to allow more realistic assessment of the temporal relations, and therefore potential interaction, among the regionally defined groups of Neolithic cultures. The temporal boundaries of "early" and "late" Neolithic used throughout this and other chapters is indicated in the right-hand margin of Figure 2.

Interpretations of the nature of early Neolithic farming have changed dramatically in the past decades. Nevertheless, a uniform adaptation is still posited for this period over much of central Europe. In contrast, a unified perspective on agricultural strategies for the late Neolithic is still lacking, largely because of the variable nature of the evidence upon which reconstructions have been based. Specific characterizations of the animal component of the subsistence economy vary accordingly for each period.

The Early Neolithic Expansion

Much attention has been devoted to trying to understand the nature of the early Neolithic adaptation in Europe, particularly the mechanisms by which food production spread throughout the continent. The distinctive distribution of Linearbandkeramik sites is well known: throughout most of central and western Europe, groups of settlements are situated on loess or similarly fine-grained soils in close proximity to watercourses. The settlements themselves are either villages or homesteads, with the outlines of multiple rectangular structures, often oriented northwest-southeast, interspersed with the remains of numerous pits. The surfaces of these sites are usually heavily eroded, leaving no intact floor assemblages. The characteristic spiral-meander decorated ceramics and polished stone tools are recovered from refuse pits at these sites or associated with burials from the graveyards occasionally located nearby. Organic remains which could yield the most direct evidence of subsistence practices were unevenly recovered until systematic sampling began in recent decades. Evidence for grain cultivation consists of carbonized seeds and impressions or inclusions in ceramics, in addition to tools for the harvesting and preparation of plant foods. Where available, pollen sequences have been used to infer more detailed patterns of land clearance and use. Bone preservation at these sites is often poor, largely because of the decalcification that loessic soils have undergone for the last few millennia. Not surprisingly, interpretations of the nature of the early farming adaptation have traditionally relied more heavily upon the material culture and settlement evidence than the plant and animal remains.

The broad similarities in material culture and settlement structure within the Bandkeramik have often been taken to indicate homogeneity in subsistence strategies across Europe in the early Neolithic. This can be seen in the reconstructions of Neolithic economy reviewed in the last chapter: the idea of an extensive, shifting cultivation system for the early Neolithic has been replaced by the idea of a land-intensive horticultural system focusing on cereal cultivation. Both reconstructions describe a single, although different, subsistence strategy for the early Neolithic rather than attempting to identify the range of variability in plant and animal management which may have characterized different periods or regions.

A system of shifting cultivation, incorporating land clearance by burning and a long-fallow regime, has been variously considered a universal stage of primitive agriculture (eg. Boserup 1965), or a specialized adaptation to areas with low soil fertility, particularly under conditions of abundant available land and relatively low population levels (Grigg 1974:72). If the former is true, then the identification of such a shifting cultivation system in the archaeological record is most pertinent to the question of subsistence economy in the early Neolithic; the latter situation may suggest the presence of a system of shifting cultivation in the late Neolithic, for instance, in association with the expansion of farming to the heavier soils of the Alpine foreland and northern European plain. Given its potential significance to multiple periods in the Neolithic, it is worth tracing the lines of investigation which led to the long-held assumption that Bandkeramik

farming was largely a slash-and-burn system.

The classification of early Neolithic farmers as highly mobile groups practicing shifting cultivation seems to have been based upon three major lines of evidence. In at least the early years, the absence of tells in the temperate zone was enough to imply a very temporary form of settlement in comparison with that identified for the Near East (eg. Childe 1929). Second, the uniformity in material culture and the broad geographic distribution of the Linearbandkeramik suggested a rapidly dispersing population. Finally, ideas about the nature of early agriculture were related to paleoecological reconstructions of postglacial Europe.

The original misidentification of pits as habitation features at the earliest excavated LBK site, Köln-Lindenthal (Buttler 1936), fit the picture of short-term settlements which would be expected with shifting cultivation. Corroborative evidence seemed to come from analysis of the ceramic designs from this site, which yielded a series of discrete groups assumed to represent chronological phases separated by gaps. The eventual recognition of timber longhouses from posthole patterns was taken to indicate some degree of residential stability, but still not on the same scale as the housing compounds and tells known from southeast Europe and the Near East.

Post World War II excavations at Bylany and nearby sites in Bohemia produced multiple lines of evidence interpreted as supporting regular cyclical shifts among series of sites in one local area. Incremental pit linings, the thicknesses of postholes from house outlines and discontinuities in local ceramic design sequences were used to construct a model of repeated occupations of each site in the microarea for 10 to 14 years, separated by periods of abandonment of 30 to 50 years. Decreasing soil fertility after about 10 years of cultivation was considered the major factor limiting occupation (Soudsky 1973; Soudsky and Pavlu 1972).

Paleoenvironmental data were even more important in initial attempts to reconstruct early Neolithic agricultural systems. An association between modern areas of relatively open vegetation and prehistoric farming settlements was noted early (eg. Gradmann 1900). This gave rise to the theory that these regions were not forested in the past, and thus presented easily occupied and cultivable areas. Detailed pollen studies in the early twentieth century forced modification of this view somewhat: reforestation after the last glacial was seen to be relatively complete, with no evidence of open steppe areas as relict habitats (Firbas 1949, 1952). The recognition that the primary Neolithic expansion coincided with the dense, climax forests of the warm and moist Atlantic period required some explanation of prehistoric methods of land clearance.

Evidence for prehistoric land clearance was identified in pollen cores from southern Scandinavia in the 1940s.

Danish cores showed phases of open vegetation containing cereal pollen and charcoal, interpreted as intentional clearing of forest patches by burning (Iversen 1941). Although Iversen originally emphasized that these clearances were aimed primarily at creating grazing areas and were not to be compared with the swidden cultivation of historic Finland (Troels-Smith 1984:14), his observations were soon elaborated into an expansive system of slash-and-burn agriculture to explain the spread of early farming across Europe (eg. Clark 1945, 1952). The model was further supported by both ethnographic analogy with tropical systems (Sangmeister 1951) and evolutionary models of agricultural development (Boserup 1965). The observation that few of the shifting cultivators studied ethnographically keep livestock (Grigg 1974:58) suggested that prehistoric systems were similarly focused on crop cultivation. This generalization seemed to be re-enforced by the relatively small amounts of animal bones recovered from LBK sites, especially in comparison to assemblages from later periods of prehistory.

A model of shifting agriculture in the early Neolithic was originally attractive because it combined an explanation of settlement pattern features with a plausible mechanism for the rapid dispersal of agricultural communities throughout Europe. Dissatisfaction with the model began to arise in the 1960s, after investigations at the Dutch LBK sites of Sittard, Geleen and Elsloo. Elsloo in particular appeared to have been occupied for a long time - a period of about 500 years (Modderman 1975:264). The close proximity of the Dutch settlements to each other seemed to contradict the idea of an extensive, shifting agricultural system (Waterbolk 1962:235).

The ethnographic and historical analogies which were used to support the idea of an initial phase of shifting cultivation across Europe in the early Neolithic were also re-evaluated. Slash-and-burn regimes in historic times were restricted to limited areas of Europe - areas which are even today considered marginal for agriculture. This suggests that a long-fallow system incorporating periodic clearance by fire is more an adaptation to regions with low soil fertility than the remnant of an earlier universal stage of agriculture (Rowley-Conwy 1981). Regarding soil fertility in general, the thick, rich soils associated with most Linearbandkeramik sites are hardly comparable to the thin, easily depleted soils of the tropical areas to which swidden cultivation is best adapted. It has been pointed out that the soils available to early Neolithic farmers were probably richer than soils in those same areas today (Modderman 1971). Long-term continuous cropping experiments on unfertilized fields with modern strains of wheat and barley have not shown the drastic declines in yield which would require a long-fallow regime (Lüning and Meurers-Balke 1980: 307-309).

Radiocarbon dating of palynological sequences has suggested that widescale land clearance did not occur until the later Neolithic. The period of clearance by burning identified in Iversen's original sequence has been radiocarbon dated to 3800-3400 BC, with comparable sequences in central Europe and Switzerland dating to about 2500 BC, associated with the Corded Ware culture (Troels-Smith 1984:18). For the early Neolithic, pollen cores from the Netherlands, Rhineland and Poland indicate that LBK settlements in these areas were not accompanied by widescale deforestation, as would be expected at least periodically from a slash-and-burn system (Bakels 1982; Bogucki 1982). In addition, it is not completely clear to what extent certain pollen diagrams provide unambiguous evidence of agricultural practices rather than merely a reflection of local environmental change. Tauber's analysis of pollen diagrams from Switzerland, for example, suggested that the regeneration sequence there may indicate the lowering of lake levels rather than direct human activity (Tauber 1965).

Finally, other settlement evidence has been used to argue against the idea that swidden cultivation was probably the dominant agricultural system in the early Neolithic. Many of the interpretations made of the Bylany data have been questioned: the incremental layers in pits are not necessarily from annual relinings (Tringham 1971:118), and discontinuities in the ceramic sequence do not necessarily indicate settlement gaps (Bogucki 1982:35). The Aldenhovener Platte project has provided evidence of long-term development of microregional settlement systems. Concentrations of farmsteads or hamlets have been identified which appear to have been maintained and re-built over periods as long as 500 years (Kuper et al. 1974). In general, processes of drift or local population expansion and contraction have been cited as more appropriate than cyclical movement to explain variability in housing patterns and material items of LBK sites (Hamond 1981; Stehli 1989).

The model of an inherently expansive slash-and-burn agricultural system for the early Neolithic has been generally rejected, and a consensus is slowly emerging regarding alternative subsistence strategies which may have characterized this period. Regional settlement pattern studies have probably contributed the most to the construction of a new model. Kruk (1980) and Sielmann (1971a) have provided perhaps the best documentation of the close association of Bandkeramik sites with particular ecological zones. Their work, and that of some of their contemporaries, differs from previous research in the integration of multiple environmental variables, for instance, precipitation and temperature, rather than a simple association of sites with soil types. Kruk in particular emphasized the location of Bandkeramik sites in low-lying zones adjacent to watercourses. He suggested that these zones were the primary loci of both occupation and crop cultivation, which was carried out in small, relatively permanent fields. Nearby valley bottoms and more distant uplands were presumed to be important for domestic stock keeping (Kruk 1980).

Paleobotanical and experimental data both support the idea that Bandkeramik cultivation was carried out in small forest clearances, and that use of these fields was relatively long term (eg. Bakels 1982; Knörzer 1972; Lüning and Meurers-Balke 1980). More detailed processes of crop rotation or seasonal cycles of plant and animal use are difficult to identify. It is unclear whether LBK cereal cultivation followed a spring or winter growth cycle (Willerding 1986). Early models assumed the predominance of winter-sown crops (eg. Jankuhn 1969), presumably on analogy with modern cereal strains grown in northern latitudes. Now, however, a cycle of spring planting and late summer harvesting of cereals is generally accepted, with the suggestion from some weed assemblages that both spring sown and winter sown varieties of cereals were cultivated (Groenman-van Waateringe 1971). Implicit in this inference is the assumption that early cereals had already undergone a shift in their growth cycle from a long (winter) growth period characteristic of their natural state in a dry environment to an accelerated (spring) growth cycle viable in the alluvial zones of a temperate environment. Whether this shift occurred before farming expanded beyond the eastern Mediterranean (Sherratt 1980:317), or represented the main change in LBK farming north of the Carpathians (Butzer 1971:580) is still a point for debate. Nevertheless, the adaptive advantage of such spring sown varieties of cereals in a temperate climate are clear: difficulties of winter cold are avoided, and the spring precipitation can be efficiently used, especially on soils which allowed the drainage of excess water. In addition, it is easier to envision the integration of domestic animals into a summer crop regime. After harvesting, fields become available for limited stubble grazing, providing nearby forage for part of the winter, and allowing the land to be at least minimally weeded, broken up, and fertilized between plantings (Barker 1985:146-147).

Sherratt has suggested that this early system of intensive cultivation could have supported relatively high local population levels, but was ecologically restricted by its simple techniques of hoe cultivation. Its expansion across the continent would have involved a constant fission of small segments of local populations, and their relocation in nearby patches of appropriate habitat (Sherratt 1980:318). The impetus for expansion in this new view is not the predatory nature of shifting cultivation, but still involves the acquisition of new agricultural land under conditions of population growth.

Although this general picture of Bandkeramik farming has gained broad acceptance, the related issues of permanence of settlement and integration of plant and animal resources into the economy remain problematic. In areas such as Bohemia, a cyclical pattern of residential mobility is still posited. This mobility, however, is not based upon the assumption of shifting plot agriculture, but relates to other (as yet unnamed) social or economic factors (Pavlu 1982). Regarding the initial expansion of farming onto the northern European plain, the hypothesis of a transhumant strategy has been presented, with seasonal or even shorter-term occupations of sites (Bogucki 1982). In other areas, arguments have been made for long-term occupation of individual settlements. This is based on the amount of effort invested in the construction of site features at Eilsleben in central Germany and Köln-Lindenthal (Kaufmann 1982). In the Dutch Limburg and Aldenhovener Platte sites, long-term occupation of settlement zones with only minor spatial shifts through time in household location has been inferred (Boelicke et al. 1988; Farrugia et al. 1973; Kuper et al. 1977).

Finally, a new view of resource use in the early Neolithic has emerged from evaluation of recent data from central Europe as a whole. The need to recognize regional and temporal variability in early Neolithic settlement and subsistence patterns, particularly in the non-loess areas, has been stressed by Bogucki (1982:41). In all likelihood, a mixed farming economy depending upon both domesticated plants and animals was present from the start. But the combination of plant and animal resources in temperate Europe represented a very different system compared to the Near Eastern pattern from which it was ultimately derived. Cattle and pigs supplemented sheep and goat in importance from the very earliest stage, though there was undoubtedly a certain degree of variability due to local conditions. This variability could have resulted in economic specialization within certain regions, even during the Bandkeramik occupation. Sielmann has identified two economic facies, one possibly oriented more toward stock keeping, for the later Bandkeramik sequence in the upper Rhine based on environmental parameters of site locations (Sielmann 1971a). Kaufmann has postulated that the presence of enclosed ditch sites in the western and northwestern range of the LBK distribution is related to a greater emphasis on cattle-keeping in these areas (Kaufmann 1982). The possibility of a transhumant component based on cattle for the Bandkeramik of central Poland has already been mentioned.

These interpretations modify the view derived from Childe's synthesis that crop cultivation was dominant in the early Neolithic, and that animals had only a limited role as meat sources. The potential significance of domestic animals in the management of fields has been pointed out by several authors (eg. Barker 1985; Rowley-Conwy 1981). Zooarchaeological analyses from LBK sites have long provided additional evidence of a higher level of animal management than previously thought. The central role of cattle in early Neolithic economy has been repeatedly noted. Overlap in size between domestic and wild taxa has been interpreted as local domestication of indigenous fauna, for example in central Germany (Müller 1964) and at Müddersheim (Stampfli 1965). Castrated cattle have been identified in central Germany (Müller 1964), indicating their use for draft purposes or fattening to enhance meat yield. The possibility of a dairying economy has been suggested for LBK sites in Poland based on both cattle remains and the presence of ceramic sieve fragments (Bogucki 1984).

Fewer detailed interpretations have been made concerning the roles of pigs and ovicaprines in Bandkeramik sites. There does seem to be some patterning in the relative abundance of these taxa through time. It has been suggested that ovicaprines shift from second to third place in order of importance from the early to the later Bandkeramik (LBK to SBK) (Nobis 1984:76). No evidence for the use of either sheep or goat milk or wool products in the early Neolithic has been described. Some local domestication of pigs seems likely, again mostly for the central German area, based on metric observations (Müller 1964). Most of these animals were slaughtered young (Nobis 1984:76).

The above discussion illustrates the considerable changes which have taken place in the interpretations of the economic importance of animals, particularly domesticates, in the early Neolithic. However, with some exceptions (eg. Polish lowlands, Paris basin), it is still common practice to assume that most Linearbandkeramik settlement and subsistence systems reflect a similar strategy of land selection and use. According to current ideas, this strategy was related to a stable, long-term agricultural system in a forested environment, incorporating both domestic plants and animals and, to some degree, their wild relatives. There are indications that this stable pattern may have been preceded in some areas, such as the Polish plain and Bohemia, by a period of exploration characterized by short-term occupations of LBK farmers in a variety of habitats (Bogucki 1979; Rulf 1986). In the late Bandkeramik, there is again increased variability in location of sites. However, there seems to have been the attempt to remain in areas with environmental parameters most closely resembling the primary settlement zones (Sielmann 1971a).

The Nature of the Late Neolithic Transition

Childe's Period III represented a major break in the Neolithic continuum of central Europe. With the application of radiocarbon dates, the timing of this "break" has become attenuated, and is now seen to extend from the early fourth millennium to the middle of the third millennium BC. Beginning at about 4000 BC, significant differences can be observed in the patterning of settlements across central Europe. These differences are of two kinds: 1) the first major occupation of large regions not formerly used by farmers, for instance the Alpine foreland and the northern European plain; 2) ecological infilling, or exploitation of local environmental zones not previously used. This included, for example, settlement expansion to different soil types and different elevations. These changes were coincident with the formation of new regional associations after the disintegration of the relative uniformity of the Bandkeramik tradition. Somewhat later, the third millennium BC witnessed even more

dramatic changes in the character of cultural groupings. With the Corded Ware cultures of central and northern Europe, and the Bell Beaker groups in central and western Europe, there is the reappearance of broad, geographical similarities in material culture. In contrast to the Bandkeramik situation, however, it becomes more difficult to trace general strategies of settlement and subsistence in the latest Neolithic. For large parts of central and western Europe, cultural remains are restricted to burial contexts, with little evidence of settlements per se.

Cultural Classification in the Fourth and Third Millennia BC

A variety of taxonomic schemes have been used to classify the archaeological cultures associated with the geographical expansion of farming economies in the fourth and third millennia BC. Consequently, there is a considerable amount of confusion when terms like "middle Neolithic" or "late Neolithic" are used to compare interregional cultural developments. Some cultural classifications attempt to integrate a particular region into the Neolithic sequence of the continent as a whole, while others were developed only for very local use. For instance, the contemporaneity of Baalberg in central Germany and western Czechoslovakia, with Altheim in southern Germany, Pfyn in southwestern Germany and Cortaillod in northeastern Switzerland is generally acknowledged (eg. Breunig 1987; Driehaus 1960; Ottaway 1986; Suter 1985). However, cultural taxonomies place Baalberg of central Germany in the middle Neolithic (Behrens 1973); Baalberg in Bohemia belongs in the older Aeneolithic (Neustupny 1981). Altheim and Pfyn are classified as belonging to the "Jungneolithikum" or younger Neolithic (eg. Driehaus 1960; Strahm 1987). Cortaillod, representing the earliest farming culture in much of northeastern Switzerland was referred to as "Neolithique ancien" (Vouga 1929), or early Neolithic.

This terminological confusion has resulted largely from the non-synchronous nature of Neolithic development. Additional confusion surrounds the initial introduction of copper metallurgy and its significance. The recognition of a qualitatively different period of copper use in southeastern Europe, especially Hungary, seemed to justify the creation of a Copper Age - the Aeneolithic - as a transition between the Neolithic and Bronze ages. The distribution of copper-using groups further west is somewhat more complex. There is evidence for the coexistence of copper-using and non-copper-using groups, especially in Alpine foreland. In addition, some copper-using groups were followed by groups only rarely possessing metal artifacts (eg. Altheim is succeeded by Cham in Bavaria). The addition of copper metallurgy was not a uniform development throughout central Europe, and the construct of the Aeneolithic is at present not ordinarily applied further west than Bohemia. In any event, the use of copper does not seem to have had a substantial effect on the technological system associated with the subsistence economy (Neustupny 1981).

The temporal framework for the research presented here includes a number of cultural groups associated with the settlement changes of the fourth and early third millennia BC. Collectively, these cultural groups will be referred to as "late Neolithic" in opposition to the early Neolithic, largely Bandkeramik tradition described above (see Figure 2 for identification of early and late groups of cultures). The very latest Neolithic horizon, dominated by the Corded Ware and Bell Beaker groups, is not dealt with directly in this work. The lack of settlement evidence and limited organic remains associated with these groups is a major methodological hindrance to the comparison of faunal data. The aim here is to detail changes hypothesized for the period immediately preceding the latest Neolithic, which is itself identified by dramatic changes in settlement, and presumably in social and economic relations.

Environmental Change in the Fourth and Third Millennia BC

The original definition of a late Neolithic crisis was predicated on the idea that the Atlantic/Subboreal transition identified in pollen sequences was accompanied by a significant degree of climatic change in central Europe. Specifically, this transition is supposed to have heralded the beginning of a warmer, drier period with increased continentality, lasting from about 3800 BC until the beginning of the Subatlantic phase around 800 BC. The concept of a dry Subboreal for most of Europe now appears to be unfounded, rather, climatic change in the fourth and third millennia BC was quite variable in nature according to geographical region (Frenzel 1976). There does seem to have been a decrease in mean summer temperatures for much of central Europe following the thermic maximum of the late Atlantic. This decrease seems to have been relatively minor and, based on the continued presence of pond turtles in Neolithic sites, summer temperatures were probably in the range of 18 to 20 degrees C., slightly warmer than today (Barthel and Cott 1977). In the past decade, it has been assumed that environmental change in the fourth millennium BC was more likely a result of human settlement and agricultural activity than dramatic shifts in climate (Frenzel 1977; Patzelt 1977; Rösch 1987). As a result, early theories which hypothesized a breakdown of agricultural systems in the later Neolithic because of severe alterations in climate have generally been disregarded.

Recent intensive paleoecological investigations of the Alpine foreland have reopened the question of climatic change in the fourth millennium BC. Numerous palynological cores from Switzerland, Austria and southern Germany show shifts in the relative abundances of either beech or fir pollen at about 3600 BC, suggesting regional expansion of these species possibly related to a general shift in climate. On the Bodensee, evidence of economic change around 3700 BC is followed by a decrease in local site density, suggesting the possibility of an ecological crisis during the late Pfyn occupation of this area (Rösch 1990). Corresponding changes in other regional settlement systems have not yet been described, but it seems that the relative effects of climate versus human activity at the old Atlantic/Subboreal transition must again be reevaluated.

Economic Evidence in the Late Neolithic

Unlike the earlier Bandkeramik period, there is no uniformity in the interpretations of subsistence economy made for the fourth and third millennia BC. The picture for west central Europe is particularly confused. For this area, a pattern must be built up by a consideration of the data and interpretations for each culture in turn. There is tremendous variability in terms of the amount of evidence available for analysis: the rich organics at many waterlogged sites in the Alpine foreland are difficult to compare with the poorer remains further to the north and east. It is unclear how much the broad spectrum of resources recovered from these contexts is attributable to better preservation conditions versus different subsistence practices. There is evidence of broad settlement changes here as in the rest of Europe, but no real idea as to what these imply in terms of changes in the subsistence systems. A general trend of ecological infilling of settlement zones has been repeatedly documented for the later Neolithic in western central Europe, as elsewhere (eg. Rulf 1979; Schier 1985; Sielmann 1971a; Starling 1983). An increase in the number of sites located in defensible positions, often surrounded by massive ditch systems, has contributed to the impression of social unrest in this period.

Early Fourth Millennium Groups

In the absence of a unified interpretation for the late Neolithic, the data used to reconstruct subsistence economy, particularly those pertaining to animal management, are reviewed for a range of archaeological cultures in west central Europe. This review is limited to those cultural groups which fall within the late Neolithic as identified in Figure 2, and for which faunal data have been analyzed (see Chapter 5). Groups of the early fourth millennium BC include Cortaillod, Pfyn, Altheim, Mondsee, Baalberg, Michelsberg, Schussenried, and Polling. For the late fourth to early third millennium BC, Horgen, Auvernier, Lüscherz, Cham, Rivnac, and Bernburg are addressed. General spatial and temporal placement of each of these cultures is shown in Figure 2.

Cortaillod

The Cortaillod and Pfyn cultures of Switzerland and southwestern Germany are considered first because of the qualitatively different evidence they contain, and their potential for more detailed interpretations of subsistence economies. Since their discovery in the mid-1800s, evidence from these sites has contributed more toward a knowledge of general Neolithic lifeways than any other group of sites throughout the continent. Although they represent some of the earliest examples of interdisciplinary investigation, the original reports (eg. Keller 1866) are confusing because of the identifications of multiple forms of domesticates and the mixing of temporal and cultural strata. Understanding of these sites was clarified considerably after the centennial symposium of the mid-1950s (Guyan 1955) and with the numerous excavations of the 1970s and 1980s.

Cortaillod is the Swiss expression of the Chassey-Lagozza cultural horizon within the greater Windmill Hill cultural sphere (Winiger 1981:99), and shows a closer affiliation to western rather than eastern material culture complexes. Cortaillod sites are found throughout central and western Switzerland, located almost uniformly on lakeshores. They appear earliest in the west, perhaps by 4200 BC, but classic Cortaillod as identified at Twann on the Bielersee is dated from 3838 to 3768 BC (Suter 1985).

The early model of Cortaillod subsistence economy proposed by Welten (Welten 1955) was one of shifting cultivation incorporating some degree of domestic animal keeping. This cultivation system was very similar to the traditional LBK model described above with two modifications. The wealth of structural evidence at many Cortaillod sites was interpreted as indicating relatively lengthy occupation periods (eg. 100-120 years at Burgäschisee-Süd), and leaf foddering and stalling were suggested as techniques of domestic stock keeping. Still, the contribution of animals to the diet was considered minimal and occasional high percentages of wild animals were attributed more to the elimination of crop robbers than to an emphasis on hunting (Boessneck 1963:202).

Higham presented an interpretation of Cortaillod subsistence economy based on site locational information and analyses of faunal assemblages from seven sites (Higham 1969). He noted a high degree of variability in predominant species among sites, and pointed out that Cortaillod sites contain some of the highest percentages of wild animal bones recovered from Neolithic sites in general. The location of settlements was related to specific characteristics of the lakeshore environment: slightly lower and warmer, more open land, and an abundance of fodder plants.

Higham attributed broadly similar strategies of domestic animal management to all of the Cortaillod sites he analyzed. Cattle mortality data indicated selective slaughtering was practiced to obtain meat from young males, while allowing more females to mature for breeding stock and possible use of milk. Young steers were often killed in late fall to eliminate the need to overwinter large number of stock. Overwintering practices, such as the collection of adequate fodder and indoor stalling of stock, were undoubtedly known but probably undesirable because of their labor-intensive nature. Small numbers of ovicaprines were kept, with a high proportion of goat to

sheep because of their more advantageous browsing adaptation. Ovicaprine age curves suggested primary use of these animals for meat, perhaps some use of milk products of adult females. No evidence of wool industry was indicated. Pigs were apparently killed at one of two ages, either at one year of age or between 18-30 months. Hunting of wild animals helped minimize competition with domesticates for favorable pasture, and was necessary in order to control crop-robbing red deer. A highly mobile settlement system was assumed, and considered viable only as long as land was plentiful and local population levels low (Higham 1966, 1969).

More recent analyses of site duration and economy have also suggested the kind of frequent settlement shifts which may be associated with true shifting cultivation. Egolzwil 5 is estimated to have had an occupation period of only 15 years (Stampfli 1976a:133), and multiple sequential occupations have been differentiated throughout the course of the Cortaillod settlement at Twann (Becker and Johansson 1981:103). The local area around this latter site offers only limited possibilities for farming, leading to at least one suggestion that animal keeping was predominant (eg. Sakellaridis 1981). The variability in animal use in the different settlement phases of Twann and the striking differences in taxonomic composition between Burgäschisee-Süd and Südwest (closely related in both time and space) (Stampfli 1964) contribute to the impression that Cortaillod faunal assemblages reflect relatively short-term, local subsistence decisions. A general pattern has been abstracted from these data, in which cattle are the most important domestic taxon, yielding meat, milk, manure and skins. Sites with high percentages of wild fauna may reflect periodic subsistence stress, and there is a possible increase in the relative importance of ovicaprines through time (Becker and Johansson 1981:103-105).

Pfyn

The Pfyn culture is the earliest farming group in northeastern Switzerland, centered on the Zürichsee and Bodensee. Originally subsumed under the Michelsberg culture, the distinguishing features of Pfyn were noted by both Scollar (1959) and Driehaus (1960). There has been a significant increase in knowledge about Pfyn settlement distribution and density in recent years as a result of the Bodensee Project (Landesdenkmalamt Baden-Württemberg 1984, 1985, 1990). Although at least partially contemporaneous with Cortaillod, the origins of Pfyn have long been associated with Funnel Beaker (TRB) related cultural groups, for instance Altheim and Baalberg (Driehaus and Behrens 1961). Recent excavations on the Bodensee have led to the identification of the Hornstaad group. Beginning about 4000 BC, Hornstaad precedes Pfyn in this area and shows definite material culture ties to the south and east (Dieckmann 1987). The faunal inventory of Hornstaad-Hörnle shows the high use of wild taxa often hypothesized for the initial settlement of a new area (Kokabi 1985, 1987).

The Pfyn culture itself has been dated from about 3850 to 3500 BC (Rösch 1987; Suter 1985). Similar to Cortaillod, the best known settlements are on the shores of large lakes or swamps, with multiple houses oriented toward the water and frequently a fence or palisade to the landward side (Wyss 1970). Pfyn sites exhibit a certain amount of variability regarding the degree of settlement permanence and types of agricultural strategies (Liese-Kleiber 1987). The weed spectrum and ruminant manure layers discovered at Thayngen-Weier have been interpreted as indicating cultivation of permanent fields closely integrated with domestic stock keeping. Animals were kept in the settlements for at least part of the year, fed with collected leaf-fodder, and their manure presumably used for field fertilization (Troels-Smith 1984; Winiger 1971). On the other hand, a number of sites show clear evidence of periodic abandonment and reoccupation although it is unclear whether this is due to some intermittent phenomenon like periodic flooding (Wyss 1970), or a pattern associated with agricultural cycles. Periods between occupations seem to be on the order of 30 to 40 years (Sakellaridis 1979:127). The type of agriculture hypothesized for the Bodensee sites is an extensive one based on periodic shifting of fields, possibly every 20 years, with use of fallow lands for wild plant procurement or domestic stock keeping (Rösch 1987). Animal keeping seems to have been focused on cattle, with small domestic pigs second in importance (Sakellaridis 1981:157). Age distributions of these two taxa from a site near Zürich (Utoquai-Seehofstrasse) confirm year-round occupation, with regular annual killoff of pigs, and the suggestion of a milk economy of cattle (Jacomet and Schibler 1985). The location of sites in areas not immediately adjacent to prime agricultural land has been cited as evidence of primary dependence on stock keeping (Sakellaridis 1979:127). However, an attempt at a dietary reconstruction for one Pfyn site suggests a more equal contribution of plant and animal resources (Jacomet and Schibler 1985). The presence of sites without immediate field areas is more likely an indication of an increase in population in the course of the Pfyn sequence (Schlichterle 1987:40-41).

Altheim

Ceramic typological traits have long suggested that Altheim and Pfyn, along with Baalberg, belong to the same broad cultural horizon (Driehaus and Behrens 1961:245). The distribution of Altheim sites is centered on southern Bavaria, with the southeastern border at the Salzburg basin, the northwestern one at the Nördlingen Ries (Driehaus 1960) and some mixed Pfyn/Altheim assemblages from the Federsee (Köninger 1986). No uniform choice of site locations is recognizable. In lower Bavaria, site location sometimes follows that of previous Neolithic groups: on the edge of loess patches above stream channels. Altheim sites are also located in areas

not formerly colonized by farmers: on a variety of substrate types and elevations (Driehaus 1960:92; Schier 1985). Altheim sites have also been found on low-lying lake or marsh edges, similar to Pfyn sites in southwestern Germany (eg. Ottaway 1983). Compared to Cortaillod and Pfyn, little is known about the details of Altheim settlement organization. There are no known analogs for the complex ditch system identified at the type site and only a few isolated house outlines are known from Altheim, Goldberg, and the Fischergasse site (Aitchison 1989).

It is unclear how much economic variability is to be associated with this variability in choice of settlement location. There are no clear ideas of the length of site occupation or the nature of Altheim farming systems. Driehaus's assumption of an equal importance for plant and animal resources was based mostly on Childe's generalization about the increased use of animal resources in the later Neolithic rather than on comparative botanical and faunal analyses (Driehaus 1960). Although some macrofossils and ceramic impressions indicate the cultivation of crops, there is a general paucity of plant remains from Altheim sites. Recently analyzed paleobotanical samples from the Fischergasse site included both emmer and einkorn, as well as some remains of cereals less commonly found in this time period, such as millet, spelt and barley. Wild fruits and nuts rounded out the spectrum of plants used at this site (Küster 1989). The animal economy was originally summarized by Boessneck: cattle were the most important taxon, followed by pigs and ovicaprines. Age profiles suggested the primary yield of the domesticates was meat, but the use of cattle for milk production or traction was not ruled out (Boessneck 1956). Subsequent analyses have not substantially altered this picture.

Mondsee

The Mondsee culture was first identified over 100 years ago in the great rush to find lake-side dwellings similar to those discovered in Switzerland. It is now known from approximately 20 lake-side sites and hilltop sites, centered on the Mondsee, Attersee and Traunsee in upper Austria. Culturally, Mondsee appears to have developed under the same general Funnel Beaker influences as Altheim and Baalberg. Recent investigations have divided Mondsee into two chronological phases with a total of five typological stages: the Mondsee group of the late Neolithic/Copper Age is followed by a 500-year gap, then the Bronze Age Attersee group (Ruttkay 1981). Although there was originally strong disagreement with radiocarbon dates in the range of 3800 to 3600 BC for the earliest Mondsee group sites (Pittioni 1980:67), additional determinations have strengthened this chronological placement (Offenberger 1981; Ottaway 1986).

Generalizations about Mondsee agricultural practices have so far been based only on the lake-side villages. A pollen core near See has indicated land clearance associated with the occupation of this site, although there is relatively little suitable agricultural land in the immediate vicinity. A variety of clearance techniques have been hypothesized, including burning and field rotation possibly accompanied by frequent settlement shifts. Cultivated crops included cereals (emmer, barley and millet), oil plants (flax and poppy) and vegetables; an assortment of wild fruits, nuts, and herbs were collected (Offenberger 1981).

The animal component of the economy is best known from See, the nearby site of Scharfling having possible sampling problems. See contained a relatively high percentage of wild animals, possibly hunted to minimize competition with domesticates. Among the domesticates, cattle were most important, primarily as a meat source. Some adult females were kept, as well as male castrates. Stock could have been stalled in winter, and allowed to graze in unplanted fields in summer. Ovicaprines were next in importance, and the presence of castrated sheep suggests adult males were kept for wool. The relative unimportance of pigs has been related to the composition of the forests in this area: the lower percentage of beech as noted in the pollen spectrum indicates a less favorable environment for this taxon. Most pigs were killed very young, in their first fall or winter (Wolff 1977).

Baalberg

Baalberg represents an early culture within the main Funnel Beaker tradition of north and east central Europe, now thought to have developed from the cultural fusion of hunter-gatherers and agriculturalists in a broad band along the northern and eastern margins of the early Neolithic groups. Baalberg itself was probably derived from southeastern influences (Behrens 1973; Preuss 1966), and is restricted to central Germany, Bohemia, and southern Poland.

Baalberg settlement pattern shows some continuity of earlier Neolithic site locations on the terraces above water courses. In addition, there is the first appearance of hilltop enclosure sites, which may have served ritual as well as defensive functions (Pleslova-Stikova 1985). In the western half of the Baalberg area, settlements and house remains are rare. Most finds consist of plain earthen or wood-lined graves. These structures link the development of this area with the monumental mortuary tradition of northern and western Europe. Some areas of low site density in central Germany may be related to local population decline resulting from the initial colonization of the northern plain (Starling 1983). Farther east, for example in Poland, there is the inverse pattern of more settlements and fewer graves (Preuss 1966).

Plant remains from Makotrasy in Bohemia in the form of both impressions and carbonized fragments indicate cultivation of the suite of Neolithic crops usual for this area: emmer, einkorn, barley and millet. In addition, the varieties of weed remains recovered show that probably both summer and winter varieties of cereals were grown

(Tempír 1985). Conclusions about Baalberg faunal economy are somewhat contradictory. In general, the composition of faunal assemblages seems to differ from the earlier Bandkeramik tradition in the area. There is a stronger predominance of cattle (80% of the domesticates), followed by ovicaprines and dog (at 10% each) (Preuss 1966). Makotrasy also shows the predominance of domestic stock, especially cattle. However, Clason states that this assemblage shows little difference in the overall patterning of animal exploitation when compared to either earlier or later cultures in this region (Clason 1985:150).

Michelsberg

The Michelsberg culture has long been plagued by difficulties in understanding both regional and temporal variability. The origins of the group remain unclear: the major dispute has revolved around the relative importance of western European influence versus the contact with emerging Funnel Beaker groups, especially in the north (Driehaus and Behrens 1961:237). Lüning created a developmental sequence for Michelsberg (Lüning 1967), but his chronological phases have been criticized for at least partially confounding contemporaneous regional groups (Pape 1978:33). Michelsberg sites are distributed throughout an area from the Netherlands and Rhineland in the west, to eastern extensions in southern Bavaria, Bohemia and central Germany. The definition of Altheim and Pfyn in the 1960s has resulted in the absence of true Michelsberg in Switzerland and the Bodensee area (Winiger 1981:124). The earliest radiocarbon dates are for the late fifth millennium BC in Rhineland, and Michelsberg in general lasts until the latest Neolithic. Munzingen has been recognized as a regional, late Neolithic Michelsberg group with connections to Pfyn and Cortaillod, and similarities to the Danish early Neolithic (Raetzel-Fabian 1986:62).

The preoccupation with time and space parameters has resulted in comparatively little discussion of economic characteristics of Michelsberg sites. For southwestern Germany, Sielmann (Sielmann 1971a, 1971b) has documented a settlement shift from the Bandkeramik occupation of dry loess zones (with optimal conditions for cereal cultivation) to Michelsberg occupation of loess zones with higher precipitation, or non-loess zones with moister soils. The number of settlements in these zones doubled, sometimes tripled by the time of the Michelsberg occupation of the central and southern Rhine. These zones, while considered unfavorable for crop cultivation, could have offered excellent conditions for stock keeping, especially a forest-fodder system of cattle and pig management. He further associates this trend with an increase in the number of pits in excavated settlements which contain animal bones to infer intensification of the economy through a greater emphasis on animals (Sielmann 1971b:67). In the Danube valley near Regensburg, a similar study shows the first settlement of interfluvial zones in Michelsberg times, also implying an increase in the relative importance of animals (Schier 1985).

Hilltop enclosure sites are characteristic of Michelsberg, and have long fueled an argument regarding whether these are defensive or related to stock keeping. Two sites in particular have yielded large faunal assemblages. Munzingen was originally thought to be very late, lasting until the early Bronze Age. The almost completely domestic fauna recovered from this site was used to support a young age, based on the evolutionary assumption that a general trend in prehistoric economy involved a shift from hunting to the exclusive use of domesticates (Schmid 1958). The other site, Hetzenberg, also showed a very high proportion of domestic taxa (Beyer 1970).

Schussenried

Originally restricted to the Federsee basin (Driehaus and Behrens 1961) Schussenried sites are now known from the middle Neckar drainage southward to the Zürichsee. Temporally, Schussenried overlaps classic Pfyn and Pfyn-Altheim (Keefer 1983), and is contemporaneous with late Michelsberg in the Rhine valley (Lüning 1976). It is probably best understood as a local group heavily influenced by the advanced stages of the adjacent Michelsberg and Cortaillod cultures (Pape 1978; Winiger 1971).

Few, if any, recent generalizations have been made about Schussenried settlement and economy. The lake-side village of Ehrenstein is the best known site. Its multiple occupations seem to have been separated by burning episodes, obscuring the question of periodicity of occupation. Less than 50% of the bone fragments recovered were from domestic animals, and a great variety of wild taxa was also found (Scheck 1977). Other Schussenried assemblages have shown the opposite extreme, with few taxa overall, and over 90% domesticates (eg. Hartmann-Frick 1960; Nobis 1977).

Polling

Polling was first identified as a single ceramic assemblage at one site in the upper Danube drainage. It was later elaborated by Lüning into a "group" with a number of findspots showing comparable ceramic assemblages (Lüning 1971:87). Its temporal position has altered somewhat, from initial placement at the end of the Neolithic (Driehaus 1960) to a slightly earlier position in the later Neolithic, contemporaneous with Michelsberg II and early Schussenried, preceding Altheim (Lüning 1976).

The lake-side eponymous Polling site exhibited numerous anomalies in general material culture, especially the stone tool inventory. Agriculture was inferred from the presence of grinding stones, but the typology of these pieces is problematic, and quantities unusual. The structural evidence at the site was also confusing in its lack of daub,

a common construction material at most Neolithic sites (Müller-Karpe 1961). The high proportion of wild animal bone is also unusual, and was originally attributed by Boessneck to the unexploited nature of the local environment (Boessneck 1956). The possibility has also been raised that Polling was a seasonal station. In this case, the few domesticates present would have been kept for consumption during the occupation of the site, or captured from the local forests (Blome 1968:53-56).

Late Fourth/Early Third Millennium Groups

Archaeological groups of the late fourth and early third millennia BC can be divided into two broad cultural horizons. The western one, in Switzerland, includes Horgen, Auvernier and Lüscherz, most closely related to the traditions of eastern France (Winiger 1981). Southern and central Germany, Czechoslovakia and Austria contain a series of cultural groups - including Cham, Bernburg, and Rivnac - with material culture heavily influenced by Baden groups of southeastern central Europe, and with hilltop settlements a typical feature (Zapotocka and Zapotocky 1986:57).

Horgen, Auvernier, Lüscherz

Horgen spans a period from about 3400 to 2900 BC. (Suter 1985), and is known from 80-100 settlements in northern and eastern Switzerland, and southwestern Germany (Sakellaridis 1979). It is closely related to the contemporaneous cultures of eastern France (Winiger 1981:154). Pollen spectra show geographical variation in the plant economies of Horgen sites, and generally indicate greater land clearance than in previous periods (Liese-Kleiber 1987:59). Within Horgen faunal remains, domestic taxa dominate, though there are also frequently high percentages of wild taxa. The importance of pigs is inferred from both the number of bone fragments and the large body size of individuals (Sakellaridis 1981; Winiger 1981). These observations have led to a model of specialized pig keeping for Horgen (Stampfli 1980).

Lüscherz and Auvernier are both classified as western Swiss variants within the larger cultural region of the Saone-Rhone culture (Winiger 1981:166). Lüscherz, roughly contemporaneous to Horgen (Pape 1978:48), has yielded two faunal assemblages for comparison. The number of wild animal remains approaches that of domesticates, within which cattle, then pigs are most important (Winiger 1981). The percentages of wild grasses in pollen samples indicate an increase in settlement activity, possibly the formation of pastures (Liese-Kleiber 1987:59).

Auvernier may or may not be partially contemporaneous with Horgen, and does seem to at least partly overlap with Corded Ware (Pape 1978:50). Of the 30 or so sites scattered throughout the Swiss Jura lakes, (Sakellaridis 1979), the location at Auvernier la Saunerie has the best reported faunal evidence. Domestic animals account for about two-thirds of the assemblage, with pigs followed in abundance by cattle and ovicaprines. Elements of the wild fauna, as well as the spectrum of weedy plant remains, suggest the surrounding region was undergoing rather extensive land clearance (Stampfli 1976b; Winiger 1981).

Cham

The Cham group of Bavaria, Bohemia and Austria dates to the late fourth and early third millennium BC (Ottaway 1986; Ruttkay 1987). Stimulus for its origin has been traced to southeastern Europe, from within the greater cultural realm of Baden. At a more specific regional level, Cham can be derived from western Moravia and probably followed a dispersal route up the Danube into lower Bavaria (Burger 1988). In Bavaria, Cham sites appear throughout the region formerly inhabited by the Altheim group, apparently after an occupational hiatus (Matuschik 1985). A rather complicated pattern of cultural diffusion has been presented to account for the distribution of Cham sites and their similarities with adjacent groups. From a core area in eastern Bavaria, Cham appears to have spread into western Bohemia, where it is partially contemporaneous with both Rivnac and Globular Amphorae ceramic groups. A later, renewed period of movement in the opposite direction has been postulated to account for ceramic traits in the Franconian uplands which seem to be derived from Cham in Bohemia (Pleslova-Stikova 1969). In particular, the Goldberg III group of adjacent portions of Baden-Württemberg and Hessen seems to be a closely related phenomenon (Spenneman 1984). A later Cham expansion also seems to be responsible for a more southern group of sites in the Alpine foreland, extending at least as far into Austria as the Salzburg basin. Late Cham probably overlaps partially with early Corded Ware, at least within Bavaria (Burger 1988).

The locations of many Cham sites do not appear to have been chosen for proximity to those soil types best suited for cereal crop cultivation: most are hilltop sites surrounded by ditches, often located on poor soils (Rulf 1986; Schier 1985). The topographic situation of a settlement, on an elevated point, with some natural protection and often between two converging streams, seems to have been more critical than the actual quality of soil in the immediate vicinity (Burger 1988). Few attempts have been made at possible reconstructions of Cham subsistence practices. Plant remains are rare, and evidence of agriculture is mainly derived from grain impressions in ceramic and daub, and the presence of grinding stones. The limited data available suggest a greater reliance on barley than in the previous Altheim culture. A relatively mobile, pastoral economy focused on sheep or goat keeping has been suggested for late Cham in upper Bavaria, based on the limited faunal remains available at one site (Dobl [Uerpmann 1988]) and on the repeated appearance in numerous Cham sites of large spindle whorls and loom weights, suggesting a weaving industry (Burger 1988).

However, other faunal analyses show a broader range of domestic animals more typical for the later Neolithic. Cattle and pig seem most important among domesticates, though they are accompanied by a relatively high proportion of wild taxa (Busch 1985). The Galgenberg site has yielded a somewhat surprising abundance of horse remains. Preliminary analyses support the identification of these animals as domesticates, and their exploitation seems to have resulted in relative decreases in all other domestic taxa: cattle, ovicaprines, and pig (Glass 1988). The possibility of spatial and temporal differences in Cham subsistence pursuits, as suggested by Burger (1988), remains to be adequately tested.

Rivnac

Rivnac arose in the northwestern part of central Bohemia under the strong influence of Baden cultures from east. Temporally, it belongs in the first half of the third millennium BC, chronologically overlapping both Corded Ware and early Bell Beaker groups in the same region. Topographically, sites have been recorded from hilltops, gentle slopes, flat ground, and caves. It is presumed that the fortifications of many hilltop sites were maintained as protection against the culturally different adjacent groups (Pleslova-Stikova 1968, 1969).

Homolka is the best reported Rivnac site (Ehrich and Pleslova-Stikova 1968). Domestic animals dominate the faunal remains: cattle and pig seem to be first and second, respectively, in importance. Some interbreeding of both these taxa with wild relatives has been suggested based on osteometric observations. Individuals of both taxa were slaughtered by about two years of age. The possibility that cattle were kept for milk, and sheep for wool has been mentioned (Ambros 1968).

Bernburg

Bernburg is a later culture in the TRB tradition in central Germany, dated to about 3200-2700 BC (given as 2550 bc to 2200 bc in Breunig 1987). It is closely related to Walternienburg - the two are now considered associated ceramic styles, which may occur separately or together. Settlement evidence includes fortified sites with post and semi-subterranean structures, and the presence of some collective graves shows a connection with megalithic cultures (Behrens 1973:100-110). Bernburg is at least a partial development from a Baalberg foundation (Preuss 1966), combined with influence from Rivnac. It is also partly contemporaneous with the Globular Amphora culture, better known from further north and east.

Bernburg faunas show a predominance of domesticated animals, especially cattle. Many lived to an adult age, and sex ratios suggest both milking and use for traction. Sheep and goat follow cattle in importance, and the presence of castrates under sheep may indicate exploitation for wool (Barthel 1985; Müller 1978, 1985).

The End of the Neolithic in Central Europe

The transition to the latest Neolithic begins by about 2800 in Switzerland (Suter 1985), southern Germany and Czechoslovakia (Raetzel-Fabian 1986). The Corded Ware groups may have coexisted with some of the groups listed above, for example, Rivnac, Cham, and Bernburg. Slightly later, the appearance of Bell Beakers in a horizon beginning ca. 2500 BC provides a transition to the early Bronze Age.

Corded Ware groups of northern and central Europe share settlement characteristics, or rather, the lack of them - most finds relate to burial contexts. The few settlement areas known exhibit a highly dispersed pattern of sites across the landscape. To archaeologists in the early part of this century, the broad distribution of Corded Ware groups throughout the continent and the lack of settlements seemed to show great mobility, the presence of numerous graves with "battle axes" was taken as evidence of warfare, and the appearance of horse and other animal remains in graves completed the picture of mounted warlike nomadic herders. All this evidence fit in with the results of philological studies, which had reconstructed a nomadic pastoralist economy for Indo-Europeans. Corded Ware seemed to provide the archaeological manifestation of the Indo-European dispersal (Neustupny 1969).

Each of these lines of evidence supporting nomadic pastoral warriors has been refuted, and replaced by the interpretation that Corded Ware groups practiced a mixed agricultural subsistence strategy (Neustupny 1969). The relative lack of settlements is still problematic, particularly as our knowledge of the immediately preceding cultural groups is derived almost exclusively from analyses of settlement debris. The few inferences that have been made concerning Corded Ware agricultural strategies suggest a high degree of continuity with the late Neolithic cultures. At the same time, the grave assemblages seem to show the emergence of a new concern for symboling material wealth and social prestige (Shennan 1986). It is these social changes which are supposedly rooted in the changes in subsistence economy of the preceding millennium.

Reconstructing Diet at Neolithic Sites

A variety of analytical techniques have been used to try to estimate the relative contribution of animal resources to the subsistence economies of particular Neolithic sites. These have been based on a number of different kinds of evidence, and yield somewhat contradictory results on the nature and scale of animal use. The traditional reliance in European archaeology on a general developmental model of prehistoric subsistence has already been mentioned in Chapter 2. It is sufficient to point out in this context that the idea of a unidirectional progression from the use of wild to domestic resources, or from plant to animal products, has been implicit in many investigations of

Neolithic subsistence. The use of settlement pattern data to address the question of subsistence changes from the early to the later Neolithic has been described in this chapter. In summary, there has been a general trend noted from a close association between settlement location and good agricultural areas in the Bandkeramik period to a broader use of geographical regions and environmental zones in the fourth and third millennia BC. This has usually been interpreted as indicating a shift in the resource base, possibly toward a greater dependence on domestic animals. However, localized demographic processes and the emergence of ritual and/or defensive sites have also been implicated in these settlement pattern changes. While the relationship between subsistence practices and site location may be relatively clear in the early Neolithic, there is sufficient evidence to suggest that this relationship is not as straightforward in later periods. A final line of research which has attempted to elucidate the relative importance of particular resource groups involves the reconstruction of paleodiet through the direct analysis of animal and/or plant remains from a small number of sites.

Three brief examples can serve to illustrate the ways in which dietary reconstructions have been used to estimate the scale of animal use in Neolithic subsistence strategies.

The first example is the Cortaillod site of Burgäschisee-Süd, which was almost completely excavated. Boessneck (Boessneck 1963) saw a contradiction in the results of pollen studies, which indicated a heavy use of cereals, and the idea that an abundance of wild taxa in the fauna indicated economic dependence on hunting. He calculated the number of wild animals hunted per year from the MNI figures for each taxon and the estimated period of site occupation (100-120 years). An annual use of two animals per year was estimated for the most abundant taxa (red deer and wild pig), with others exploited at a rate of one animal every three years (aurochs) down to one every 10-12 years (bison and bear). Similar killoff rates were estimated for the domestic animals at the site. All of these summed together suggested a yearly exploitation of a total of only 7.38 animals. Boessneck took this as an indication that the importance of animals to the overall diet must have been relatively minor. He did, however, acknowledge a problem with the killoff rates calculated for some of the domesticates, which contradicted the age profiles as inferred from bone fusion. For example, a killoff rate of one pig every three to four years had been estimated, yet epiphyseal fusion studies showed pigs only rarely lived to an age of two years. This led him to question the continuity of site occupation, but does not seem to have altered the conclusions about the relative unimportance of animals to the subsistence economy of the site. He concluded that wild taxa were probably hunted to minimize crop damage rather than as part of a heavy economic emphasis on animal use in general.

In his analysis of fauna from the Cortaillod site of Egolzwil 5, Stampfli (1976a) pointed out the relationship which exists between length of occupation of a site, the number of inhabitants and their nutritional requirements. If two of these values are known, the third can be calculated. Egolzwil 5 was completely excavated and a 12-year occupation indicated for the site, with a total of 35 inhabitants, 10 of which were hypothesized to be children or juveniles. Stampfli suggested that animals were the main source of dietary protein (there is little evidence for legumes or other significant sources of plant protein), and assumed that an estimate of the protein requirements of the inhabitants would at the same time approximate the degree of exploitation of animal resources. The total amount of protein per day needed to sustain a village of this size was calculated, based on the requirements of individuals in different age categories. The amount of protein delivered by one cattle (or red deer of approximately the same size) was estimated as the percentage of body weight, based on an average individual weight of 250 kg. This suggested that the village needed 26 cattle or red deer per year, or 312 large mammals for a 12-year occupation by 35 people. Comparisons with the faunal data yielded only a small proportion of the quantity of bones which would be expected from the use of over 300 animals, and this was interpreted as reflecting biases in disposal and recovery processes. Particular calculations made at every step of this analysis may be questioned; however, the underlying assumption is that animals were the most important protein source, and animal exploitation, here phrased solely in terms of meat exploitation, represented a substantial portion of the economic pursuits at this site. This is quite a different assumption from that described above for Burgäschisee-Süd.

The final example comes from an analysis of the Pfyn occupation at the Utoquai-Seehofstrasse locale on lake Zürich, also more or less completely excavated. An estimated length of occupation (20 years) and number of inhabitants (25-30) were derived from the excavation. The plant-animal ratio in the diet was investigated through reconstructing first, protein needs of the inhabitants and amounts supplied as identified through plant and animal remains, then similar reconstructions of more general caloric needs of the same population. The amount of meat needed for the village per year was calculated on the basis of these requirements, the population, and duration of site occupation. The actual percent contribution of each taxon was taken from the faunal data at the site. Both methods suggested a comparable dependence on plants and animals for nutrition, with possibly a slight predominance of plants. The average number of animals hunted or butchered each year was estimated as 11 domestic animals (six cattle, two ovicaprines, four pigs) and three large wild mammals (two red deer and one wild boar). The authors point out that this conclusion contradicts previous statements of economy in the area, which

had been based solely on site catchment data (Jacomet and Schibler 1985).

These three examples demonstrate the drastically different impressions that exist regarding the scale and intensity of animal use, even within one rather narrow temporal and spatial context of the Neolithic. Faunal data can and have been manipulated to support the idea that 1) animal resources were of minor importance; 2) animal resources were of major importance; and 3) animal resources were of equal importance relative to plant resources in the subsistence economies of particular sites. One possibility is that these reconstructions illustrate the real range of variability in animal use characteristic of the fourth millennium BC in the Swiss area. Alternatively, they may merely reflect shifting assumptions about the importance of animals in Neolithic economy over the past 20 years.

Evaluating Evidence for Animal Management in the Neolithic

A number of observations can be made regarding the evidence for subsistence economies of the Neolithic groups reviewed above. The first concerns the uneven nature of the data, especially for the later period. Based on the literature used for the above review, it is difficult to derive a picture of the complete subsistence economy for any one time and place. It is particularly difficult to generalize about the relationship between plant and animal resources to gain an overall understanding of land use. The preservation of organics, especially plant remains, deteriorates rapidly with distance from the Alpine foreland, exaggerating any economic differences and masking any similarities which may exist between these groups and adjacent, contemporaneous ones. There is considerably more variability both in the types of sites which exist in the later Neolithic, and in their distribution across the landscape. Decisions regarding site placement cannot be assumed to have been primarily related to aspects of the subsistence economy, as is the case with the Bandkeramik. For example, intergroup conflict and local population pressure seem be factors important in the selection of specific sites described for Rivnac of Bohemia and Pfyn on the Bodensee. Given these biases which exist in the data base, the comparison of faunal assemblages from later Neolithic contexts may be expected to offer a better understanding of the animal component of the economy than site locational studies.

A second observation which must be made about the kind of data available from the later Neolithic concerns the spatial and temporal relations of the groups involved. The absolute chronology of later Neolithic cultures is still under construction - some of the groups listed above have only been radiocarbon dated in the past few years. A complete overview of chronological relations remains difficult because of the problems involved in reporting absolute dates: there are inconsistencies among the various labs in use, and few attempts at calibration outside the Swiss area. In addition, many sites have been excavated more than once, and their contents analyzed by multiple authors. Socioeconomic conclusions are always made in the context of the spatial-cultural framework available to analysts at the time. It follows that any changes in ideas about cultural relations in the Neolithic may require re-evaluation of the original conclusions. Interpretations are similarly guided by the theoretical framework in which analyses have been carried out. Many inferences about animal use appear based on a priori notions actually derived from traditional views of Neolithic agricultural development rather than specific analyses of data. These include, for instance, simplistic statements about the relative importance of wild animals in the economy.

A third and final observation about economic interpretations for the later Neolithic relates to the cultural classifications of groups in this period. The above review of settlement and subsistence evidence was organized according to archaeological cultures, largely in order to facilitate presentation. These entities have been defined along criteria typical for the culture construct which has long served as the major organizational tool of European prehistory. The main discriminating criteria between all of these groups are usually aspects of ceramic typology. It has been pointed out that the relationship between groups constructed this way and real ethnic or cultural entities is unknown (eg. Driehaus and Behrens 1961). It follows that there is no reason to assume that economic systems are completely isomorphic with these archaeological entities. The differential scale or magnitude of later Neolithic cultural entities provides an additional source of confusion. Groups vary in scale from Michelsberg, a somewhat diffuse culture which covers a relatively large geographical area and a long time span, to Polling, which is an extremely localized phenomenon in both time and space. This observation alone should suggest the futility of searching for a Michelsberg or Polling subsistence economy. This is not to say that subsistence economy, and animal management, should not be expected to vary in culturally meaningful and patterned ways, only that archaeological cultures may not be the best indication of these groups.

Finally, some comparisons may be drawn between the interpretations made for animal management in the early Neolithic and observations made for the later Neolithic groups. There appears to be a progression through time away from an animal economy in which cattle is always the most important taxon, to an increased emphasis on other taxa. Some of these emphases on particular taxa may be culturally specific as, for instance, in the case of pig keeping at Horgen sites. Other examples of taxonomic dominance are site specific in nature, such as the appearance of horse at the Galgenberg Cham site.

Regarding specific management techniques, there is evidence since the earliest Neolithic for the use of selective breeding strategies (castration), and the use of milk from cattle. By the later Neolithic, there is evidence for additional methods of domestic stock management: some indoor stalling, and suggestions from age curves and sex ratios that small ovicaprine use is oriented toward specific body products. There is possibly less emphasis on domestication of indigenous cattle and pigs in the later Neolithic. This implies greater separation of wild and domestic populations, either by physical restraint of the domesticates, or elimination of the local wild relative.

The presence of sites in the later Neolithic with high percentages of wild taxa is still puzzling. This apparent increase in the use of wild animals has been explained in two ways, based on slightly differing assumptions about the implications of long-term human settlement for local animal populations. One assumption in many of the analyses reviewed above is that the presence of human agriculturalists led to a decrease in local wild animal density through the course of the Neolithic. Based on this assumption, the high percentages of wild animals at some sites have been related to the lack of former Neolithic occupation in the area - the fauna is in a denser, more "natural" state. On the other hand, cleared agricultural plots create new habitats attractive to a variety of wild fauna, in particular deer. One consequence of human settlement, then, could have been an increase in the relative abundances of certain taxa, perhaps requiring more intensive hunting as a crop protection measure. Full assessment of these somewhat contradictory assumptions depends upon a more detailed knowledge of local settlement sequences than is presently available for most of the areas discussed above.

In conclusion, qualitative differences in subsistence economy between the early and late Neolithic are indicated by both settlement and faunal data. However, it is not clear to what extent a model of major shifts through time in the economic emphases associated with domestic animal keeping is supported by these observations. This requires the reanalysis of presently available faunal data with specific predictions in mind regarding the correlates and implications of agricultural intensification. Differences in the intensity of animal management can best be examined by the study of faunal data from a wide range of later Neolithic sites, and comparison with the more patterned early Neolithic remains. One prerequisite for such a comparison is a better understanding of animal production as an integral part of an agricultural system, as well as a knowledge of the kinds of parameters which affect the maintenance or intensification of specific production strategies.

Chapter 4

PARAMETERS OF ANIMAL PRODUCTION IN NEOLITHIC EUROPE

This chapter will construct a set of expectations regarding the general parameters and scale of animal management in Neolithic Europe. An initial discussion concerns the general economic characteristics of subsistence agriculture. The following section relates these general traits to the more specific context of animal production with particular attention to identifying types of land use and labor requirements which may be expected, as well as the most important biological and behavioral attributes of major animal taxa. Finally, ways in which animal production may be increased are considered.

Agricultural systems can be classified according to a number of parameters, including land use, resource manipulation, labor input and total productivity. A general process of intensification is often subjectively identified on the basis of relative increases in the amount of effort or energy directed toward any or all of these parameters. Ethnographic data from around the world suggest that there is a substantial amount of variability possible even within small-scale agricultural systems. It is useful at this point to review some basic observations about subsistence agricultural production that have emerged from ethnographic studies and relate some of the terms and concepts to the more specific realm of animal production.

Subsistence agriculturalists are generally dependent almost entirely on the produce of their own fields or gardens. The primary unit of organization is the household, which experiences its own demographic cycle of growth and decline (Chayanov 1966). Studies in peasant economics have pointed out that the individual household, by virtue of its fluctuations in population and wealth, is often badly matched with the labor demands of a farming economy (Fleming 1985). As a result, a secondary level of organization commonly develops, comprising a series of cooperative relationships between spatially proximate groups of households. Although this leads to some collective use of land and resources, the household usually remains the basic reference unit for discussing decision-making in agricultural production (Barlett 1980).

It is reasonable to expect that subsistence agriculturalists are capable of producing a surplus of food in normal years, at least enough to ensure their food supply in an occasional season of poor yield. However, as has been pointed out for many traditional African systems, small-scale cultivators are often not interested in productivity much above the level needed to ensure security against periodic shortage, or in producing very large surpluses which cannot be stored (Allan 1965). At first glance, this seems to contradict one of the basic tenets of economic theory that, given adequate information, humans will seek to maximize their gains by obtaining the highest possible return for any given resource or else will seek to economize (minimize) using the smallest quantity of a resource to obtain a given return. The problem, however, is one of identifying the kind of gains, or levels of return, acceptable for a whole spectrum of resources within specific cultural contexts. Much economic decision-making seems to be oriented toward a multiplicity of goals, rather than a single-return strategy (Chibnik 1980).

Levels of agricultural production are tied to aspects of the local environment, technology, social organization of the groups involved, and demographic processes, both at the household and regional levels. These factors interrelate in a complex causal nexus, with the proximate point of systemic change often difficult, if not impossible to isolate. Ignoring these causal links for the moment, specific aspects of changes in production can be discussed.

Agricultural production can be increased in two ways: by increasing the amount of land under management, or by increasing the yield per unit land. Both options are associated with increasing costs. For instance, one consequence of increasing the geographical extent of an agricultural system was noted early by economic geographers: the expense of managing additional land increases as a function of the distance of that new land from the center of production (Chisolm 1979; von Thünen 1910). Without substantial changes in at least transportation efficiency, capability for geographical expansion of agricultural systems is very limited. This option becomes even more unrealistic under conditions of environmental heterogeneity and a limited labor force. In comparison, higher yield per unit land can be achieved either by direct increases in the amount of human labor, or by improvements in or modifications of technology. Modern peasant situations show that recourse is most often to increased labor input (Barlett 1980). This suggests that technological change is often expensive in itself, involving either the acquisition of capital equipment, or the reorganization of work forces.

Finally, there is some information to suggest that, even under conditions of increasing production, the minimization of labor may be an important consideration. Among subsistence agriculturalists, the yield per unit land is often less important than yield per unit labor (Clark and Haswell 1967:35-36). Given the above discussion, we might expect that if an increase in production is required, geographical expansion would be the optimal solution until transport costs outweigh those involved in adding labor to raise the yield per unit land. Of course an additional requisite behind such an assumed option is the availability of land.

These are the basic characteristics generally accepted for subsistence-level agricultural production. There is considerable disagreement among economists and anthropologists about how to model the actual decision-making processes that create change or stability within a particular economic system. An assumption of complete economic rationality, which posits that primitive farmers work to get the maximum return for minimum effort, appears difficult to support. In contrast, risk minimization, entailing strategies which ensure survival of the population at environmental low points, may be a more appropriate concept for understanding decision-making in subsistence agriculture (Netting 1974:39).

Systems of Animal Production

For purposes of discussion, animal production can be considered as a subsystem within the larger context of subsistence agriculture practices. In reality, animal management in a mixed agricultural economy cannot be easily separated from crop cultivation: the two are mutually dependent. Nevertheless, it is heuristically useful to consider them separately in order to better understand the options and constraints inherent in the use of each resource class. Most of the general tenets of subsistence agriculture already stated above also apply more specifically to the management of domestic animal resources. However, it is not always obvious how concepts like production costs and goals and risk minimization pertain to animal production without a review of the basic features involved. The three major components of any system of animal use include: land, labor, and the animals themselves.

Land Use

Variability in land use associated with animal management is best phrased in terms of an extensive-intensive continuum. Following modern animal production literature, "extensive" refers to free-ranging behavior, "intensive" refers to conditions of higher animal density created by maintenance in enclosures (eg. Arnold and Dudzinski 1978). Extensive animal husbandry describes the practice of allowing animals to forage for themselves over an area of land. In the most extreme sense, this implies no control over movements of stock, rather, animals determine their own range and density based on specific patterns of social and feeding behavior. This extreme should really be considered a hypothetical one - even hunter-gatherers influence the distribution and density of their prey species through manipulation of the environment, and more complex methods of animal control are at the very heart of the domestication relationship.

Minimally, two kinds of interactions may be expected in early systems of animal management: protection of domestic stock from predators and increased access to food (either indirectly, through the creation of suitable forage areas, or directly, by supplementary feeding of gathered or cultivated fodder). Both of these tasks may be more easily accomplished through a more intensive use of land, that is, by keeping larger numbers of animals on smaller areas of land. This often involves the use of some sort of enclosures, which may range in complexity from brush or deadfall fences to structures like stalls and barns. Obviously, the more intensive use of land for domestic animals may limit the use of this space for other taxa. Even forest grazing severely impacts the local wild mammal population by increasing competition for forage, usually to the disadvantage of the wild species (Sukachev and Dylis 1968:351). Grazing of domesticates can, in short order, lead to rapid changes in the natural environment which may be undesirable in economies at least partially dependent upon wild animal resources.

Strategies of extensive and intensive land use can clearly be combined, as was first recorded for Roman animal husbandry (Baranski 1971), and in the infield-outfield system characteristic of much of late medieval Europe. With domestic animals, this often occurs on a seasonal basis, enclosing animals in periods of natural food shortages or at times when they are particularly vulnerable to predation (eg. birth season). The observation that land use is closely related to systems of land tenure (Boserup 1965; Netting 1974), suggests that the limits of intensification are often defined by cultural as well as purely economic factors. The specifics of land use can also vary widely according to the characteristics of particular taxa, aspects of the local environment, and the amount of time and effort invested by the human group involved.

Labor

The type of labor input required by animals is best characterized as of low intensity, but continuous. In this sense, domestic animals are rather inflexible in that there is always a certain minimum amount of effort which must be devoted to their maintenance and care (Behnke 1980). Two basic types of control may be expected in any system of animal management: manipulation of feeding and breeding. Control over these two classes of behavior can be discussed in terms of major points at which human labor is needed in traditional animal management tasks.

Feeding

Movements of stock still need to be controlled to some degree even when feeding takes place under free-ranging conditions. Spatial considerations might include proximity of grazing areas to ultimate use area of animals or animal products. In the case of lactating females, for example, it is often desirable to graze them as close as possible to a milking facility in order to minimize costs of transporting milk. Additionally, it is probably undesirable to separate females from their young for long periods early in life. Similar considerations might be important in the season of birth, especially to minimize loss of neonates from predation.

Control over stock movement during grazing may be very loose, resembling herd following or observation rather than formal control. Accompaniment of herds may be necessary on a daily, seasonal or permanent basis, depending on the scale of movement needed to ensure adequate grazing requirements and the presence of carnivores or human predators. These types of animal management are particularly amenable to cooperative effort: one individual may be able to direct movements of a large number of domestic stock. In addition, it can often be arranged that this individual is in an age or sex grade which may have little other productive value.

Movements of animals may also be directed in concert with techniques of field management. This may require restriction of animals to specific areas of land to control shrubbery, loosen earth, and distribute manure. Greater supervision of movement may be necessary for other reasons as well, for instance, to keep animals from damaging crops and/or houses in intensive cultivation or contiguous homestead situations (eg. Fel and Hofer 1969; Rappaport 1968).

Other types of labor associated with animal feeding surround periods of environmental stress. Movement of stock and the collection and storage of fodder can be viewed as alternative strategies to food shortage (Behnke 1980). In this context, it becomes obvious that land-intensive animal keeping techniques often require an intensification of labor. If fodder is collected, the collection and storage of substantial amounts of forage must take place during the active growth period of plants, while they have some nutritional value (Perry 1984). Fodder may also be taken from cultivated plants, either in the form of field stubble for grazing or crops specifically grown as fodder plants. In this case, the number of animals that can be kept becomes directly dependent upon the amount of cultivated land. This can be contrasted to free-ranging conditions, in which herds are limited by the minimum level of nutrition provided by winter pasturage (Eadie 1969:17).

Feeding in seasons of stress is undoubtedly the most substantial cost associated with domestic stock keeping. This is evident in the continuing debate about the necessity of autumn stock killoff, a pattern best known from the Middle Ages and often assumed characteristic of earlier periods (Slicher van Bath 1963:297). Methods of overwintering stock, in terms of the skill and technology required, are really very simple. The actual ability to collect and store fodder may have been more influenced by labor requirements (Higham 1969), which possibly interfered with cultivation tasks such as weeding and harvesting (in the case of spring-sown crops) or field preparation and sowing (in the case of autumn-sown crops). In winter, the feeding and care of stalled animals may represent the most substantial form of economic labor, as cultivation remains more or less at a standstill. The provisioning of even small numbers of stock combined with minimal stall maintenance may require several hours of labor a day (Fel and Hofer 1969; Netting 1981).

Breeding

Control of breeding of stock animals is associated with considerably fewer labor-intensive tasks. The breeding of most domestic animals is simply controlled by manipulation of the sex ratio of the herd: males are usually killed off in juvenile or subadult stages, leaving only a few breeding individuals and their replacements (Hafez 1968). Elimination of males also frequently lessens both intra- and interspecific agonistic behavior, thereby easing problems of management in general. If domestic breeding is controlled at all, either for purposes of trait selection or timing of birth season, additional tasks surround the separate herding or housing of males and females for most of the year.

Although negligible labor is often associated with the breeding of most domesticates, particular difficulties may be encountered with animals that have wild relatives in the area. In the context of Neolithic Europe, the wild relatives of both pig and cattle were present in the local environments of most sites, and are commonly identified in faunal assemblages. It is often possible to distinguish between wild and domestic individuals of the same species on the basis of size and other morphological criteria. This may indicate that these animals were under more strict control than other taxa, such as sheep and goat, which had no wild counterparts in the surrounding forests. Some greater degree of attention was probably given to pig and cattle breeding in order to prevent complete feralization of domestic stock.

Control over domestic stock is often increased in the season of birth, when added shelter and protection may serve to offset infant mortality. There is also the suggestion that some physical contact and socialization between humans and animals is crucial to maintenance of the domestic relationship. This is easily accomplished through increased handling at birth (Albright 1969). The post-birth season is associated with substantial increased labor input if milking is practiced: separation or early weaning with supplemental feeding may be required for infants, and milking itself must be done frequently for the duration of the lactation period.

Finally, the control of wild animals may entail a considerable amount of effort. Obvious concerns include the prevention of stock loss due to carnivore predation, and the loss of cultivated crops by wild ungulate feeding. In addition, the hunt may provide important food and other animal products. Not much is known about hunting in the Neolithic, although surrounds and stalking have both been suggested (Blome 1968). Collective techniques are particularly effective in order to selectively cull certain taxa, for instance deer. Stalking of individual ungulates could represent a winter occupation, when it may be advantageous to gain meat in periods during which domestic stock are under food stress. Fur animals, in particular carnivores, may also be more easily hunted in the winter or breeding season, when their location is restricted and easier to predict (Edlin 1960).

The Animals

Finally, the needs and productive capabilities associated with each species of domestic animal must be taken into account in the functioning of any subsistence system. Certain characteristics of domestic animals can be summarized with respect to features important to their exploitation. These include: general feeding and reproductive behavior, approximate body size as a correlate of meat yield, milk yield, reproductive capacity as an indicator of the potential for herd growth, and the contribution of other kinds of energy to the human system, for example, additional body products or power. The emphasis here is on the taxa important in Neolithic Europe.

Aurochs/Cattle

The biological and behavioral characteristics of the aurochs (*Bos primigenius* Boj.) are poorly known since the last individual was killed in Poland in 1627. Some inferences can be drawn from general bovine trait complexes and a few historical references. Aurochs populations underwent a strong decline with the widescale deforestation of the early Middle Ages. There is no good estimate of prehistoric population densities for this animal. *Bison bonasus*, a more selective grazer than *Bos*, is kept at stocking rates of two individuals per 100 ha in modern forests, or approximately .2 per square km (Grzimek 1972:393). This may give a minimum figure for aurochs. Their preferred habitat is thought to have been lightly forested areas, valleys and water meadows - basically areas where open patches were adjacent to scattered trees, offering a variety of forage. In spring and summer, aurochs probably fed on grasses and tree foliage, on acorns in autumn, and on dried leaves from forests in winter. They are thought to have lived in small herds of one bull with several cows and their young. Skeletal remains of aurochs show great sexual dimorphism, with males up to 25% heavier and larger than females. Adult body weight has been estimated at 800-1000 kg. Mating occurred during the rut in August or September, with young born in May or June after a nine-month gestation period. Longevity of most wild cattle is approximately 20-25 years (Grzimek 1972:369-370).

In some ways, it is just as difficult to describe early forms of domestic cattle (*Bos taurus*) as it is to describe the extinct wild *primigenius* form. Modern breeds highly selected for meat or milk production are poor analogs, and even today's "unimproved" varieties have undergone millennia of adaptation usually to arid or tropical environments, which bear little resemblance to environmental

conditions in the temperate forests of Neolithic Europe. Disagreement exists about basics like body size: liveweights of small varieties of modern cattle average about 700 kg (Clason 1973; Grzimek 1972), reconstructed weights of archaeological specimens from the Neolithic generally average between 200 and 300 kg (Barthel 1985; Jacomet and Schibler 1985; Müller 1985; Stampfli 1976a). Some diminution and lessening of sexual dimorphism is a recognized consequence of domestication (Herre and Röhrs 1973), still, these differences in estimated bodyweights for *Bos primigenius* and Neolithic *Bos taurus* seem excessive.

It might be assumed that food requirements of Neolithic cattle were roughly similar to those described above for aurochs. When discussing domestic stock, however, it may be more meaningful to phrase these food requirements in terms of estimated stocking rates per unit area, or quantities of fodder per unit time in order to more easily visualize the management requirements with respect to land and labor. Despite a long history of forest grazing in Europe, there are remarkably few estimates of this kind. In oak forests of the Ukraine, uncontrolled grazing results in average densities of .8 ha per head (Sukachev and Dylis 1968:350) or approximately 13 animals per square km. Bogucki (1982) estimates land requirements on the order of 4 sq. km.\50 head for an eight-month grazing period for Bandkeramik sites in the Polish lowlands, based on Adams's (1975) stocking estimates for forests of 1 ha\head\month. Finally, Fleming (1972:182) suggests that herds of 20-30 cattle per square km probably represent a maximum capacity for most forest pastures.

There is even less information on the quantities of leaf fodder required for overwintering of cattle. It is generally assumed that domestic stock would have needed stored food resources for a period of four to six months for survival during the winter, although, given the apparent success of aurochs in the same environment, this assumption may be unwarranted. Sjöbeck's estimate of 1000 sheaves of 1 kg each for a 150 kg cattle to survive a Swedish winter is most often cited (eg. Clark 1952). Fleming gives additional estimates: roughly 1 square km is needed to supply enough fodder for 50 head in Belgium, while the same land may provide for only 22 head in the coniferous forests of Finland (Fleming 1972:182). Together with the grazing estimates above, we might expect that 30 cattle could be supported year-round on approximately 2 to 4 square km in a mixed forest environment. Thirty head may also represent a minimum viable size for reproductive maintenance of a herd composed primarily of females and young (Bogucki 1982:109). In addition to food, cattle also require substantial amounts of water. Daily consumption in temperate climates can range from a minimum of 16 kg to as much as 30-83 kg (Hafez, Schein and Ewbank 1969:252).

The reproductive behavior of early domestic cattle may

also have resembled that of its wild relatives. It is unclear whether or not the breeding cycle was seasonally restricted. If so, the schedule presented above for aurochs may be appropriate, with birth occurring in May or June. Even if breeding were possible at other times of the year, it is likely that a pattern of autumn mating with spring births was encouraged, as was the case in Roman times (Baranski 1971).

Additional data on fertility and fecundity have been reported for a number of African groups practicing mixed subsistence agriculture and cattle pastoralism. They may be considered generally representative of other bovines as well. First parturition occurs anywhere from age two to five years, depending on food conditions and the health of stock (Dahl and Hjort 1976:33). Calving rates, that is, the percentage of cows giving birth in one year out of the total number of cows in a herd, can be as low as 40% among sedentary groups, but more often range from 50% to 80% for pastoralists. Significant calf losses often take place in the first year of life, with mortality as high as 40% in sedentary herds. Most cows can bear young once a year and remain fertile until 10 years of age, yielding potentially six to eight calves in a lifetime (Dahl and Hjort 1976:35-38).

Lactation in African cattle generally lasts from seven to nine months. Not all cows produce milk in excess of the needs of their own calves. Among the Karimojong, only 48% of cows yielded approximately 1.5 kg per day for human consumption (Dyson-Hudson and Dyson-Hudson 1970). It must be stressed that it is very tenuous to extrapolate directly from the milk productivity of modern African breeds to prehistoric European domesticates. Lactation is directly related to amount of water intake, which is almost always limited under conditions of African husbandry. Still, these figures may be useful in a relative sense when discussing milk yields of different domestic taxa.

Two final possibilities should be mentioned in the context of cattle exploitation. Cattle are often important as providers of traction, and not necessarily only in the context of plow agriculture. Finally, their contribution in terms of dung useful in fertilization is anything but negligible: one animal can provide up to 10,000 kg of manure in a year (Slicher van Bath 1963:293).

Wild Boars/Pigs

Modern wild pig (*Sus scrofa ferus*) body sizes vary along a cline of increasing size from western to eastern Europe. Weights of up to 250-350 kg have been recorded for adult males in the Polish Carpathians, with a corresponding value of 100 kg in the Rhineland. Weight differences between males and females may be on the order of 20% (Oloff 1951:51). Reasonable estimates for liveweights of wild swine in the Neolithic range from 80 to 100 kg (Clason 1973; Jacomet and Schibler 1985). As omnivores, swine consume a variety of nuts, ferns, roots, tu-

bers, grubs, insects, and even carrion and refuse. Wild pigs remain in a loose home range, although this range varies with the season. Social groups often consist of several females with their most recent litter and the young of one previous season, usually at least six to 10 animals. Males remain solitary for most of the year. Both males and mothers with young can be extremely aggressive in the wild (Grzimek 1972).

The autumn mast of acorn and beechnuts is the most important time in the food cycle of pigs, allowing them to build up energy for reproduction, and fat for maintenance through the winter. The rut occurs between November and January; in very good years there may be two ruts, one in autumn (October-November) and a second one in March and April. After a gestation period of about four months, sows deliver an average litter of five to six piglets. Infant mortality is very high under natural conditions due primarily to harsh weather and predators. Frequently only two young per female survive their first year. Breeding is possible at an early age, often within the first year. In favorable years, up to 50% of females younger than one year reproduce, 10% in an average year. No data are available on the length of the breeding life of an individual, but the average lifespan of wild pigs is 15 years (Grzimek 1972).

The capacity for growth in pig herds is very high. Annual increases of up to 100% have been recorded for an average year in post-war Germany, though this high figure is, in part, due to an absence of natural predators, decreased hunting pressure and a series of good years (Oloff 1951:60). Information on population densities can be taken from records of the late seventeenth century in Saxony, where forests carried .3 swine per 1000 ha or approximately .03 animals per square km. In contrast, modern stocking rates of four to 12 animals per 1000 ha or .4 to 1.2 pigs per square km, proved unmanageably high in post-war Germany, and resulted in widescale field damage (Oloff 1951:77-79).

Early domestic pigs (*Sus scrofa domesticus*) are derived from *Sus scrofa*, probably interbred easily with local wild populations (Teichert 1969), and shared many traits with their wild relatives. The body size of domestic pigs is highly variable depending mainly upon the nutritional status of the animal. The absolute size of early forms was probably smaller than that of wild conspecifics due to restricted feeding under management conditions: 50 kg seems a reasonable estimate (Jacomet and Schibler 1985; Müller 1985).

One point which should be highlighted with regard to the management of pigs is the relative ease with which they can be fed and controlled. Pannage systems of the late medieval and early historic periods, in which pigs foraged freely in the forests then were collected after the mast season, are a good example of the loose kind of management which is possible (Grigson 1982). Even when left to forage freely, the proximity of pigs to human settlements is comparatively easy to encourage and maintain (Rappaport 1968). Pigs can be herded to some extent and are often moved on a daily basis to control feeding, but they are generally not amenable to the scale of movements typical of and often necessary for ruminant ungulates.

Domestic pigs are characterized by high reproductive capacity similar to the wild taxon. Herd size is likely even easier to increase under minimal control. For instance, much infant mortality which is due to exposure and predation can be avoided by the provision of shelter. Data on optimal spacing of domestic animals are rare in general, but there is some evidence to suggest that pigs suffer under very intensive conditions (Arnold and Dudzinski 1978:168). Stocking pigs at very high densities can also have a severe impact on agricultural fields and settlements. With adequate control, however, these animals can certainly be kept at higher densities than their wild counterparts.

Sheep and Goats

Neither sheep (*Ovis aries*) nor goats (*Capra hircus*) are represented by wild progenitors within temperate Europe. As such, these taxa are the only true animal imports to the region. Ease of adaptation of these animals to a temperate forest environment is unknown, although it is unlikely to have been too difficult. Physiological adjustment is easier with a move from warm to colder climates than vice versa (Hafez 1968:10). It is, however, impossible to replenish stock from the natural environment in case of a disaster, suggesting that herd maintenance may have been a more central concern with small ovicaprines than for other domesticates.

Detailed information on body product yields and management considerations is only available for ovicaprines under extensive husbandry conditions in the Middle East and Africa. Liveweight estimates for unimproved breeds of sheep average 40 kg for ewes and 68 kg for rams (Redding 1981:143). *Ovis ammon musimon*, the moulfon, smallest subspecies of modern unmanaged sheep, averages 35 kg for females, and 50 kg for males (Grzimek 1972:496) and may be more similar to prehistoric breeds. Liveweights of modern goats are 35 kg for females, 65 kg for males (Redding 1981:148). Estimates for the wild ancestral form *Capra aegagrus* range from 25 to 40 kg (Grzimek 1972:486). Body weight estimates ranging from 25 to 40 kg are used for both sheep and goat in the interpretation of archaeological remains in Europe (Clason 1973; Jacomet and Schibler 1985; Müller 1985).

Sheep prefer grass and succulent herbage, but will eat leaves in forest situations. They are more selective than goats, which preferentially browse leaves and twigs. Ovicaprines in general are very destructive in forested environments; sheep prevent regeneration of seedlings through close cropping of ground foliage, goats eat away new foliage, preventing seed generation.

Wild and feral ovicaprines naturally show segregation of the sexes for most of the year. Males form bachelor flocks or remain solitary, joining groups of females and young during the rut. In extensive herding situations, males are often allowed to range with females since breeding is very seasonally restricted even in modern domestic breeds (Behnke 1980:29). In the wild, the rut occurs in late autumn (October or November) and birth takes place in March or April after a five-month gestation period (Grzimek 1972:490; Gwynne and Boyd 1969:310). It is possible for both sheep and goats to bear young in their first year. Multiple births are rare for sheep, while goats may twin or even bear triplets.

Sheep lactate three to four months, and produce an average of 45 kg of milk per lactation (essentially per year). The period of lactation for goats is somewhat longer, it may be as long as seven months, with an average yield closer to 77 kg. Goats also produce a daily milk yield up to .05 kg more than sheep (Redding 1981:169). It should be mentioned that these values represent the total yield from which young must be nourished, leaving any excess for human consumption. There are no good data on the amount of surplus milk available for human consumption. Overall, goats produce greater quantities of milk than sheep. Sheep produce lower volumes of milk, but this milk has a higher percentage of butterfat, which may be more crucial in terms of nutritional value.

Other Taxa

Two other domestic animals present in the Neolithic include dog and horse. Both show up often in small frequencies, rarely in amounts characteristic of the above taxa. Debate surrounds the wild or domestic nature of the horse in this period. Because of their low frequencies, the reproductive and maintenance parameters for managing these taxa will not be discussed here.

The environmental and behavioral characteristics of wild animals are also important for understanding their exploitation. The integration of wild animals into an agricultural system is confusing, largely because of their destructive impact as competitors for forage and scavengers of cultivated cereals versus their value as an important food resource. In addition to aurochs and pigs described above, a number of wild animals were exploited in the Neolithic, as indicated in numerous faunal samples. A brief list of the most important taxa might include bison, elk, roe deer, bear, fox, and beaver. By far the most important wild mammal is the red deer.

Red Deer

Red deer (*Cervus elaphus*) have undergone marked diminution since the medieval period. The principal factor in this size reduction seems to have been the poor quality of food available in areas to which deer were gradually restricted (Lowe 1960). Modern weights vary tremendously, 75 to 340 kg (Grzimek 1972:175), although it should be stressed that these figures do not represent variation within a single population. A figure of 250 kg is often used as an average body weight estimate for red deer in the Neolithic (eg. Jacomet and Schibler 1985; Stampfli 1976a).

Red deer combine browsing and grazing in their feeding strategies. Their preferred natural habitat of open areas with scattered trees provides a variety of brush, grasses and forbs (Grzimek 1972:175). There are dramatic differences in the behavior of males and females (Clutton-Brock, Guinness and Albon 1982). Males often associate together and spend their summers concealed in the forest. Females and immature males band together into small herds of six to 12 animals. Red deer have characteristic seasonal movements: in the summer, deer are distributed throughout higher ground, in winter to spring they congregate on lower slopes of hills by day, moving downward with nightfall. Herding is especially marked after snowfall (Lowe 1960).

The rut takes place in early autumn, and is generally over by mid-October. Does give birth in May or June, after an average gestation period of about eight months. Single births are the norm, with twins occurring only rarely. Young nurse for nine months to a year, and young males may remain with females through their second year (Grzimek 1972:175-180).

Successful exploitation of red deer as a source of meat and other body products involves a basic knowledge of the characteristics described above. Little is known about the hunting methods used in prehistory although stalking, trapping and some collective hunting may be expected based on analogies with later periods. Collective hunting of small groups of animals may have been most effective in the autumn or winter, when the animals tend naturally to congregate.

The second major type of labor associated with the management of red deer surrounds their competition with domestic fauna. Red deer are generally at a disadvantage when in competition with domestic ungulates, which forage in a more concentrated fashion and leave little foliage untouched. As a response to competition by domesticates, deer may increase browsing on trees and shrubs; in the Ukraine, it has been noted that deer damage to forests increased directly with an increased abundance of meadows and pastures. Another consequence is that deer often increase scavenging of cultivated crops under conditions of competition (Sukachev and Dylis 1968:351). The protection of agricultural fields from these creatures may require minimally an increased vigilance by hunters, maximally, the construction of fences or traps.

Increasing Animal Production

The above review has indicated some of the types of land use and labor that are associated with animal production,

as well as the biological needs and capabilities of the major animals important in the context of Neolithic Europe. It is useful at this point to discuss how the management of animals may be intensified in a general sense, that is, how production may be increased.

Decisions on how to increase production will be based on two types of information. First, given the characteristics of the taxa involved, we need some idea of the relative contribution of various body products of each animal. Some idea of the relative amounts and scheduling of labor involved in exploiting animals in different ways is also necessary.

Energy

The energy contribution of animals to an agricultural system is a complex subject. In addition to the basic meaning in terms of protein contribution to diet, animals supply energy in the form of transport or draft ability, fuel and fertilizer, and the physical manipulation of soil and plant communities through grazing. Although these multiple forms of energy benefits may be explicitly recognized by a farmer, they cannot all be adequately quantified. The most important energy contribution of domesticates to subsistence economy of agriculturalists is generally assumed to be their provision of a reliable source of animal protein. For some domesticates, this protein contribution includes a combination of meat and milk products. Table 1 presents the four major domestic taxa ranked in descending order by their relative contributions of these two types of protein. The quantity of meat per animal is based on the body weights given in the above descriptions. Meat yield is basically a function of body weight, minus a certain percentage lost in carcass preparation. Milk yields in this table for sheep, goat and cattle are ordered according to absolute yield per female per lactation. They are also ranked according to the percentage protein in milk (from Grzimek 1972:272-273), which may be more important than absolute quantity, at least in the context of selection between small ovicaprines. A more detailed comparison of the amounts of meat and milk (eg. calculation into standard units with respect to one animal - livestock units) is not practical because of the discrepancies in absolute body yield which undoubtedly exist between original sources of information, largely African and Near Eastern taxa, and Neolithic animals.

Herd Security

Herd security is also an important concept in any discussion of maximization of yields, or optimization of multiple goals in animal production (Redding 1981:267). Herd security refers to the minimization of fluctuations in herd size, especially those that may result in a reduction of annual yield (Dahl and Hjort 1976). Herd security can be related to the general strategy of subsistence agriculturalists identified at the beginning of this chapter, in which production levels are kept somewhat above the level of

Table 1. Major domestic animals in descending rank order according to different types of energy yields.

Meat yield	Milk Yield (Absolute)	Milk Yield (%Protein)	Reproductive Capacity
Cattle	Cattle	Sheep	Pig
Pig	Goat	Cattle, Goat	Goat
Sheep, Goat	Sheep		Sheep
			Cattle

immediate need to ensure supplies in times of shortage. It may be quantified as the reproductive capacity of an animal combined with the absolute number of individual animals kept. There are no good estimates of minimum breeding population sizes or herd sizes for the taxa reviewed above, with the possible exception of cattle. Therefore, only reproductive capacity will be considered.

Reproductive capacity is considered here to be basically identical to fecundity, or the power of a species to increase. This power is dependent on the age of breeding, frequency of breeding, length of breeding life and number of viable offspring produced each time an animal breeds successfully (Moule 1968:353). Most of these data have been presented in the taxonomic review above, although coverage of the individual animals is by no means even. Aspects of fecundity which can be uniformly taken into account for all taxa include length of gestation period, frequency with which young are borne and the number of young at birth. Table 1 also presents the four domestic taxa ranked in descending order according to reproductive capacity. This provides some idea of the relative ability of each taxon to increase its numbers.

Scheduling of Labor

Much of the pertinent information regarding the potential labor requirements associated with each of the major domestic taxa discussed above is summarized in Figure 3. The points at which human labor might be expected to have the most effect on levels of production include the time of parturition, and the periods of lactation, fodder collection and overwintering. Two observations may be made concerning the distribution of these potential tasks throughout the year. First, labor requirements are present all year round, assuming some minimal attention to animals in the reproductive season and some supplemental feeding in winter. Second, periods of potentially high labor input overlap for many of the taxa. This suggests that, under conditions of labor shortage or if labor is to be minimized, a farmer may have to choose between exploiting the full range of body products of one or two taxa, or using multiple taxa at lower levels. This brings up two possible strategies for increasing animal production: specialization and diversification.

Specialization

Specialization refers to concentration on one taxon, or a very limited range of taxa. The economic focus may be on animals with greater productivity in a local environment or on animals with specific desired yields. Specialization is often a risky strategy to pursue, since all stock may be affected by localized disease or disaster. The relative expense of maintaining exclusively one kind of stock might be expected to decrease with larger numbers of animals primarily by facilitating the organization of labor, which is aimed at the rather predictable requirements of only one taxon. There is, however, an upper threshold of herd size beyond which a significantly higher labor input is often required (Dahl and Hjort 1976:205). This maximum herd size varies by animal, perhaps also according to local environmental conditions.

Specialization is a common response of subsistence agriculturalists to the introduction of a market economy (Clark and Haswell 1967). For this reason, it has generally been regarded as representing a late development, facilitated mainly by the establishment of interregional economic systems integrated into the world market. On a smaller scale, some degree of specialization was undoubtedly possible in prehistory as well. Strong connections among prehistoric groups may have been dependent upon networks of social relationships to either exchange produce, or spread risk by intergroup redistribution of animals.

Diversification

Diversification refers to a strategy in which multiple kinds of animals are kept, and are usually managed for different products. It often provides a way to retain a high degree of flexibility as required, for instance, by instability in the natural environment. In contrast to specialization, risk is often lessened - disease or disaster are less likely to affect all taxa. However, diversification is fairly expensive in terms of land and labor. Most combinations are only successful if an owner has a complete herd of one animal, plus a sizable number of individuals of one or more other taxa as an investment (Behnke 1980:73). Diversification is also dependent on the ability to combine different animals and may require a more extensive use of land if animals are incompatible or have different ecological requirements.

According to the criteria presented above, Sherratt's secondary products revolution, discussed in Chapter 2, can be identified as a model positing a process of diversi-

	Mar	Apr	May	Jun	Jul	Aug	Sep	Oct	Nov	Dec	Jan	Feb
Sheep	Birth	⊢ Lactation ⊣										
Goat	Birth	⊢──── Lactation ────⊣										
Pig	Birth						Birth(?)					
Cattle		Birth	⊢────── Lactation ──────⊣									
Feeding	First Browse		⊢ Collect Fodder ⊣			⊢ Mast ⊣── Over Winter ──⊣						

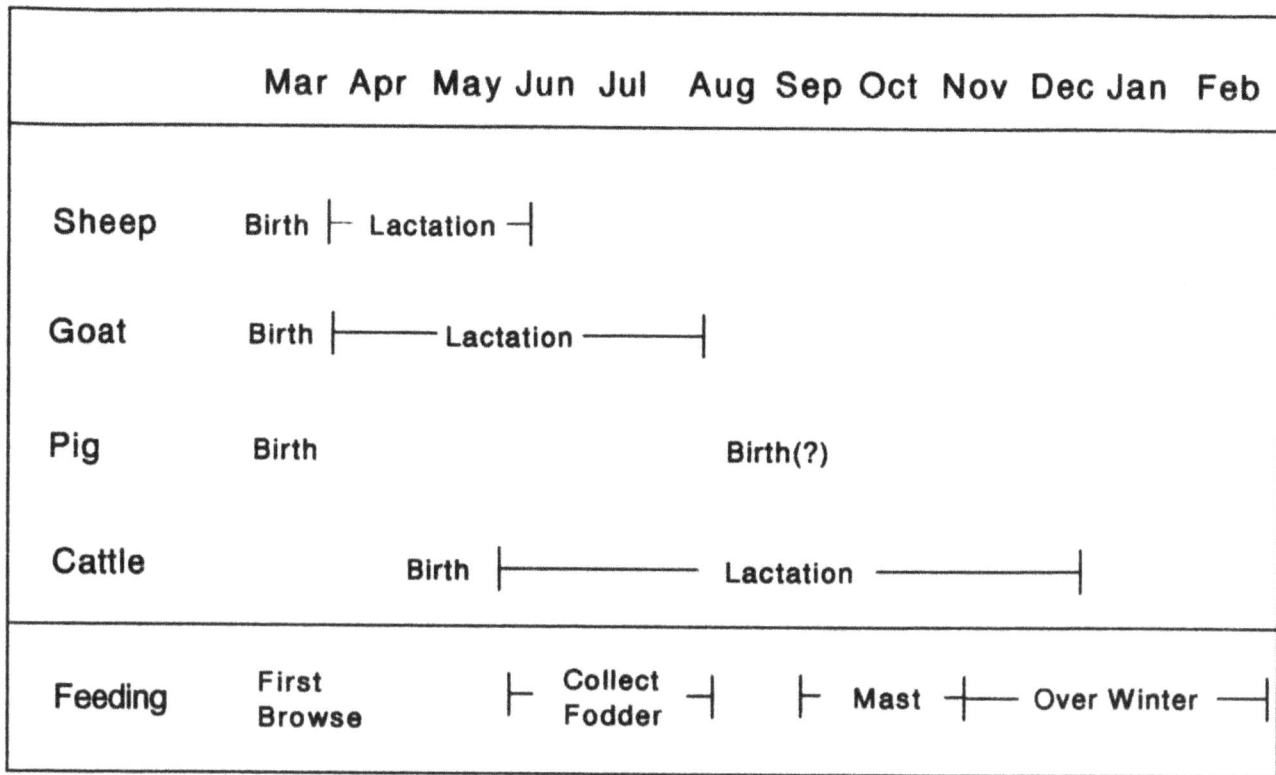

Figure 3. Estimates of seasonal labor and food requirements associated with domestic animal production.

fication in the animal economy during the course of the Neolithic. According to this model, domestic animal exploitation up to the fourth and third millennia BC across most of Europe and the Near East was mainly concerned with meat use. Beginning around the mid-fourth millennium BC, a series of changes involving the exploitation of taxa for different body products is hypothesized. These include the development of milking, the use of draft animals, wool sheep, etc.. Phrased in the context of general decision-making in subsistence agriculture, it becomes obvious that such a strategy of diversification entails a host of corresponding changes in both land use and the organization of human labor.

Specialization and diversification should be viewed as different degrees of resource selectivity, rather than mutually exclusive, non-overlapping alternatives. In attempting to balance the concerns of risk minimization, labor minimization and multiplicity of goals identified for subsistence agriculturalists at the beginning of this chapter, a strategy of diversification of animals and/or animal products appears to present a better solution than specialization in situations where increased production is required. This may be especially true in the absence of strong interregional exchange systems. However, a move toward diversification is not necessarily a universal trend, nor an irreversible one. It depends, rather, on the availability of land, labor, and the characteristics of the particular resources at hand. As in the case of the implementation of specific management techniques, one must test for either specialization or diversification in particular cultural contexts rather than assuming a universal tendency in either direction.

Chapter 5

NEOLITHIC FAUNAL ASSEMBLAGES

Faunal data collected from a number of Neolithic contexts can be compared in order to test hypotheses concerning changes in strategies of domestic animal management during this period. One problem to be addressed is the nature of the difference between early and late Neolithic faunal assemblages. How do samples from these time periods differ, and can these differences be related to an intensification of animal use? A second question surrounds the greater variability which has been identified for the later Neolithic. Does this variability reflect a general process of diversification in the use of animals and animal products? Is there any indication of selective manipulation of a narrow portion of the faunal spectrum which might suggest economic specialization?

The first two analytical chapters focus on comparisons between early and late Neolithic assemblages. Assemblage composition is compared in terms of general structure, as well as the relative contribution of major taxa. In the final analyses, emphasis is on types of variability within the late Neolithic assemblages which reflect specific strategies of domestic animal management. These include age and sex profiles and osteometric observations for the major taxon: cattle.

A total of 59 faunal assemblages from the western portion of central Europe have been chosen for analysis. Twenty-four samples are from early Neolithic sites, Bandkeramik or closely related cultures, the remaining 35 are from late Neolithic contexts as identified in Figure 2. These faunal data are derived from a number of different sources. I identified three of the assemblages used in these analyses: the Fischergasse assemblage, and the bones from the Altheim and Cham contexts at the Galgenberg site. The rest have been collected from published reports gathered during an extensive survey of literature on Neolithic Europe, and include analyses published up to 1988. With a few exceptions (in cases when original articles or reports proved inaccessible), only primary data have been used. That is, original faunal reports were consulted, and data from these reports abstracted and reorganized by me for use in specific analyses. An obvious problem with such an approach is the comparability of identifications performed by a variety of analysts. Most analysts within

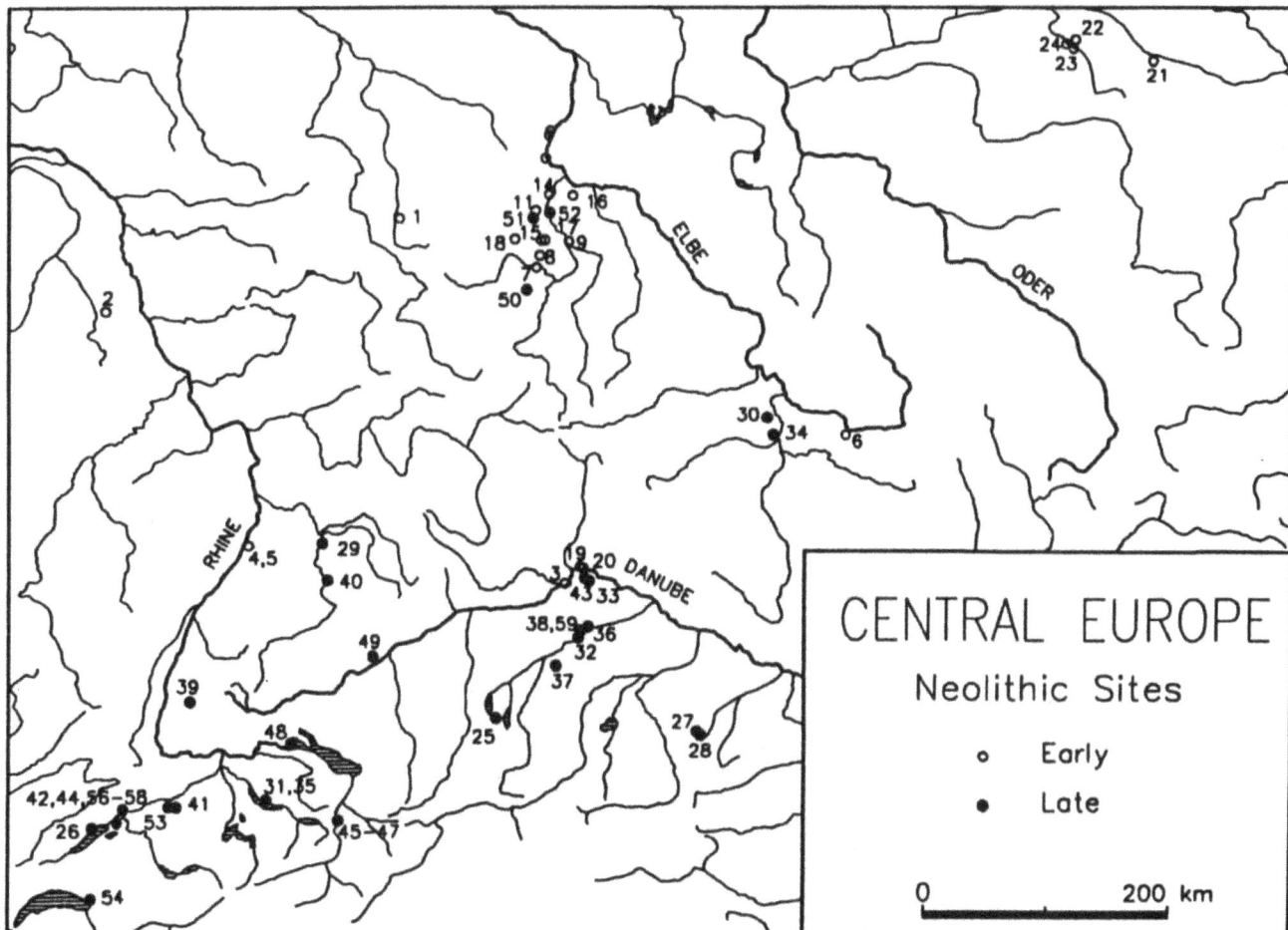

Figure 4. Map of west-central Europe showing distribution of Neolithic sites.

Table 2. List of assemblages used in analyses with cultural affiliation and bibliographic references.

NO.	SITE	CULTURE	REFERENCES
1	Rosdorf	LBK	Reichstein 1977
2	Müddersheim	LBK	Stampfli 1965
3	Hienheim	LBK	Clason 1977
4	Kraichtal-Gochsheim 12	Hinkelstein	Boessneck 1982
5	Kraichtal-Gochsheim 3	Grossgartach	Boessneck 1982
6	Bylany	LBK-SBK	Clason 1970
7	Tröbsdorf	LBK	Müller 1964
8	Dammendorf	LBK	Müller 1964
9	Halle-Trotha	LBK	Müller 1964
10	Gatersleben Akademie-Institut	LBK	Müller 1964
11	Cochstedt	LBK	Müller 1964
12	Barleben Schweinemästerei	LBK-SBK	Müller 1964
13	Magdeburg-Prester	SBK	Müller 1964
14	Barleben-Hühnerfarm	LBK	Müller 1964
15	Grossörner	LBK-SBK	Müller 1964
16	Köthen-Geuz	LBK-SBK	Müller 1964
17	Hettstedt	LBK	Müller 1964
18	Hohlstedt	LBK	Müller 1964
19	Regensburg-Pürkelgut	LBK-SBK	Boessneck 1958
20	Regensburg-Kumpfmühl	Oberlauterbach	Boessneck 1958
21	Brzesc Kujawski	LBK	Bogucki 1982
22	Miechowice	LBK	Bogucki 1982
23	Lojewo	LBK	Bogucki 1982
24	Strzelce	LBK	Bogucki 1982
25	Polling	Polling	Blome 1968
26	Auvernier	Auvernier	Stampfli 1976b
27	Scharfling	Mondsee	Wolff 1977
28	See	Mondsee	Wolff 1977
29	Hetzenberg	Michelsberg	Beyer 1970
30	Makotrasy	Baalberg	Clason 1985

(continued...)

this area of central Europe share a common tradition emphasizing detailed osteological observations and exhibit similar approaches to the investigation of prehistoric faunas. Because of this, there is considerably more uniformity in data collection and presentation than might intuitively be expected. Nevertheless, interobserver bias must be acknowledged as a possible source of error in interpretations of these faunal collections.

All assemblages were screened for obvious inconsistencies by the comparison of taxonomic abundances quantified in different manners. In addition, element frequencies of the most important taxa were compared for any possible discrepancies in identifiability which may have affected the calculation of taxonomic abundances. Assemblages which remained after this intensive, albeit subjective, scrutiny have been used in this research. Figure 4 shows the distribution of the selected assemblages throughout the study area. Table 2 lists the cultural affiliations for each assemblage and the major bibliographic references from which data were derived.

Interpreting Economic Strategies From Faunal Remains

There are many problems involved in the attempt to reconstruct economy from faunal assemblages. These have been pointed out by multiple authors in a number of contributions that need not be reviewed here (eg. Lyman 1982; Meadow 1980; Rackham 1983; Uerpmann 1973). However, two of these problems pertain directly to the type of investigation attempted in this dissertation and so are addressed briefly. Other interpretive difficulties will be mentioned in connection with their specific analytical contexts.

The identification and comparison of productive strategies is obviously dependent upon the analysis of remains from analogous contexts which reflect economic activity. Contextual problems can be somewhat controlled by the judicious selection of appropriate samples. In this case, analysis has been restricted to assemblages which have been characterized as occupational debris at sites identified as settlements. That is, there is reason to believe that these were habitation loci for some period of time in prehistory. However, there is no clear idea of the range of settlement variability within either the early or late

Table 2 (Continued).

NO.	SITE	CULTURE	REFERENCES
31	Feldmeilen-Vorderfeld	Pfyn	Eibl 1974; Förster 1974
32	Fischergasse	Altheim	Glass 1987
33	Riekofen	Cham	Busch 1985
34	Homolka	Rivnac	Ambros 1968
35	Feldmeilen-Vorderfeld	Horgen	Eibl 1974; Förster 1974
36	Altheim	Altheim	Boessneck 1956
37	Altenerding	Altheim	Boessneck 1956
38	Galgenberg	Altheim	Glass (this study)
39	Munzinger Berg	Michelsberg	Schmid 1958
40	Ludwigsburg	Schussenried	Nobis 1977
41	Burgäschisee-Süd	Cortaillod	Boessneck
42	Twann US	Cortaillod	Becker 1981
43	Mintranching	Altheim	Boessneck and Schäffer 1985
44	Twann	Horgen	Stampfli 1980
45	Eschner Lutzengüetle	Pfyn	Hartmann-Frick 1960
46	Eschner Lutzengüetle	Schussenried	Hartmann-Frick 1960
47	Eschner Lutzengüetle	Horgen	Hartmann-Frick 1960
48	Hornstaad-Hörnle	Hornstaad	Kokabi 1985
49	Ehrenstein	Schussenried	Scheck 1977
50	Grossobringen	Bernburg	Barthel 1985
51	Schalkenburg bei Quenstedt	Bernburg	Müller 1985
52	Dölauer Heide	Bernburg	Müller 1978
53	Burgäschisee-SW	Cortaillod	Josien 1956; Stampfli 1964
54	Yvonand III	Cortaillod	Chaix 1976
55	Lüscherz	Lüscherz	Josien 1956
56	Twann MS1	Cortaillod	Becker and Johansson 1981
57	Twann MS2	Cortaillod	Becker and Johansson 1981
58	Twann OS	Cortaillod	Becker and Johansson 1981
59	Galgenberg	Cham	Glass (this study)

Neolithic, much less between them. This lack of knowledge about settlement variability reflects an even greater ignorance about social organization in the Neolithic. The most crucial effect this has on the interpretation of economic strategies is in the identification of the basic unit of production. As mentioned in the last chapter, the primary production unit in most subsistence agricultural systems is the household, usually bound to adjacent primary units through a complex web of kinship and other reciprocal social relationships. By analogy, the basic economic unit of the Neolithic is assumed to be the household. The need to pool labor and resources was probably also characteristic of Neolithic farming systems, although the precise nature and degree of complexity of these collective economic entities is unknown. The presence of a tertiary, or regional level of political control in the Neolithic is very much a matter of debate, although it has been inferred in some instances (Fleming 1985; Milisauskas and Kruk 1984; Sherratt 1982). It is worth emphasizing in this context that these multiple levels of organization are difficult to discriminate archaeologically. Neolithic sites, by virtue of their structural remains, are usually thought to represent multiple households. Remains from these sites have probably resulted from both individual household and collective decisions regarding agricultural production. It is unclear how economic reconstructions at the level of the site are representative of strategies initiated at the household level.

The second set of problems are taphonomic ones, which pose considerable difficulties for all archaeological interpretations. Problems surrounding the interpretation of faunal remains relate to the different ways that animals may enter the archaeological record and the fact that their remains are differentially affected by postdepositional processes. Taphonomic problems like differential fragmentation and preservation of taxa and elements remain largely unaddressed in Neolithic assemblages, with a few notable exceptions (eg. Becker and Johansson 1981; Stampfli 1976a, 1976b). The effects of these processes are impossible to assess in the comparison of published reports unless they have first been tackled at the level of the individual site analysis.

In addition, there are unique problems surrounding the interpretation of the domestic animal contribution to a particular system. Domesticates are economically important for their entire lives, and the economic roles fulfilled by animals often change within their lifetimes. Faunal assemblages combine animals that have died at different points along their economic trajectories. This is quite a different situation from that of a wild animal, whose economic contribution is more closely associated with its point of entry into the archaeological record. A number of investigators have attempted to deal with this phenomenon in recent years (Chang and Koster 1986; Cribb 1985). There is a pressing need to develop ways of modeling the processes which accompany the transition of domestic animals from a behavioral to an archaeological context.

These problems in reconstructing prehistoric economy are ones which need to be resolved in the long run, by the gradual accumulation of data which have been systematically collected and analyzed. Although they must be explicitly recognized, they do not completely prohibit the use of faunal data for such general questions as have been posed above.

Chapter 6

TAXONOMIC DIVERSITY IN NEOLITHIC FAUNAL ASSEMBLAGES

Faunal assemblages from early and late Neolithic contexts exhibit differences in the numbers of taxa they contain, as well as in the relative contributions of major taxa. One way of investigating these differences is through an analysis of assemblage diversity.

Diversification of the resource base is thought to have played an important role in both the initial development of food-producing systems and in the ability of these systems to support subsequent increases in population (Christenson 1980; Cohen 1977; Flannery 1968; Redding 1988). Christenson has presented a general model of changes in resource selection which might be expected in a subsistence economy under conditions of population growth (Christenson 1980). Initially, increasing the number of exploited food resources would be the most efficient way to meet the increased energy needs of a group. However, this process of adding resources is only possible up to a certain point. Eventually, the limit of the local resource base is reached - it becomes either too costly to add new resources or additional resources are simply not available. After this point, change will have to proceed by intensifying use of one or more existing resources. This intensification process may, in turn, lead to a reduction in the number of resources exploited because of environmental change, overexploitation or readjustments in scheduling (Christenson 1980:36).

This hypothetical sequence has most often been applied in attempts to explain changes in the subsistence economy associated with the shift from hunting and gathering to agriculture. Empirical data from the Tehuacan Valley and the Midwestern United States (Christenson 1980), and from the Iberian peninsula (Clark and Yi 1983), appear to follow the expected pattern of increasing resource variety followed by selective intensification as outlined above. This sequence of general resource change with the origin of food production can also serve as a point of departure for a detailed investigation of diversification in animal use through the Neolithic.

Differences between early and late Neolithic animal economy have often been informally phrased in terms of differences in diversity. Low amounts of bone and a predominance of domestic animals have repeatedly been noted for Bandkeramik sites throughout Europe (Clason 1967, 1977; Müller 1964; Reichstein 1977; Stampfli 1965). This has been interpreted as representing an economy in which animal resources in general were subordinate to plant resources, and in which hunting of wild animals played only a negligible role in subsistence strategies.

In contrast, late Neolithic sites are often characterized by larger faunal assemblages overall, with occasionally very high abundances of wild animal bone (eg. Blome 1968; Boessneck, Jequier and Stampfli 1963). These larger assemblages have been considered indicative of an increased emphasis on animal use in the economy in general. More specifically, the greater number of wild animals bones recovered from late Neolithic sites has been used to infer an increase in hunting activity. This increased hunting activity has been related to the colonization of new territory both directly and indirectly. Expansion of an agricultural economy may have brought farmers into direct contact with richer, less exploited animal populations (Boessneck 1956; Driehaus 1960:90). Increased hunting activity could be related to this greater availability, as well as the need to protect agricultural fields from crop-scavenging fauna. Indirectly, an increased use of wild animals has been postulated as one of the consequences of the secondary products revolution (Sherratt 1981). The use of domestic animals for purposes like draft, traction, and dairying made them more valuable alive than dead, necessitating an increased exploitation of wild fauna to cover protein needs.

Measuring Diversity

All investigations of assemblage variability involve at least implicit consideration of the concept of diversity. Diversity indices provide a convenient way to summarize the kinds of qualitative variability characteristic of collective entities, in much the same way that statistical variance provides a measure of variability in a parametric variable (Pielou 1975:5). Following general ecological usage (eg. Odum 1971; Pielou 1975), diversity can be broken down along two dimensions: richness and evenness. *Richness* simply refers to the number of discrete classes present in an assemblage, while *evenness* describes the relative proportion of each class. These may be analyzed separately or simultaneously through the use of composite measures. Because archaeological usage of the term diversity has been applied inconsistently to analyses of either richness, evenness or both, Dunnell (1989) and Bobrowsky and Ball (1989) have recommended that the term *heterogeneity* be used for indices which specifically combine richness and evenness into a single statistic. Diversity is used here in its most general sense, referring nonspecifically to richness, evenness and/or heterogeneity.

Richness

Many investigations of community variability in ecology and assemblage variability in archaeology consider only the number of classes of information. Differences in sample size pose one significant problem associated with the measurement and consequent analysis of richness. The relationship between richness and sample size has been thoroughly discussed in the context of general archaeological analyses (eg. Jones, Grayson and Beck 1983; Kintigh 1984) and in the context of the analysis of archaeological and paleontological faunas (eg. Grayson 1978, 1981, 1984). Basically, the number of discrete classes of data is logarithmically related to the total number of items in the sample under investigation. That is, the number of classes increases at a decreasing rate as sample size increases. In populations where samples containing drastically different numbers of items are compared, some caution has to be used if variation due to sample size differences alone is to be excluded.

Evenness

At first glance, evenness describes a quality which is easily and intuitively recognizable as important: the relative proportion contributed by each category, in this case, taxon, to the assemblage as a whole. Methodologically, however, there is considerably more difficulty in isolating and analyzing evenness as a dimension of variability. This difficulty surrounds the fact that there seems to be no satisfactory way to measure evenness which does not incorporate richness. All statistics designed to measure evenness rely on some knowledge of the total number of classes present in the population, which is rarely attainable (Pielou 1977:307-309). In the absence of this knowledge, the number of classes in each sample is often substituted, which is dependent on sample size as discussed above. Beyond this, it is also questionable whether or not an independent measure of evenness is at all desirable, since it places as much weight on rare classes as on the more abundant ones, possibly leading to interpretive difficulties (Pielou 1977:309). Given the methodological and interpretive difficulties described above for the measurement of evenness, analysis of this component of diversity will be left until a more detailed discussion of taxonomic abundance.

Heterogeneity

A number of measures of heterogeneity have been adapted from ecology to the study of human subsistence systems. The one used here is a statistic called diet-breadth introduced to human ecology studies by Hardesty (Hardesty 1975). It may be described as the reciprocal of the sum of the proportional contribution of different food resources (Clark and Yi 1983:183) The diet-breadth index can be recognized as a modification of the Simpson index, originally designed as a measure of concentration or dominance of a many-species community. It varies from 1 to a maximum value equal to the richness of the sample. Low values signify assemblages with fewer taxa and low evenness, high values signify richer assemblages more evenly distributed among their member taxa. It is important to remember when interpreting diversity (richness, evenness or heterogeneity) that only the structure of an assemblage (the number of taxa and/or the pattern of abundance) is compared (Bobrowsky and Ball 1989; Dunnell 1989). There may still be major differences among the sites regarding the particular taxa which appear in the various rank categories.

Measures of both richness and heterogeneity, specifically the diet-breadth statistic, were used by Christenson to illustrate the sequence of changes in resource use described at the beginning of this chapter. The analysis of both richness and heterogeneity in faunal assemblages from early and late Neolithic contexts yields results which can then be related to this hypothetical model of general resource use.

An analysis of diversity requires consideration of two basic properties of the data under investigation (Pielou 1975:6). First, the boundaries or parameters of the collection must be specified. Archaeological assemblages, like ecological communities, can be defined along a number of lines. This analysis of diversity will deal with mammalian taxa recovered from archaeological sites. Non-mammalian taxa have been excluded because of their small quantities, and the problems associated with their recovery and identification. Second, a method of measuring the contribution of each taxon must be chosen. There are three basic ways of quantifying faunal remains: number of identified bone fragments or specimens (NISP), minimum number of individual (MNI), and bone weight. Most ecological studies of diversity use the number of individuals or some measure of biomass, depending on characteristics of body size and species distribution. Unfortunately, all three measures of archaeological relative abundance are severely biased by various taphonomic or analytical factors, and cannot be directly related to individual counts or biomass measures as used in ecology. A more detailed discussion of these relative measures will be carried out in the context of evaluating taxonomic abundance; for purposes of this analysis, the number of identified specimens was used because it is the only relative measure of abundance provided in all reports.

Analysis of Neolithic Faunal Diversity

There are several interrelated hypotheses embedded in the general trends in Neolithic faunal assemblages described above. These can be rephrased in a more specific manner to emphasize their relation to particular dimensions of diversity in order to facilitate testing. One question to address is the difference between early and late assemblages in the importance of wild animals. Both early and late assemblages usually contain the same basic core of domestic animals (cattle, sheep, goats, pig and dog), albeit in varying percentages, and the presence of wild animals almost always represents an increase in the total number of taxa. An assumption which may be made here is that a greater economic emphasis on hunting, for whatever reason, will result in a higher number of taxa in an assemblage, or in other words, an increase in richness.

A second question which may be addressed concerns the relative degree of specialization evident in faunal assemblages from the early and late Neolithic. Current reconstructions characterize the early Neolithic as land intensive, oriented predominantly toward crop products, and later systems as land extensive, with an increase in the importance of the animal component. Within the animal component specifically, early Neolithic animal use is thought to have emphasized domestic taxa, with perhaps the most importance placed on cattle. Later economic systems have been pictured as often specializing on one domestic taxon, frequently but not exclusively cattle, and exploiting a greater variety of other species (both domestic and wild) as well. The identification of such differences in combined richness and evenness is best approached through the use of a heterogeneity measure. If the trends described above for the different periods are valid, early and late Neolithic assemblages should show clearly different values.

In summary, two specific questions are addressed here. First, late Neolithic sites are expected to show greater taxonomic richness than early Neolithic sites as a reflection of an increased exploitation of wild animals. And second, early and late assemblages should show significantly different heterogeneity values, given the different strategies of domestic and wild animal use hypothesized for each period.

The Problem of Sample Size

Variability in sample sizes among sites presents one of the most obvious difficulties in comparing early and late Neolithic faunal assemblages. Table 3 presents the number of taxa and sample sizes for the 59 Neolithic faunal assemblages introduced in Chapter 5. The first 24 samples are from the early Neolithic sites, followed by the assemblages from the 35 late Neolithic contexts. Sample sizes for the early contexts range from 88 to 1500 bones, later assemblages contain anywhere from 200 to 17,000 fragments.

Two methods have been used for analyzing assemblage diversity and testing the relationship between it and sample size in archaeological data: regression analysis and simulation. Grayson (1984) presents the most thorough discussion of the use of regression analysis to address taxonomic richness in archaeological faunas. Kintigh (1984), in the context of dealing specifically with richness, introduced a simulation, or randomization, approach which has been adapted here to the analysis of taxonomic diversity in faunal assemblages. This involves constructing a background distribution of species frequencies from a group of assemblages. This

hypothetical parent population is then randomly sampled a set number of times at various sample sizes. Finally, a mean value and confidence interval are calculated for each sample size, providing a range within which a specified proportion of the simulation trials have fallen. Each individual assemblage can then be compared to this mean and confidence interval, and the likelihood that it derived from the background population can be evaluated.

In this study, the background population was constructed using a variation of Kintigh's procedures described in McCartney and Glass (1990). Species were sorted in descending rank order by NISP for each assemblage. Totals for each rank (ignoring taxonomic identification) were derived and divided by the number of assemblages. Random samples were then drawn from these ranks up to the designated sample size for the specified number of iterations. This method was chosen over a simpler approach of summing the frequencies of each species to derive their proportions. A background distribution derived from the straight sums of each discrete category pools evenness values across those categories. If there is a lot of variability in the rank order of categories among assemblages, this variation is smoothed, resulting in a background distribution which has greater evenness than any of the individual assemblages which went into its construction. Because a comparison of the underlying diversity, and not species content, of faunal assemblages in the early and late Neolithic is of primary interest here, the sorting procedure has been used. Comparisons of the relative abundances of specific taxa will be addressed separately.

The randomization method summarized above presents certain advantages over regression analysis for investigations of diversity, and for examining the relationships between diversity and sample size. In particular, randomization allows one to compare the assemblage under investigation with a parent population which has been constructed with a specific hypothesis in mind, rather than forcing comparison to a linear, or transformed linear, model. Second, randomization allows one to investigate the effect of sample size on diversity in isolation from other variables. And finally, a level of confidence may be calculated to evaluate the significance of the deviation of each observed sample from its expected score. This is important because of the observation derived from randomization studies of richness and sample size: the amount of random error varies with sample size, and must be evaluated separately for each assemblage (Kintigh 1984, 1989). Assuming a standard range of error across different sample sizes, as, for example, in an analysis of residuals, is not always valid.

Simulations of Neolithic Faunal Richness and Heterogeneity

Appendix 1 presents the raw data used for the richness and heterogeneity simulations. Some adjustments have been made to the bone counts derived from the original

Table 3. Sample size, richness and heterogeneity values for Neolithic faunal assemblages.

NO.	SITE	NISP	RICHNESS	HETEROGENEITY
1	Rosdorf	107	6	1.86
2	Müddersheim	217	10	2.78
3	Hienheim	147	11	4.43
4	Kraichtal-Gochsheim 12	188	5	1.79
5	Kraichtal-Gochsheim 3	1019	9	2.94
6	Bylany	571	10	1.51
7	Tröbsdorf	372	10	2.65
8	Dammendorf	221	7	2.04
9	Halle-Trotha	364	7	1.38
10	Gatersleben Akademie-Institut	310	6	2.77
11	Cochstedt	152	3	2.06
12	Barleben Schweinemästerei	523	10	2.37
13	Magdeburg-Prester	768	10	1.88
14	Barleben Hühnerfarm	171	5	2.07
15	Grossörner	297	8	1.62
16	Köthen-Geuz	187	8	2.43
17	Hettstedt	113	3	1.80
18	Hohlstedt	357	8	2.68
19	Regensburg-Pürkelgut	459	11	5.01
20	Regensburg-Kumpfmühl	117	8	5.16
21	Brzesc Kujawski	653	9	1.74
22	Miechowice	1503	7	2.05
23	Lojewo	620	8	1.86
24	Strzelce	88	5	1.51
25	Polling	2958	12	2.02
26	Auvernier	11711	23	5.18
27	Scharfling	522	11	2.41
28	See	1954	19	4.88
29	Hetzenberg	3344	9	2.28
30	Makotrasy	2383	14	1.85

(continued...)

reports in order to enhance comparability among sites. Where necessary, worked bone and shed antler fragments were subtracted from the taxonomic counts given by each author. In general, the categories used in the following analyses comprise the number of bone fragments identified to the species level. However, some modification was required in the case of bone identified as *Sus* sp. and *Bos* sp. Most Neolithic sites contain representatives of both wild and domestic forms of cattle and pig in their faunal assemblages: many also contain bones which, due to high fragmentation and/or intermediate size, can only be identified to genus. Omission of these bones does not seem appropriate, given the importance of these taxa for the Neolithic as a whole. In addition, the indeterminate fragments were already subsumed under their domestic counterparts in some cases. In order to increase the comparability of samples, bones identified as *Bos* sp. or *Sus* sp. were counted as *Bos taurus* and *Sus domesticus*, respectively, for purposes of this analysis. For the same reason, bones identified as *Ovis aries*, *Capra hircus* and "*Ovis* or *Capra*" were lumped together as ovicaprines.

Two separate analyses were performed: one on richness, and one on diet-breadth. The null hypothesis of each test

is that all assemblages belong to the same parent population, which has been estimated from the species frequencies of all the sites in the manner described above. In each simulation, 500 random samples were drawn from this estimated population at sizes corresponding to those of each assemblage. A mean value and 95% confidence interval were calculated for each sample size. This is considered to be the range within which an assemblage should fall if the null hypothesis is true. The lines connecting these points (mean, $z = +1.96$, $z = -1.96$) can be thought of as the values predicted if the same population were sampled at different sizes.

Richness

Figure 5 presents the results of the richness analysis. These can be interpreted with reference to two features of the graph: the slope of the line representing the mean expected richness calculated from the background population and the width of the 95% confidence interval along this line. The slope of this line shows that a high amount of variation in richness can be expected to occur with variation in sample size. The line of mean expected richness does not begin to level off until sample NISP reaches or exceeds 10,000 fragments. The width of the

Table 3 (continued).

NO.	SITE	NISP	RICHNESS	HETEROGENEITY
31	Feldmeilen-Vorderfeld	4303	16	2.91
32	Fischergasse	851	14	4.21
33	Riekofen	10423	20	4.81
34	Homolka	1381	14	2.93
35	Feldmeilen-Vorderfeld	4718	16	4.40
36	Altheim	336	8	2.09
37	Altenerding	585	9	2.56
38	Galgenberg	400	5	3.08
39	Munzinger Berg	559	8	2.44
40	Ludwigsburg	664	8	2.63
41	Burgäschisee-Süd	17289	21	3.34
42	Twann US	13979	21	4.98
43	Mintranching	359	10	3.98
44	Twann	2918	15	2.74
45	Eschner Lutzengüetle	1822	13	3.10
46	Eschner Lutzengüetle	1148	10	2.54
47	Eschner Lutzengüetle	701	16	4.29
48	Hornstaad-Hörnle	521	10	2.76
49	Ehrenstein	10272	18	3.64
50	Grossobringen	4612	15	2.13
51	Schalkenburg bei Quenstedt	3075	18	2.89
52	Dölauer Heide	217	10	3.16
53	Burgäschisee-SW	4708	16	5.70
54	Yvonand III	225	7	3.71
55	Lüscherz	1035	11	3.22
56	Twann MS1	2957	17	3.82
57	Twann MS2	13809	23	3.43
58	Twann OS	3665	22	5.52
59	Galgenberg	2070	17	7.04

95% confidence interval decreases slightly from the left to the right side of graph, showing that somewhat higher amounts of random variability are to be expected at lower samples sizes than at larger ones. The scatter of points showing actual values of the archaeological assemblages roughly reflect these same characteristics: they fall in a relatively steeply sloping linear band, which is broader at its lower end. The points do not all fall within the limits defined by the 95% confidence interval for each simulated point. Thus, the null hypothesis can be rejected: the assemblages are probably not derived from this parent population. All but one of the points representing early Neolithic assemblages lie beneath the 95% confidence band, while almost one third of the late assemblages lie within or above the band. This further suggests that these assemblages may be derived from more than one parent populations. There may be at least two separate patterns of relatively higher and lower richness in the late and early Neolithic, respectively.

The general results of the simulation suggest that much of the variability observed in taxonomic richness found in Neolithic faunal assemblages is related to differences in their sample sizes. It also indicates that the assemblages (or at least most of them) cannot be assumed to come from a single population, or at least not from one resembling the test population. It is apparent from Figure 5 that most of the early Neolithic sites tend to be characterized by small sample sizes and low richness values, but that the later assemblages are more scattered along both axes. In order to more fully investigate possible differences in richness between early and late assemblages, the effects

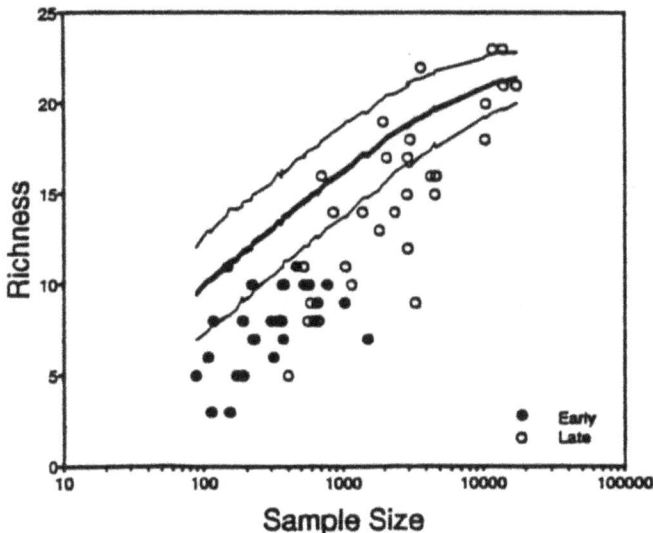

Figure 5. Results of richness simulation.

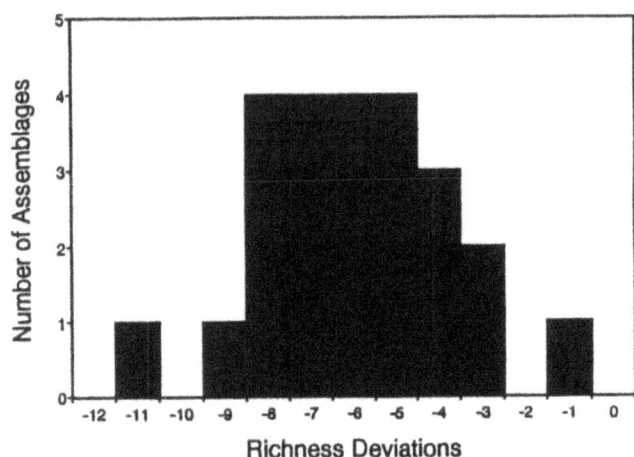

Figure 6. Histogram of deviations of richness scores for early Neolithic faunal assemblages.

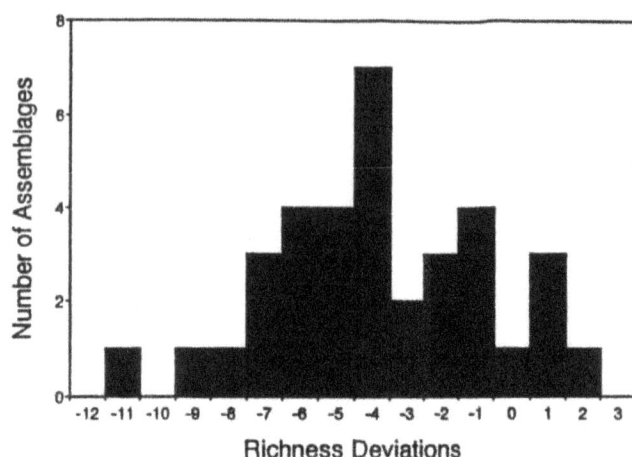

Figure 7. Histogram of deviations of richness scores for late Neolithic faunal assemblages.

of sample size indicated here may be factored out. This can be done by an analysis of the deviations between the richness value observed for each assemblage and the expected value obtained for that sample size by the simulation. Because the width of the confidence bands remain relatively stable across all sample sizes, the deviations, rather than z scores, were used. For this purpose, the line of mean expected richness is taken to represent a heuristic construct to which the real assemblages can be compared in a relative manner.

To test the differences between early and late Neolithic suggested by Figure 5, separate histograms of deviations from the mean were produced for the early and late Neolithic assemblages (Figures 6 and 7). The range of both of these distributions are the same. In addition, there is only a slight difference between the means of these two distributions, corresponding in real values to an average difference of about two more taxa per assemblage in the late Neolithic. A t-test yielded a score of 2.768 ($p = .008$). This confirms that there is a significant difference between taxonomic richness in late Neolithic sites compared to early Neolithic sites. However, the scale of these differences is drastically reduced when the effects of sample size have been estimated and removed.

Both histograms show the presence of a few assemblages with extreme richness deviations. For the early Neolithic (Figure 6), assemblages 3 and 22 show low and high differences, respectively, of a magnitude greater than two standard deviations from the mean. The late Neolithic assemblage 29 also shows up as a low extreme value in Figure 7. Based on richness alone, these assemblages appear to be different from the majority of those analyzed.

Heterogeneity

The results of the heterogeneity or diet-breadth analysis, shown in Figure 8, may be interpreted in a manner similar to the richness test. The observed scores for heterogeneity are listed in Table 3. A number of characteristics of this graph are important to point out. First, the slope

of the line connecting the expected values is almost horizontal, suggesting that heterogeneity values are not severely influenced by samples of this size range. There is, however, a marked difference in the width of the 95% confidence interval across the graph. This indicates that, although the mean index values themselves are not affected, there is a much greater range of error in the values calculated for the smaller assemblages. As with the richness test, the null hypothesis can be rejected based on the observation that the values for all of the assemblages are not restricted to the band defined by the confidence interval.

Closer inspection of this pattern has been carried out using the straight values for heterogeneity calculated for each assemblage. Use of the deviation value (difference between observed and expected score) does not seem necessary in this case because of the wide differences between the standard deviations of small versus large sites. Splitting the total population into early and late Neolithic groups (Figure 9) results in a histogram in which it is clear that the distribution of diet-breadth is different for each period. Both the early and late Neolithic are charac-

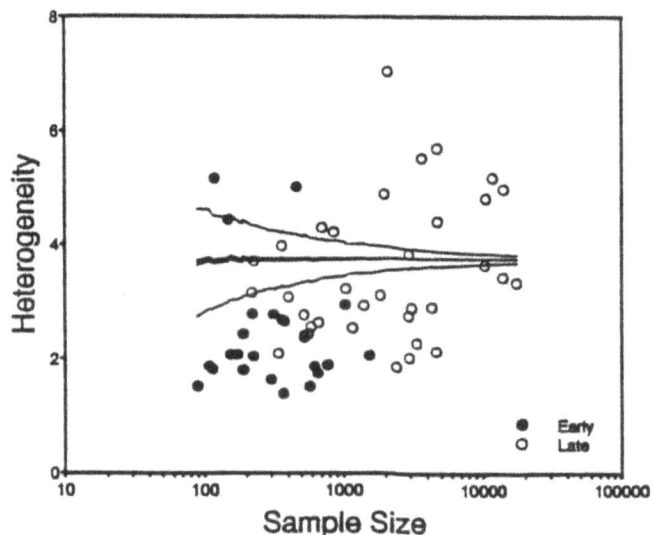

Figure 8. Results of heterogeneity simulation.

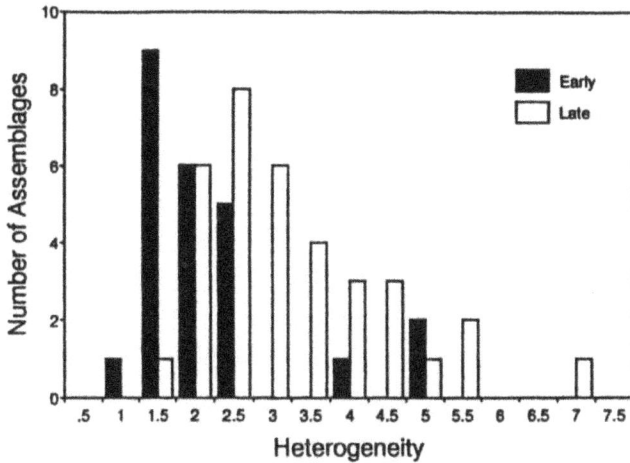

Figure 9. Histogram of heterogeneity values for early and late Neolithic faunal assemblages.

terized by a broad range of variability in terms of taxonomic heterogeneity. The distributions for both periods are skewed in favor of lower values; there tends to be a greater number of sites with low heterogeneity and fewer sites with high values. One obvious difference is the discontinuous nature of the scores for the early Neolithic: three assemblages seem to be unusually heterogeneous compared to the rest of the population. In contrast, the distribution of diet-breadth for the later assemblages appears more continuous, although somewhat skewed.

Comparisons of the heterogeneity scores of early and late Neolithic assemblages were made using the observed values because correction for bias using deviations was unnecessary. The group means for early and late are 2.4 $\pm$ 1.04 and 3.5 $\pm$ 1.21, respectively. A t-test yielded a score of $t = 3.51$ ($p = .001$), suggesting a significant difference despite the overlap in standard deviations. An alternative procedure for testing the difference between these two groups of sites allows the information contained in the confidence range derived from the simulation to be incorporated into a statistical comparison. The individual values for each group were combined using a weighted averaging technique (Long and Rippeteau 1974). Originally proposed to deal with the problem of combining radiocarbon dates with varying standard deviations, this manipulation provides a new mean and standard deviation for grouped values. When the group means are recalculated using the weighted averaging technique, group differences diverge farther and standard deviations are markedly reduced. The early Neolithic group shows a mean of 2.35 $\pm$ .05; the late Neolithic a mean of 3.72 $\pm$ .01.

It might be asked if the three early Neolithic sites with high heterogeneity should be considered as outliers. Support for this interpretation is discussed below. Without these three sites, the mean heterogeneity for the early Neolithic drops to 2.09 $\pm$ .475. Recalculation of the t-test yields a value of 5.1 ($p < .001$). The early Neolithic weighted average also drops to 2.13 $\pm$ .05. This strengthens the interpretation of higher hetero-

geneity in the later Neolithic assemblages.

Thus, although both the early and late Neolithic show sites with low and high heterogeneity, there is a greater proportion of early sites with low values. The late Neolithic shows a few more sites that are more heterogeneous. In addition, there is a tendency for the less heterogeneous sites in the early period to have lower absolute indices than the less heterogeneous sites in the later period.

To summarize, results of the two simulations show that sample size is a major factor structuring differences in taxonomic variability between early and late Neolithic faunal assemblages. The effects of sample size are fairly straightforward with respect to richness: larger assemblages contain a greater variety of animals than smaller assemblages. Since early Neolithic assemblages tend to be smaller than later ones, they also tend to be less rich. When the deviations between the observed richness scores and the scores of expected richness based on sample size are compared, these differences are shown to be significant. However, they do not appear to be particularly large and the ranges overlap extensively. Because richness is so difficult to separate from sample size in these assemblages, simplistic statements which relate increasing richness through time to shifts in animal exploitation cannot be supported. Each time period, however, does contain a small percentage of sites which differ significantly from the mean (ie, have deviations far greater or less than the mean deviation), and could be the focus of further investigation.

Sample size also affects heterogeneity, although in a different way; the degree of random error associated with a heterogeneity score is greater for small assemblages than for large ones. In both early and late groups, the majority of assemblages are characterized by low heterogeneity, with a small proportion of sites showing higher values. In addition, the early Neolithic assemblages appear to differ significantly from the later group, especially when three unusually diverse early sites are excluded. Generally, lower heterogeneity scores indicate assemblages which are relatively less rich, with a more uneven contribution of individual taxa. The richness analysis has already shown that the differences in the number of taxa in early versus late assemblages is very small (on the order of two taxa). The differences in heterogeneity values appear to be greater than would be accounted for by the observed differences in richness. This implies that there may be significant differences in evenness. The early Neolithic assemblages, with this inferred lower taxonomic evenness (ie. more unequal contribution of component taxa to the whole of an assemblage), can be characterized as more focused or specialized than the later ones.

The Meaning of Taxonomic Diversity

It must be recognized that taxonomic diversity in zooarchaeological assemblages does not necessarily reflect solely dietary diversity or, even more simply, patterns in animal exploitation. The interpretation of the meaning of a diversity statistic is subject to all the problems inherent in investigating archaeological variability in general. Preservation, sampling, and analytical or reporting biases combine to blur the patterning due to prehistoric activity, and complicate the cultural interpretations which are the goal of any archaeological endeavor. The above analyses have shown that there are significant differences between early and late Neolithic faunal assemblages in terms of sample size and a measure of general diversity. The degree to which these differences may be related to cultural as opposed to non-cultural formation processes must still be explored.

Sample Size Differences

The observation that sample size is a major factor structuring variability in both richness and diversity of Neolithic assemblages does not mean that differences among the sites in terms of absolute sample size are without meaning. The fact remains that early Neolithic settlements tend to yield smaller faunal assemblages than later sites, indicating that differences in assemblage size result from more than merely a sampling bias. It should also be pointed out in this context that the assemblages come from a variety of regions throughout west-central Europe, were excavated under diverse conditions over a number of decades and analyzed by multiple investigators. Although this does not eliminate biases due to different strategies of excavation and analysis, it does serve to homogenize their effects somewhat, lending strength to the general patterning recognized above. This suggests that differences in sample size between early and late Neolithic contexts can be related to some combination of general differences in the role of animals in the economy, the nature of site occupation (duration, intensity) and disposal patterns between the two periods.

With respect to the latter two factors, there are clear differences in the nature of the deposits yielding bone in early versus late Neolithic contexts. Most faunal remains, indeed most remains, from Bandkeramik sites have been recovered from the numerous pits distributed throughout the settlements. The principles structuring the construction and use of these pits are incompletely understood, but they do seem to have become areas for accumulation of secondary debris, at least in the later stages of their existence. Underrepresentation of bones in these contexts can often be related to decalcification of organic remains in the loess-based soils (Clason 1970, 1977; Modderman 1982). Other authors cite little or no evidence for deterioration of bones recovered from Bandkeramik sites (Müller 1964). In a number of ways, the nature of late Neolithic deposits is usually quite different. Major earthworks at some sites have acted as a repository for large amounts of general site debris (eg. Altheim, Galgenberg, Riekofen, Grossobringen). Many other

assemblages, lacking obvious spatial structuring, have been characterized by analysts as general site or kitchen refuse (eg. Fischergasse, Auvernier, Twann). Faunal remains from contexts such as these, which have accumulated over longer periods of time and probably contain refuse from a variety of activities, are expected to be both qualitatively and quantitatively different from bone deposited in smaller, special-activity-turned-refuse pits. It is possible that differential refuse accumulation between the two periods has greatly enhanced apparent differences in diversity between early and late assemblages. It could also imply the existence of significant differences in occupation duration or intensity as well, which are probably best investigated through studies of combined classes of general settlement debris.

Sources of Variability in Diversity

Putting aside the problems created by differential contexts, there are a number of potential sources of variability which have undoubtedly contributed to the taxonomic diversity noted above. It should be emphasized that neither the early nor the late Neolithic group represents a true temporal horizon or cultural entity. Rather, construction of these groups was dictated by the availability of faunal reports within the area of interest (west-central Europe). As the purpose of this analysis has been to test for general differences in strategies of animal exploitation between Bandkeramik and fourth and third millennia cultures, this level of investigation was deemed appropriate. It cannot, however, support detailed inferences about local subsistence strategies.

Nevertheless, there are some very general observations which can be made about diversity and spatial or cultural patterning. Just as there is no simple division between the diversity scores of early and late sites in general, there appears to be no way to predict, based on either cultural affiliation or geographic region, whether an assemblage will be characterized by high or low diversity. The five assemblages of the Altheim group, for example, show very different heterogeneity values. In addition, three sites with multiple cultural levels (Feldmeilen-Vorderfeld, Eschner-Lutzengüetle and Twann) show quite different values for their component assemblages. One possible exception to this apparent lack of geographic or cultural patterning may be the three early Neolithic assemblages which yielded high heterogeneity scores. The sites in question, Hienheim, Regensburg-Pürkelgut and Regensburg-Kumpfmühl, are the only early sites with faunal remains from the Regensburg-Kelheim area of the Danube valley in Bavaria. This suggests that at least in this case, the exceptionally higher heterogeneity may be related to characteristics of the local environment or settlement system. In general, though, variability in diversity does not seem to be strictly associated with subgroups of archaeological cultures and may only in some instances reflect certain characteristics of the local environment.

Finally some conclusions may be drawn regarding these results and the schemes of changing resource use described for the development of food production in general (Christenson 1980) and the fourth and third millennia BC in particular (Shennan 1986; Sherratt 1981). This requires the assumptions that the general sequence would also be reflected in the faunal component alone, and that the differences in faunal diversity do, in fact, reflect primarily dietary selection.

In general, the animal economy can be characterized as more focused or specialized in the early period, and more diversified in the later one. Some degree of diversification in the use of faunal resources is underway in the later period in the sense that each taxon may be contributing lower, and more equal, amounts to the total subsistence. There is no clear evidence of intensified use of a narrow range of taxa in the late Neolithic assemblages, at least at this scale of analysis.

Summary

The analyses of diversity lead to a number of general conclusions about the structure of Neolithic faunal assemblages. First, there is a slight trend toward an increase in the number of taxa in faunal assemblages from the early to the late Neolithic. The obvious differences in sample size between the two periods are at least partially related to differential depositional contexts of bone in Bandkeramik as compared to other Neolithic sites. It is unclear how these differences in deposition should be explained; the relative importance of factors like occupation duration, intensity, site function, etc., remain to be tested with analyses of general settlement refuse. Second, both early and late sites show a bias toward lower heterogeneity. With three exceptions, early Neolithic sites tend to have lower heterogeneity values than the sites of the later period. These sites may be characterized as more focused or specialized in terms of selectivity of faunal resources than later ones. The three early Neolithic sites with high heterogeneity are geographically near each other. Their higher scores may reflect unique characteristics of the local settlement system. Finally, the degree of emphasis on specific faunal resources is not entirely clear from an analysis of diversity alone - the scores reflect similarities and differences in the structure of assemblages, not their actual composition. The relative abundances of specific taxa are the subject of the next chapter.

Chapter 7

TAXONOMIC ABUNDANCE IN NEOLITHIC FAUNAL ASSEMBLAGES

Patterning in the relative abundances of major taxa found in Neolithic assemblages might be expected at a number of different levels of magnitude. At the broadest scale, two early systems of animal husbandry have been described for Europe in general: a Mediterranean system, with an emphasis on sheep and goats; and a central European system in which cattle were predominant, accompanied by ovicaprines (Clason 1973). This latter system can be identified as characteristic of Bandkeramik groups. By the late Neolithic, both of these patterns were supposedly present in Europe north of the Alps, with a possible area of overlap in the Swiss-south German area (Clason 1973). Differences in the abundances and characteristics of specific taxa have occasionally been related to this broad level of variability in animal keeping (eg. Busch 1985:55).

At the other extreme, a certain amount of variability is to be expected at the level of the individual site or occupation. The importance of the immediate cultural and/or physical environment has been pointed out in a number of cases. Nobis attributed much of the variability in composition among Neolithic faunal assemblages in northern Germany to local environmental characteristics (Nobis 1955). It is more difficult to explain the striking differences between the assemblages from the adjacent sites of Burgäschisee-Süd and Burgäschisee-Südwest (Stampfli 1964) in light of their shared physical setting. In addition, a number of multicomponent sites show clear differences in assemblage composition when the environmental, if not the cultural, associations of the occupations have remained the same.

Most archaeologists assume that patterning in subsistence economic practices occurs primarily at the level of the archaeological culture, conditioned by aspects of the local environment. Many analyses of faunal assemblage variability have been directed at the investigation and comparison of exploitation systems of particular archaeological cultures (eg. Higham 1966; Sakellaridis 1981; Uerpmann 1977). It has already been pointed out in Chapter 3 that this level of investigation may not be appropriate in the case of all Neolithic cultures because of their differences in temporal and geographical scale. A related problem involves the inadequate representation of sites, even within archaeological cultures of the same general duration and magnitude. In the sample of assemblages used here, there are a number of Cortaillod sites with faunal remains analyzed, but only one analysis each from Baalberg and Rivnac. An even stronger geographical bias exists in the sample of early Neolithic sites: most

of those with well-preserved and analyzed faunal remains come from the northern regions of the Bandkeramik distribution.

The preceding diversity chapter has suggested that there are significant differences in the relative abundances of particular taxa between early and late groups, and that there is greater variability among the later assemblages than is seen for the early Neolithic. The approach taken here is to compare the amount and kind of variability in the abundances of specific taxa between early and late Neolithic assemblages as a whole. In this manner, the nature of the general differences in animal use between the sixth and the fourth and third millennia BC is addressed without reference to particular cultural contexts.

Units Of Analysis

The abundances of different taxa can be compared using three basic kinds of measurements: the number of identified specimens (NISP), minimum number of individuals (MNI) and bone weight. The pros and cons of each type of measurement have been amply discussed in general literature on the interpretation of faunal remains from archaeological sites, and need only be briefly reviewed here. The relative utility of each of these measures can be evaluated within the context of quantification of data for analysis. This discussion is not concerned with problems associated with the initial identification of remains, or the recognition of site-specific taphonomic biases.

NISP

The number of identified specimens (NISP) is the starting point for all other types of quantification of faunal remains. The most critical problem associated with NISP is the differential fragmentation of skeletal elements and animals of various body sizes. In Neolithic faunal studies, there has been some attempt to adjust for this by the creation of a fragmentation index. Based on the assemblage at Egolzwil 5, Stampfli identified an average number of fragments per element for large ungulates (Stampfli 1976a). These factors were then multiplied by the frequency of each element in the body of a single individual, and the resulting figures used as expected values against which raw NISP values were compared for investigating element and taxonomic abundance. A number of subsequent investigators have adopted this technique and Stampfli's factors in their analyses of representation of Neolithic taxa (eg. Barthel 1985; Becker and Johansson 1981). The underlying assumption of this approach seems to be that fragmentation is the result of taphonomic processes of unspecified origin which do not

Table 4. NISP for nine taxa in Neolithic assemblages. 1-24 = Early, 25-59 = Late.

ASSEMBLAGE	Cattle	Ovicapr.	Pig	Horse	Dog	Red Deer	Wild Pig	Roe Deer	Aurochs
1	76	10	16	0	0	0	2	0	2
2	120	19	32	4	1	2	3	2	33
3	55	15	26	0	1	29	5	7	0
4	137	12	26	0	0	8	5	0	0
5	382	205	405	1	0	9	8	7	0
6	460	29	57	0	1	4	4	1	10
7	156	164	25	1	0	3	7	11	1
8	52	145	7	0	0	1	0	5	1
9	307	32	18	1	0	0	1	2	3
10	151	86	66	0	0	1	5	1	0
11	97	39	16	0	0	0	0	0	0
12	317	98	65	0	1	7	31	1	0
13	539	69	130	3	0	6	12	4	3
14	42	110	16	0	0	0	1	0	2
15	229	38	13	6	0	3	3	4	1
16	98	68	9	0	0	0	2	3	0
17	24	80	9	0	0	0	0	0	0
18	188	89	64	2	0	3	0	2	0
19	141	26	54	0	6	88	24	8	100
20	26	10	22	1	0	34	7	4	13
21	484	97	15	2	2	21	0	26	0
22	921	497	35	0	0	7	0	11	31
23	440	95	61	1	0	4	0	1	17
24	71	6	0	3	0	6	0	2	0
25	99	3	76	1	0	1954	702	35	8
26	1902	937	183	19	293	409	130	613	63
27	154	3	8	0	0	296	12	1	2
28	641	376	135	0	65	354	21	34	7
29	1618	1500	189	0	2	15	7	2	10
30	1699	181	376	14	50	30	10	3	5

(continued...)

vary between assemblages. This is a questionable assumption at best, especially in the light of the numerous taphonomic studies which have been undertaken in recent years (Binford and Bertram 1977; Brain 1981; Lyman 1984). Minimally, it would seem that such factors should be derived independently for each assemblage, and some attempt made to identify the human or natural agents at play in each case.

Other modifications of NISP have appeared in the paleontological and zooarchaeological literature in the context of assemblage quantification and comparison. These include the use of factors to control for different numbers of skeletal elements in various taxa (Shotwell 1955), quantification by use of diagnostic zones (Watson 1979) or the calculation of minimum numbers of elements (Binford 1984). Although all of these modifications may provide additional information about site-specific assemblage variability, they are all only infrequently used, not easily calculated on published data, and of limited use for interassemblage comparison.

MNI

The use of MNI has received perhaps the most attention in recent years. The calculation of a minimum number of individuals is usually undertaken in the attempt to facilitate comparison of the relative abundances of different taxa or assemblages which have different taphonomic histories. In this way, it may circumvent the problem of differential fragmentation. An initial set of difficulties emerges with the multitude of ways which have been proposed for actually counting MNIs, many of which are highly idiosyncratic. This, coupled with the fact that few investigators explicitly state their criteria for the identification of individuals, seriously undermines the comparative utility of MNI counts.

The most important characteristic to recognize about MNI is its relationship with sample size (Grayson 1984). MNI is related to sample size in much the same way as richness in that as the number of bones identified to a taxon increases, the number of individuals which can be identified, based on the recurrence of body parts, increases logarithmically. The effect is that the relative importance of rare taxa may be overestimated, while MNIs of taxa at higher sample sizes are almost certainly underestimates.

Beyond these problems, there is the basic question of

Table 4 (Continued).

ASSEMBLAGE	Cattle	Ovicapr.	Pig	Horse	Dog	Red Deer	Wild Pig	Roe Deer	Aurochs
31	2238	273	977	0	33	556	71	6	0
32	255	194	250	3	36	69	9	15	0
33	1991	1277	3628	312	79	1695	842	303	44
34	729	184	266	2	16	109	12	9	40
35	1054	188	1556	0	692	997	56	22	2
36	219	36	68	0	3	1	7	1	0
37	343	20	98	69	1	28	21	3	0
38	147	134	111	0	6	0	0	2	0
39	302	51	184	0	11	0	0	1	7
40	315	92	244	0	3	1	4	1	0
41	357	222	941	0	198	8849	1835	1612	1908
42	3825	3867	1069	0	332	2641	1076	387	0
43	83	119	101	2	9	31	1	7	0
44	736	261	1560	0	5	223	38	8	5
45	903	364	319	4	27	122	41	8	0
46	650	225	209	1	5	24	29	0	0
47	183	78	113	2	8	247	21	5	2
48	176	1	15	0	1	252	11	3	56
49	1683	372	2858	100	22	4182	357	408	121
50	3064	570	364	127	163	262	6	31	1
51	1568	793	405	26	105	38	27	66	12
52	106	44	35	22	2	2	3	1	1
53	1335	207	464	0	83	1136	478	368	420
54	89	49	51	0	0	26	0	6	3
55	523	122	59	0	0	136	16	24	144
56	1292	412	421	0	158	479	114	21	11
57	2551	545	866	23	794	6760	1194	233	181
58	717	517	178	1	540	1105	296	43	34
59	214	122	325	436	305	285	271	57	13

whether or not MNI represents a class of information which is intrinsically more meaningful than simple bone counts. In almost all cases, MNIs are clearly underestimates of the number of individuals originally present if, indeed, an assemblage was derived from a collection of complete individuals in the first place. An MNI estimate is certainly no closer to a representation of the "true" original population, nor is it necessarily more accurate in its reflection of the relative contribution of particular taxa to an assemblage.

Bone Weight

The use of bone weight for quantifying faunal assemblages has been harshly criticized in the American literature (eg. Casteel 1978; Klein and Cruz-Uribe 1984), and only incompletely used in the European. Bone weights have been most frequently used to calculate meat quantities and the contributions of various taxa to the subsistence economies of particular sites. Most analyses follow some variation of Kubasiewicz's method, which recognized the allometric relationship between bone weight and body weight in an individual (Kubasiewicz 1956). In the simplest application, bone weight is multiplied by an empirically derived factor to calculate the amount of meat which would have been associated with the bone.

Criticisms have surrounded the particular factor used (Casteel 1978), as well as the fact that the technique doesn't provide any idea of the number of animals or taxa represented in the assemblage (Matolcsi 1970). Such dietary reconstructions must always depend on additional knowledge from archaeological remains - eg. duration of occupation, number of occupants, knowledge of other dietary components. As has been shown in the dietary reconstructions presented in Chapter 3, interpretations are not always straightforward even when these parameters are known.

Additional criticisms of the analytical use of bone weights have focused on the instability of density and weight in many archaeological deposits: diagenetic processes can increase or decrease absolute values. Realistically, this does not present such a problem when only relative quantities from similar recovery contexts are considered and compared. Furthermore, once the notion of converting bone weights into meat weights is discarded, weight emerges as a measure of relative abundance in some ways superior to NISP or MNI. Fragmentation is ignored in the comparison of bone weights among different taxa, and the dependence on repetition of skeletal parts inherent in MNI calculations is removed. Given these obvious advantages, it is surprising

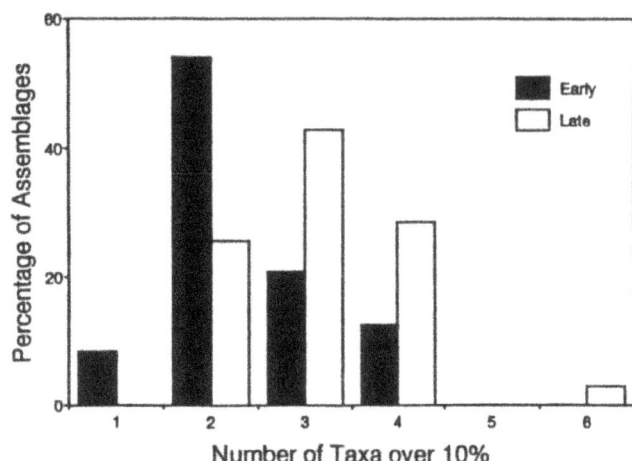

Figure 10. Histogram of taxonomic evenness.

that bone weights are so inconsistently reported and infrequently used. Their major disadvantage in the context of this analysis is that, even when reported, bone weights have rarely been broken down into useful analytical categories in same way as NISP.

These three methods of quantification each have their own set of advantages and disadvantages, and are best used in concert to explore the individual characteristics of each faunal assemblage. NISP is at present the measure most often reported in the literature, and is used in this investigation of taxonomic abundance primarily for this reason. An unfortunate consequence of this decision has been the forced exclusion of a few major works in which only MNI was reported (eg. Hescheler and Rüeger 1942; Higham 1966; Sakellaridis 1979).

It is obvious from the discussion of richness in the preceding chapter that many taxa appear only rarely in the analyzed assemblages, and can be excluded from consideration at this point. A collection of domestic and wild animals was chosen that could reasonably be expected to appear in most, if not all, assemblages. A total of 10 species have been selected: six domesticates and four wild animals. The list of animals used includes those taxa

discussed in Chapter 4: cattle, sheep and goat, pig, aurochs, wild pig, red deer. In addition, three other taxa which are often present, though usually in very low frequencies, are included: horse, dog, and roe deer. As in the diversity analyses, totals of cattle and pigs have been adjusted to include bones identified as *Bos* sp. and *Sus* sp. Sheep and goat will again be combined. Table 4 presents the number of specimens identified to these nine taxa for each of the 59 Neolithic assemblages. The only additional manipulation of these values was to sum NISP across these nine taxa and calculate the percent representation for each taxon within each assemblage.

Dominance of Taxa/Evenness

The results of the diversity analyses suggested that differences in the relative contributions of individual taxa, or evenness, may have contributed significantly to the observed differences between early and late Neolithic assemblages. This can be further investigated by a comparison of the representation of the nine major taxa in grouped early and late assemblages. Figure 10 shows the number of taxa which are present in frequencies higher than 10% for both periods. This figure illustrates the fact that early assemblages are characteristically dominated by only a few taxa, frequently two, with the remaining taxa present in low proportions. In comparison, the late Neolithic pattern appears somewhat different: assemblages often have three or more taxa contributing at least 10% each to the total sample. In general, the pattern identified in the diversity analyses of the exploitation of a broader range of animals in the later period is reflected even in this smaller taxonomic spectrum.

Species Abundance

Figures 11 through 14 present histograms of the relative abundances of the major taxa - cattle, ovicaprines, pig and red deer - for the early and late Neolithic assemblages. It is evident from the graphs of cattle and ovicaprines that these two taxa often account for high proportions of the NISP in the early Neolithic assemblages

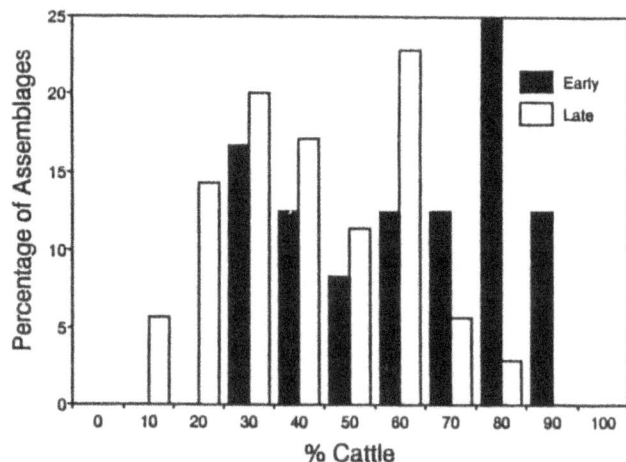

Figure 11. Histogram of cattle frequencies in Neolithic assemblages.

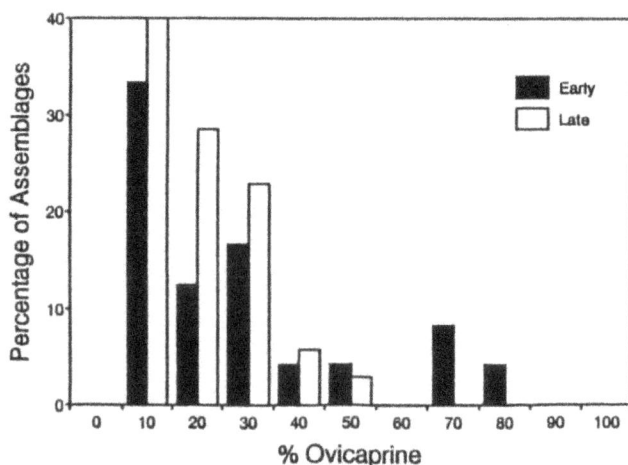

Figure 12. Histogram of ovicaprine frequencies in Neolithic assemblages.

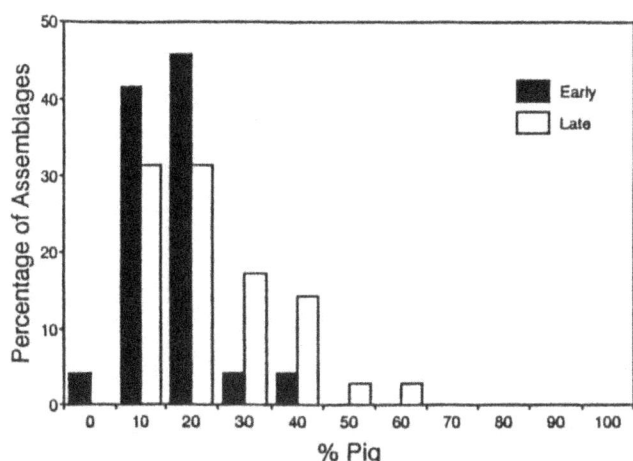

Figure 13. Histogram of pig frequencies in Neolithic assemblages.

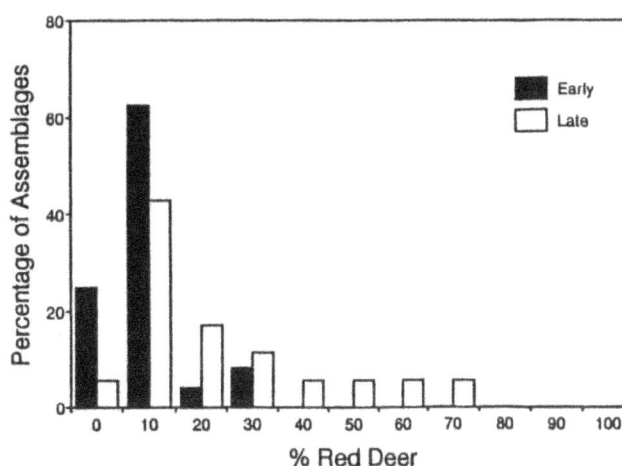

Figure 14. Histogram of red deer frequencies in Neolithic assemblages.

while their contributions in the later sample of sites is somewhat lower. Late Neolithic assemblages tend to have higher proportions of both pig and red deer. These distributions give some idea of which taxa are most dominant. However it is still not clear how early and late assemblages differ when multiple taxa are considered, or if the frequencies of taxa covary in any way.

Variance and Covariance Among Taxa

Principal components analysis has been used to identify the taxa which account for the most variance within each group of sites, and to investigate patterns of covariance among these taxa. This technique permits a simple summary of the information contained in the data by way of mathematical transformations of the raw variables - in this case, %NISP of each taxon in each assemblage. Principal components analysis was selected as a means of achieving economy of representation, and not in an attempt to represent the structure of taxonomic covariance in terms of a hypothetical causal model, as in true factor analysis (Kim and Mueller 1978:18).

The groups of early and late Neolithic assemblages have

been analyzed separately. Only components associated with eigenvalues greater than 1 are considered here. Tables 5 and 6 show the loadings for each taxon along the first three components, along with the percent variation explained by each component for early and late, respectively. In the early Neolithic, the first three components account for just over 73% of the total variance; in the later Neolithic, the first three components account for about 67% of the variance. All values given here refer to unrotated loadings. Varimax rotation was carried out in some additional runs, but did not appear to change loading values appreciably, nor contribute to the interpretability of components.

In both groups, the first component basically represents a domestic-wild dichotomy with wild taxa loading with high positive values. There are some differences in the actual sequence of specific taxa along this component, as well as the loadings of particular domesticates. For example, in the early assemblages, ovicaprines and cattle achieve only low negative values; in the late Neolithic, cattle loads with a moderately high value of -.75.

Table 5. Loadings of major taxa on first three components for early Neolithic assemblages.

COMPONENT LOADINGS	1	2	3
Red Deer	0.896	0.011	0.163
Wild Pig	0.805	-0.069	-0.226
Dog	0.795	0.050	0.022
Aurochs	0.763	0.066	-0.053
Roe Deer	0.538	0.060	0.629
Cattle	-0.393	0.846	-0.210
Ovicaprines	-0.404	-0.785	0.424
Horse	0.030	0.675	0.376
Pig	0.285	-0.287	-0.710
Percent of Total Variance Explained	37.269	20.955	14.955

53

Table 6. Loadings of major taxa on first three components for late Neolithic assemblages.

COMPONENT LOADINGS	1	2	3
Red Deer	0.860	0.138	0.152
Wild Pig	0.817	-0.255	0.085
Cattle	-0.756	0.289	0.475
Roe Deer	0.618	0.178	-0.552
Ovicaprines	-0.589	0.010	-0.289
Aurochs	0.527	0.579	-0.009
Dog	0.206	-0.739	0.034
Horse	0.088	-0.681	0.262
Pig	-0.440	-0.251	-0.690
Percent of Total Variance Explained	35.865	17.868	13.229

The next component is somewhat more difficult to interpret, and identifies those taxa which contribute most to variability among assemblages once basic wild-domestic differences have been accounted for. These taxa can be relatively clearly identified for the early Neolithic. Variability is distributed along a dimension with cattle at the high positive end, and ovicaprines at the high negative end. In the late Neolithic group, the second component is identified by moderately high loadings of two low-frequency domesticates: dog and horse.

In the third component, a moderately high negative loading is associated with the same taxon for both early and late assemblages: domestic pig. Also in both groups, roe deer shows up with moderate positive or negative loadings (ie. above absolute value of .5). Its association along this axis with pig is not easily interpretable, rather, the loading of this taxon is probably best understood as a function of its low relative abundance in both groups of assemblages.

The patterns of variance in early and late assemblages share some common features. In both groups, the most important dimension of variability involves the opposition of wild and domestic taxa. Subtle differences in the loadings of individual taxa suggest the relative abundances of wild taxa contribute slightly more to the total variability in the early Neolithic sample, while there is somewhat more variability associated with the major domesticates as well as wild taxa in the later group.

A major difference is that while the second component is made up of dominant taxa in the early group, it comprises low-frequency taxa in the later group. This reflects the greater uniformity in the underlying structure of early Neolithic assemblages: the negative covariance of cattle and ovicaprines appears to be a consistent feature at almost all sites. In contrast, the later Neolithic assemblages are characterized by relatively high and equal frequencies of multiple taxa, so that those taxa which account for the most variability in actuality represent fairly small and unequal contributions to the assem-

blages. A similar phenomenon can be seen in the third component. Pig represents a relatively low frequency taxon in the early Neolithic, while it is often present in higher frequencies in the later period.

The results of the principal components analysis complement the information already derived from the investigation of diversity. It can be seen that the more focused or less diverse nature of the early Neolithic assemblages can be attributed primarily to the dominance of domestic animals, in particular, to fluctuations in the relative abundances of cattle and ovicaprines within individual assemblages. The greater diversity of the late Neolithic assemblages results from the slight increase in the use of wild animals, and a reliance on different combinations of multiple taxa in moderately high frequencies. These emerging patterns of covariance can be further investigated by comparisons of the relative abundances of particular taxa to each other, and to the measure of hetero-

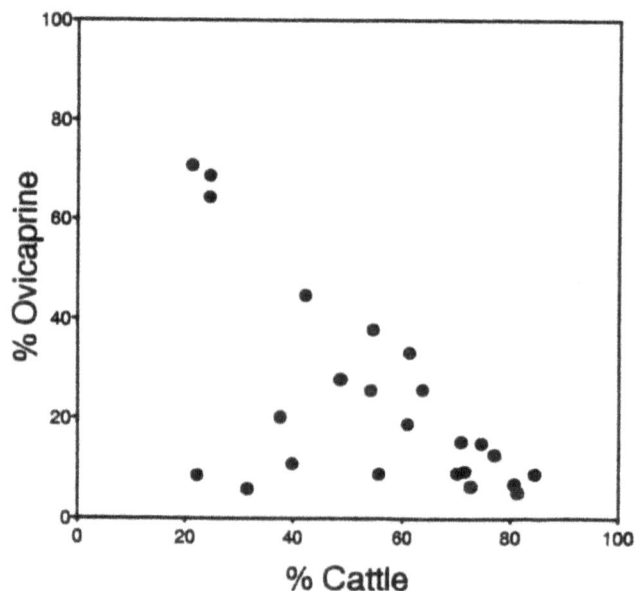

Figure 15. Plot of percent cattle and percent ovicaprines for early Neolithic assemblages.

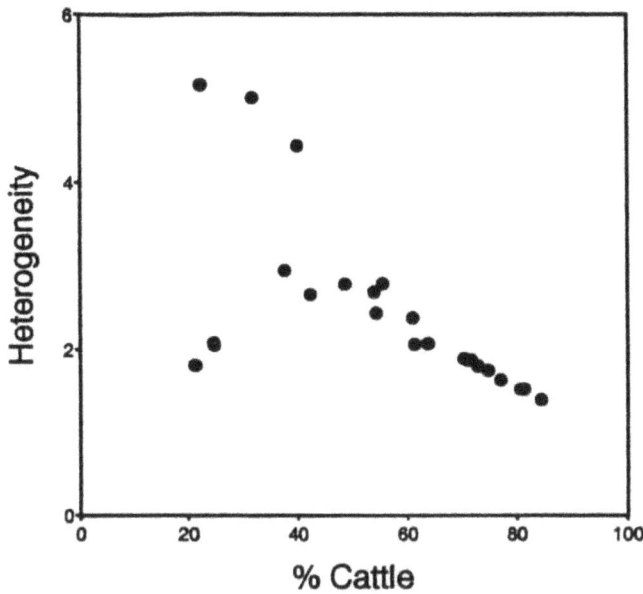

Figure 16. Plot of percent cattle and heterogeneity for early Neolithic.

geneity used in Chapter 6.

Early Neolithic

The contribution of cattle relative to sheep and goat has been isolated as an important component of variability for early Neolithic assemblages. Figure 15 shows a scatterplot of %NISP for these two taxa. Most of the assemblages fall in a linear band, illustrating a strong negative relationship in relative frequencies. Assemblages which have high proportions of sheep and goat have correspondingly low frequencies of cattle, and vice versa. There is a small group of four sites (3, 5, 19, 20) located in the bottom left portion of the plot which appear to have low frequencies of both these major taxa.

Figure 16 presents a scatterplot of %NISP cattle for the early Neolithic assemblages plotted against their heterogeneity values. The relationship between frequencies of ovicaprine and cattle is clearly mirrored in this plot. Most of the assemblages fall in a curvilinear band in the lower portion of this figure. The assemblages in the left-hand segment of this band are those shown in Figure 15 to have high proportions of sheep and goat. These assemblages are also characterized by relatively low heterogeneity values. As we move toward the right, and assemblages dominated by cattle, the heterogeneity scores increase up to a value of about three, then decrease again as %NISP for cattle approaches 80%.

Of the four sites identified as different in Figure 15, three of them (3, 19 and 20) are also set apart in Figure 16 by their high heterogeneity scores. Assemblage 5 appears more similar to the assemblages in the cattle-ovicaprine continuum, although it also shows a slightly higher heterogeneity value. Inspection of Figure 17 reveals the source of these differences for these assemblages. Sites 3, 19 and 20 all contain 20% or more red deer bones. They also constitute the only assemblages in

which four different taxa account for 10% or more of the total NISP - hence their greater diversity. Site 5 shows relatively high abundances of three major taxa, including a strikingly high proportion of pig.

These exceptions aside, most of the variability in the relative abundances of major taxa in the early Neolithic can be accommodated within one pattern. This involves a strategy of cattle and ovicaprine exploitation, in which a few sites show an extreme concentration on either ovicaprines or cattle while the majority show some combination of these taxa. In a little over half of the sites, assemblages are composed of 50% to 80% cattle, and 10% to 40% ovicaprines.

It is difficult to relate these percentages to actual numbers of stock, but some generalizations about the use of these taxa follow from the discussion of parameters of animal production presented in Chapter 4. The first thing to note is that the two major taxa are relatively compatible for combined management. Cattle and ovicaprines can often graze together, though local ecological parameters often favor the combination of cattle with only one of these taxa (ie. sheep or goat) (Dahl and Hjort 1976). The distribution of suitable forage in Neolithic forests may well have necessitated the combinations of domestic animals with as little interspecific competition as possible. However, given the problems of identifiability of ovicaprines, and our limited knowledge regarding grazing competition in mixed deciduous forests, the preference of one ovicaprine over another is impossible to predict or test.

The fact that the relative abundances of these taxa are negatively correlated may be related to a number of factors. Both cattle and ovicaprines can be expensive to maintain in large numbers, and their combination may only be possible with certain proportions to minimize conflict in labor associated with their keeping. This is especially true if either taxon is exploited for more than one body product, for instance, meat and milk. When productivity in terms of milk and/or meat yield is taken into

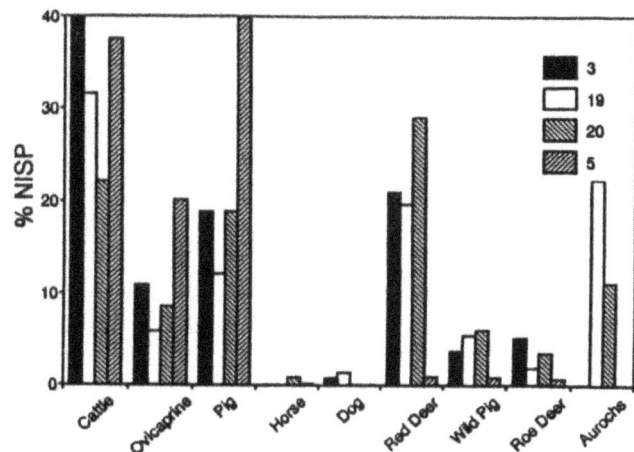

Figure 17. Representation of major taxa at sites 3, 19, 20 and 5.

consideration, it is obvious that cattle usually represent the more substantial contributors to the economy. The importance of smaller numbers of ovicaprines in this context may be related to minimizing the risk associated with a focus on large animals with a longer reproductive cycle. Sheep and goats can both increase their numbers rapidly, and may provide meat or milk at periods when cattle are less productive. Sites with extremes in either taxon may represent different functional aspects with regard to their total economic strategy, or ones at which the local environment allowed one taxon to flourish at the expense of the other. Alternatively, these assemblages could represent different positions along a boom and bust cycle of combined cattle and ovicaprine use, as seen, for instance, in modern African groups combining large and small-stock management. Among the Ariaal Rendille, periodic loss of cattle through disease, raiding or debt may be compensated for by temporary concentration on sheep or goat herding. The relatively rapid acquisition of animal wealth through small stock keeping can then lead to the acquisition of more expensive large stock (Fratkin 1988).

The picture which emerges from this discussion of taxonomic abundance in the early Neolithic is one of a largely shared strategy exhibiting a narrow range of variability. At the moment, it is unclear how the few sites which do not share this pattern should be explained. Assemblages 3,19, and 20, set apart by their highly diverse assemblages and use of wild animals, seem to represent a qualitatively different strategy perhaps related to their shared environment. Assemblage 5, with its abundance of pig, is equally difficult to relate to any additional assemblages in this period.

Late Neolithic

Unlike the case in the early Neolithic, it is not entirely

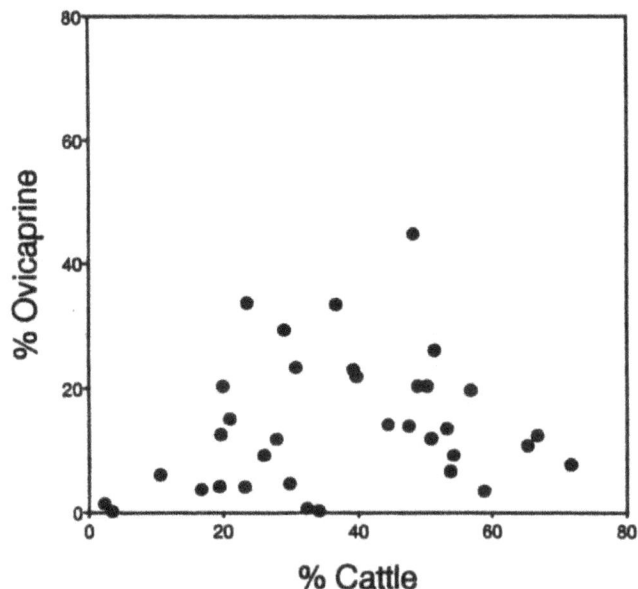

Figure 18. Plot of percent cattle and percent ovicaprines in late Neolithic assemblages.

clear from the results of the diversity and principal components analyses which taxa, if any, covary within the later Neolithic assemblages. A good place to start is by investigating some of the relationships identified among taxa in the early group of sites.

Figure 18 shows a scatterplot of %NISP for cattle and ovicaprines from late Neolithic assemblages. The strong negative relationship identified for the early assemblages is not obvious here, rather, it appears that the assemblages may be split into at least two groups based on these taxa. In the lower left quadrant of the plot, assemblages 25, 26, 27, 33, 35, 41, 44, 47, 48, 49, 53, 57, 58, and 59 constitute one group, while the remaining 21 sites can be considered a second group.

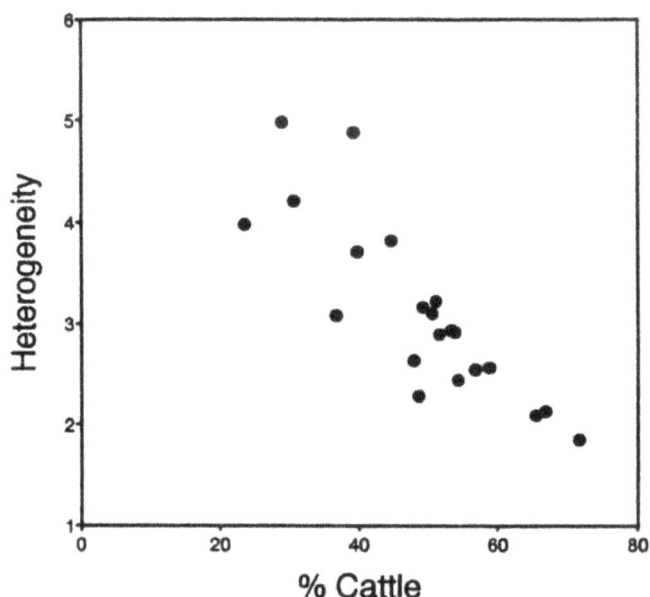

Figure 19. Plot of percent cattle and heterogeneity for 21 late Neolithic assemblages.

This second and larger group of assemblages appears to show a relationship between cattle and ovicaprine representation similar to that noted for the early Neolithic. In the early assemblages, the nature of this relationship became clear in the plot of percent cattle and heterogeneity. Figure 19 plots these two observations for the late Neolithic. It should be recalled that a curvilinear pattern in the lower portion of the plot was visible in the corresponding figure for early assemblages. The relationship between these two variables in the later samples is a linear negative one. There are a few sites of low heterogeneity which appear to focus on cattle, as in the early period. However, the early Neolithic pattern of a spectrum of cattle and ovicaprine combinations within a narrow range of heterogeneity values cannot be traced. Instead, there are a number of assemblages with high heterogeneity, containing relatively small proportions of cattle. This suggests that multiple taxa contribute in low frequencies to the greater heterogeneity of these assemblages. This contrasts with the majority of early Neolithic sites, in which the heterogeneity of assemblages has been

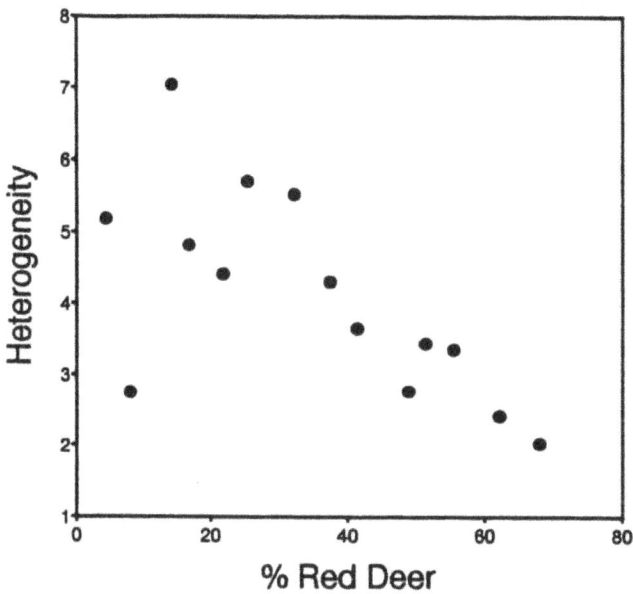

Figure 20. Plot of percent red deer and heterogeneity for 14 late Neolithic assemblages.

seen to be primarily a product of the relative abundances of only two taxa.

Heterogeneity values associated with the smaller group of 14 assemblages appear to be related to the relative abundance of a different taxon: red deer (Figure 20). Most of the points in Figure 20 fall in a linear band showing a negative relationship between percent red deer and heterogeneity. As in the case with the previous group, there are a number of assemblages of low heterogeneity in which a single taxon, red deer in this case, accounts for 50% or more of the total NISP. Sites with higher heterogeneity values of about 4 and above contain relatively smaller proportions of red deer. There are a few assemblages of low to medium heterogeneity (B<4) in which neither cattle nor red deer are the most abundant taxa. These include assemblage 44 in Figure 20 and assemblage 38 and possibly 29 and 40 in Figure 19. This suggests the presence of at least one other taxon which should account for relatively high proportions of NISP at

these sites. In addition, sites 26, 33 and 35, fairly heterogeneous assemblages, do not fit the linear pattern identified in Figure 20 all that well, again indicating the presence of one or more additional taxa in relatively high frequencies.

Figure 21 gives the %NISP for the nine major taxa at the less heterogeneous sites: 29, 38, 40, and 44. Two of the assemblages are dominated by two taxa: cattle and ovicaprines in the case of site 29, pig and cattle in assemblage 44. The other two assemblages are dominated by cattle, with ovicaprines and pigs as additional important taxa. A similar bar graph in Figure 22 presents %NISP for the major taxa in assemblages 26, 33, and 35. Pig represents the most abundant taxon at each of these sites, with various combinations of two or three other taxa also appearing in high frequencies.

The higher relative abundance of pig in late Neolithic sites is shown in both of these graphs, as well as by the high loading of this taxon on the third component of the principal components analysis. Pig, cattle and red deer, then, can be identified as the most important taxa among the sample of late Neolithic sites considered here, with a number of assemblages dominated by each taxon. In addition to these taxa, ovicaprines remain important at a number of sites although, with the exception of a few assemblages like 29 and 38, they appear in relatively lower frequencies than in the early Neolithic. Their presence and abundance seem to be governed by factors other than the corresponding proportion of cattle in the assemblage, as is the case in the early Neolithic. In a final attempt to illustrate the relationships among major taxa in the late Neolithic assemblages, the relative contributions of the three main taxa are shown in a triangle graph in Figure 23. The percentages have been recalculated for this graph so that the frequencies for the three taxa sum to 100. It is clear that, while certain assemblages are dominated by each of these three different taxa, it is difficult to identify discrete groups with similar proportions of these major taxa.

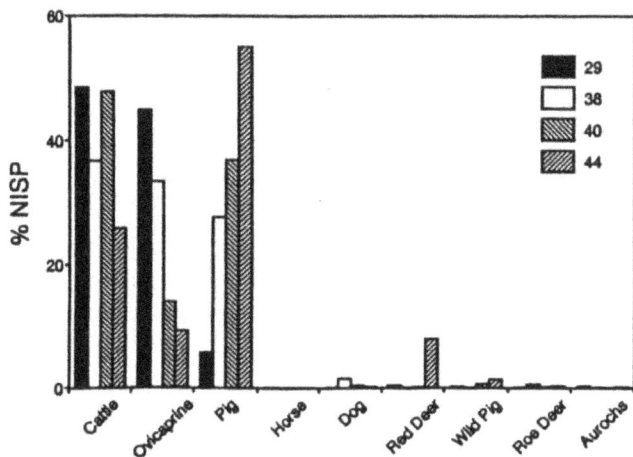

Figure 21. Representation of major taxa in assemblages 29, 38, 40, and 44.

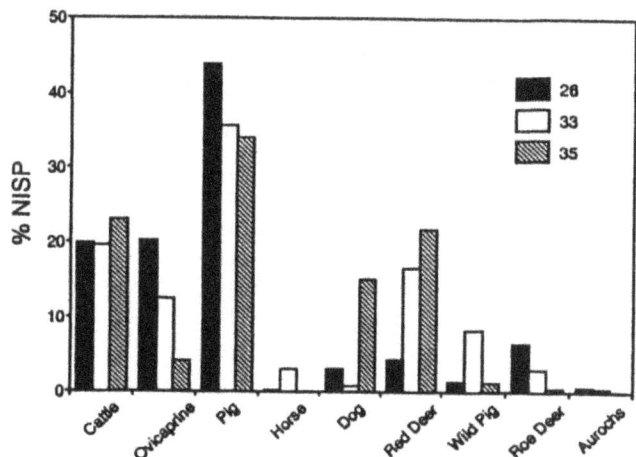

Figure 22. Representation of major taxa in assemblages 26, 33, and 35.

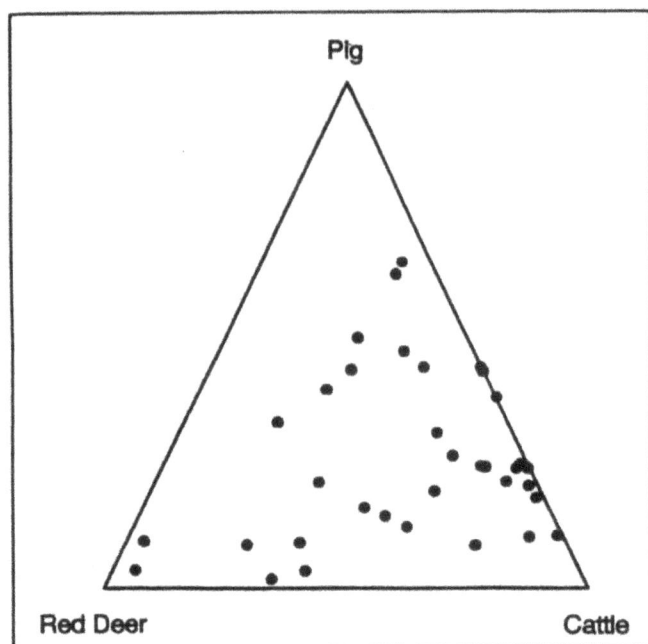

Figure 23. Triangle graph of percent cattle, percent red deer and percent pig for late Neolithic assemblages.

As in the early Neolithic, a number of inferences may be made about the management and combination of particular taxa. About one-third of the late Neolithic faunal assemblages (11) are dominated by cattle (ie. cattle contribute 50% or more to the total site NISP). One-half of these assemblages (five) have an additional 10% to 30% of their bones identified as sheep or goat. Domestic pig is the third most abundant taxon at these sites, and also occurs as the second most abundant taxon in those assemblages with fewer ovicaprines (frequencies range from about 15% to 35%). This group of sites basically represents a continuation of the pattern identified for the early Neolithic, with the addition of higher frequencies of domestic pig. Ovicaprines and pigs seem to be interchangeable as second- or third-ranked taxa, which may perhaps indicate their functional similarity in the productive systems in question. The great reproductive capacity of pigs has already been noted in Chapter 4. This, plus the minimal costs associated with keeping small numbers of pigs, makes them an ideal secondary resource in situations where the major taxon (cattle) may be more unstable.

Pig can be considered the dominant taxon in five or six assemblages, although it only accounts for more than 50% of the total NISP in one instance. In the other cases, pig is the most abundant taxon, contributing from 30% to 44% to site totals. All of these assemblages also contain 20% to 30% cattle, and generally another 15% to 25% of some other single taxon. One problem in interpreting the relative taxonomic abundances in such assemblages is the degree to which the %NISP truly reflects an emphasis on pig as the major resource. In general, when pig appears as the first-ranked taxon, there is a more even representation of other (usually domestic) taxa. This is indicated by

the heterogeneity indices for these assemblages, which, with the exception of assemblage 44, all have values greater than 4. This observation may be related to two aspects of pig management already identified in Chapter 4. The first relates to the rather unique ability of the pig to maintain and increase its numbers with little conscious effort on the part of humans. One consequence of this is that pig numbers can, in short order, grow out of control. As noted among the Tsembaga, large numbers of pigs are often difficult to control, and may wreak havoc in villages and fields if their numbers are not reduced (Rappaport 1968). This suggests that it may be advantageous to maintain relatively small numbers of this taxon, regardless of how much cultural significance may be attached to pig-keeping. The second aspect of pig management relates to the fact that pigs, while a good source of meat protein and animal fat, offer little else in term of body products. The consistent presence of cattle and sheep or goats in these sites with high pig frequencies may be inferential evidence of the exploitation of these latter taxa for purposes other than meat protein.

Finally, there is the group of assemblages in which red deer is the most abundant taxon. This includes eight assemblages with red deer occurring in frequencies from 32% to 68%. Six of these sites are ones in which wild taxa in general (including red deer) account for over 50% of the total NISP. This suggests that, rather than representing sites in which red deer procurement (or extermination) was the only concern, these assemblages indicate a primary focus on hunting rather than domestic animal keeping. Red deer may simply have been the most abundant wild taxon in the vicinity. When domestic taxa are present, they consist of low to moderate percentages of cattle or pig.

Two sites with abundant red deer (47 and 58) are ones in which domestic taxa outnumber wild taxa in the assemblage as a whole. Although frequencies of red deer are 37% and 32%, respectively, the remaining 60% of these assemblages includes cattle, ovicaprines and pig or dog. In contrast to the other six assemblages, these sites appear to have focused primarily on domestic animals, with red deer an important additional resource. It is interesting to note that the heterogeneity scores associated with these assemblages are similar to those of the early Neolithic sites with high heterogeneity (3, 19 and 20), indicating a similar composition in terms of richness and evenness.

Variance and Covariance of Assemblages

Emphasis in this chapter so far has been on identifying patterns of covariance among major taxa within the two groups of sites. In this final section, the covariance among assemblages with similar taxonomic composition is considered. The aim here is to investigate whether or not sites with similar composition can be related to aspects of cultural, regional or environmental variability.

K-means cluster analysis was used to create groups of

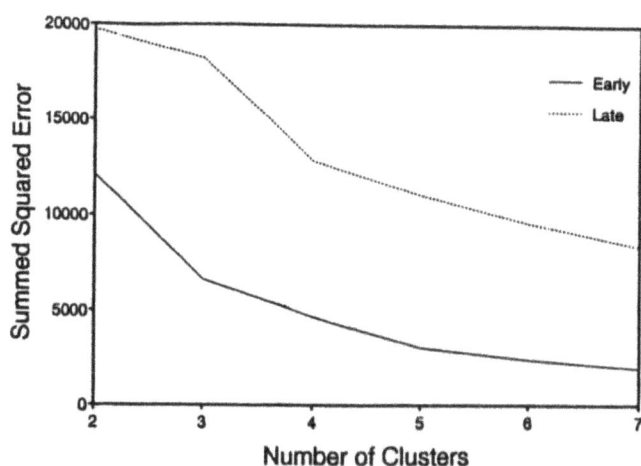

Figure 24. Plot of SSE at different cluster solutions for early and late Neolithic assemblages.

specification of a particular number of clusters for any desired solution. The number of clusters appropriate for an analysis may be derived either from a priori knowledge of associations among observations in the data, or from an investigation of the reduction in the summed square error from a series of analyses in which a succession of cluster solutions have been chosen. In this latter technique, the SSE is plotted for a number of cluster solutions, from two to N. A line connecting these points helps to visually assess the point at which SSE has been reduced to such a level that increasingly higher cluster solutions do not significantly contribute to a further reduction in error (Aldenderfer and Blashfield 1984)

sites with similar proportions of major taxa for both the early and late Neolithic. Unlike non-iterative, hierarchical clustering procedures, K-means analysis requires the

Figure 24 presents the SSE plotted for solutions of two to seven clusters for both the early and late Neolithic. It is apparent that a three-cluster solution accounts for the most variability among assemblages for the early Neolithic, while a four-cluster solution seems more appropriate for the group of later Neolithic assemblages. It

Table 7. Three-cluster solution for early Neolithic assemblages.

CLUSTER 1 Sites 1, 2, 4, 6, 9, 10, 11, 12, 13, 15, 16, 18, 21, 22, 23, 24	MINIMUM	MEAN	MAXIMUM	ST.DEV.
Cattle	48.71	67.69	84.34	10.61
Ovicaprines	5.12	16.64	37.78	9.98
Pig	0.00	10.14	21.29	6.21
Horse	0.00	0.56	3.41	0.96
Dog	0.00	0.07	0.46	0.14
Red Deer	0.00	1.34	6.82	1.82
Wild Pig	0.00	1.14	5.96	1.49
Roe Deer	0.00	0.84	4.02	1.03
Aurochs	0.00	1.58	15.28	3.65
CLUSTER 2 Sites 7, 8, 14, 17				
Cattle	21.24	28.21	42.39	8.30
Ovicaprines	44.57	62.11	70.80	10.39
Pig	3.32	6.86	9.36	2.24
Horse	0.00	0.07	0.27	0.12
Dog	0.00	0.00	0.00	0.00
Red Deer	0.00	0.32	0.82	0.35
Wild Pig	0.00	0.62	1.90	0.78
Roe Deer	0.00	1.34	2.99	1.36
Aurochs	0.00	0.48	1.17	0.43
CLUSTER 3 Sites 3, 5, 19, 20				
Cattle	22.22	32.80	39.86	6.82
Ovicaprines	5.82	11.35	20.16	5.39
Pig	12.08	22.38	39.82	10.44
Horse	0.00	0.24	0.85	0.36
Dog	0.00	0.52	1.34	0.56
Red Deer	0.88	17.66	29.06	10.33
Wild Pig	0.79	3.94	5.98	2.01
Roe Deer	0.69	2.74	5.07	1.66
Aurochs	0.00	8.37	22.37	9.27

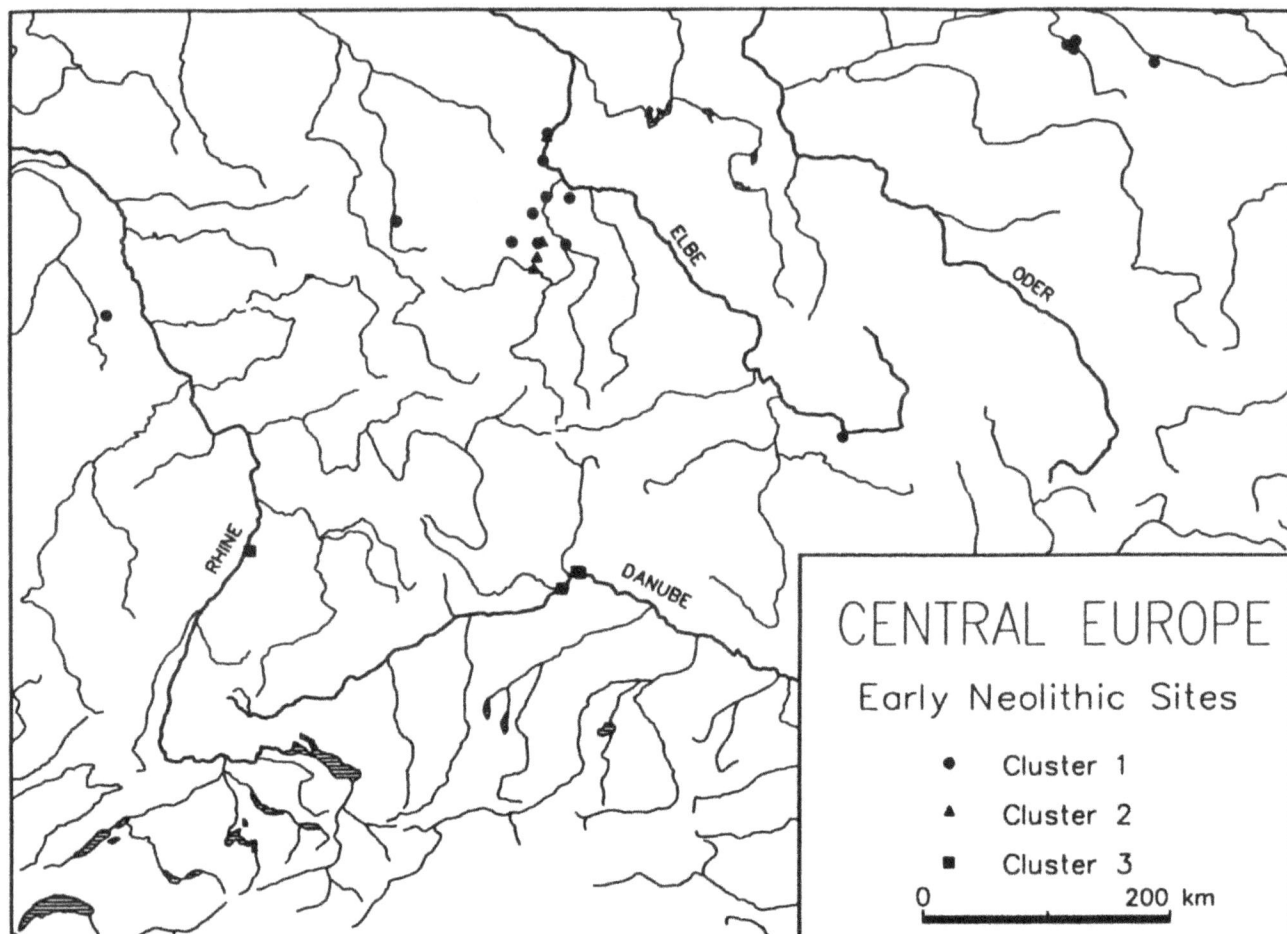

Figure 25. Geographical distribution of assemblages in each cluster for the early Neolithic.

is important to stress that clusters formed in this way are not necessarily considered to be direct representations of independent economic strategies. Rather, their purpose in this context is a heuristic one, in which groups of assemblages with similar taxonomic composition will be compared to more traditional spatial and cultural classifications.

Early Neolithic

Table 7 lists the groups of sites which resulted from a three-cluster solution for the early Neolithic. Next to each cluster are the statistics for the various taxa which determine group membership. Figure 25 shows the geographical distribution of the assemblages belonging in each cluster.

The three clusters identified by similarities in assemblage composition can be related to the results of the taxonomic analyses already presented. Group 1 includes some of the sites in which cattle and ovicaprines were identified as the major taxa, primarily those in which cattle are dominant.

These include many of the sites from central Germany, as well as assemblages recovered considerably further west, like Müddersheim, and further east, like Brzecz Kujawski. This reflects a common system of faunal exploitation in the early Neolithic over a widespread area of northern central Europe. It can be seen from the statistics

on the %NISP for each taxon that animals other than cattle and ovicaprines are frequently absent, or present in low and variable frequencies. It is interesting to note that the taxa which, after cattle and ovicaprines, contribute the most to assemblages in this group are pig and aurochs. The presence of pig in these assemblages may relate to some of the factors cited above for increasing pig use in the later period. The presence of aurochs as the most abundant wild taxon in this group possibly relates to the continued cattle domestication which has been suggested for the Bandkeramik period (Müller 1964; Nobis 1984).

The second group derived from the cluster analysis consists of the ovicaprine-dominated assemblages discussed in the taxonomic section. The accompanying statistics show that, in addition to moderate amounts of cattle, low frequencies of pig also occur in these assemblages. All four of these assemblages come from a relatively restricted area of central Germany (Müller 1964), suggesting they may represent an emphasis on ovicaprines facilitated by local environmental conditions. This could be supported by the fact that roe deer (generally considered an open-land taxon) appears as the most important wild taxon in this group, based on mean %NISP. Interestingly, this group includes assemblages dated to both early and late periods within the LBK occupation of the region, which would seem to argue against the inter-

Table 8. Four-cluster solution for early Neolithic assemblages.

CLUSTER 1 Sites 28, 29, 30, 31, 34, 36, 37, 38, 39, 40, 42, 45, 46, 50, 51, 54, 55, 56	MINIMUM	MEAN	MAXIMUM	ST.DEV.
Cattle	28.98	50.98	71.75	10.32
Ovicaprines	3.43	18.03	44.87	10.03
Pig	5.65	17.49	36.97	8.52
Horse	0.00	1.41	11.84	3.37
Dog	0.00	1.63	5.43	1.50
Red Deer	0.00	6.75	21.68	7.04
Wild Pig	0.00	1.67	8.15	1.91
Roe Deer	0.00	0.90	2.93	0.96
Aurochs	0.00	1.15	14.06	3.12
CLUSTER 2 Sites 25, 27, 41, 47, 48, 49, 53, 57, 58				
Cattle	2.24	20.74	34.17	11.08
Ovicaprines	0.10	4.63	15.07	5.04
Pig	1.68	8.97	28.29	8.17
Horse	0.00	0.17	0.99	0.31
Dog	0.00	2.94	15.74	4.86
Red Deer	25.30	46.93	67.89	13.23
Wild Pig	2.14	8.40	24.39	6.63
Roe Deer	0.21	3.13	10.12	3.42
Aurochs	0.28	4.09	11.98	4.76
CLUSTER 3 Site 59				
Cattle	10.55	10.55	10.55	0.00
Ovicaprines	6.02	6.02	6.02	0.00
Pig	16.03	16.03	16.03	0.00
Horse	21.50	21.50	21.50	0.00
Dog	15.04	15.04	15.04	0.00
Red Deer	14.05	14.05	14.05	0.00
Wild Pig	13.36	13.36	13.36	0.00
Roe Deer	2.81	2.81	2.81	0.00
Aurochs	0.64	0.64	0.64	0.00
CLUSTER 4 Sites 26, 32, 33, 43, 44				
Cattle	19.58	23.79	30.69	3.78
Ovicaprines	4.12	17.20	33.71	9.80
Pig	28.61	37.87	55.01	9.08
Horse	0.00	0.70	3.07	1.08
Dog	0.18	4.34	15.15	5.03
Red Deer	4.28	11.29	21.83	6.00
Wild Pig	0.28	2.26	8.28	2.72
Roe Deer	0.28	2.33	6.42	2.05
Aurochs	0.00	0.22	0.66	0.25

pretation of a gradual replacement of ovicaprines by pigs through time.

As already indicated in the taxonomic discussion, these two groups of assemblages should probably be considered as belonging to the same general pattern of animal use. Sites with high ovicaprine frequencies may merely indicate ecological or social conditions making it necessary or possible to keep more of these animals. Sites dominated by ovicaprines cannot be separated either geographically or temporally from the cattle-dominated ones in the first cluster, suggesting they are extremes within one behavioral system.

The third early Neolithic cluster comprises those assemblages with high heterogeneity values. These three sites, Hienheim, Regensburg-Kumpfmühl, and Regensburg-Pürkelgut, are spatially adjacent to each other, or at least

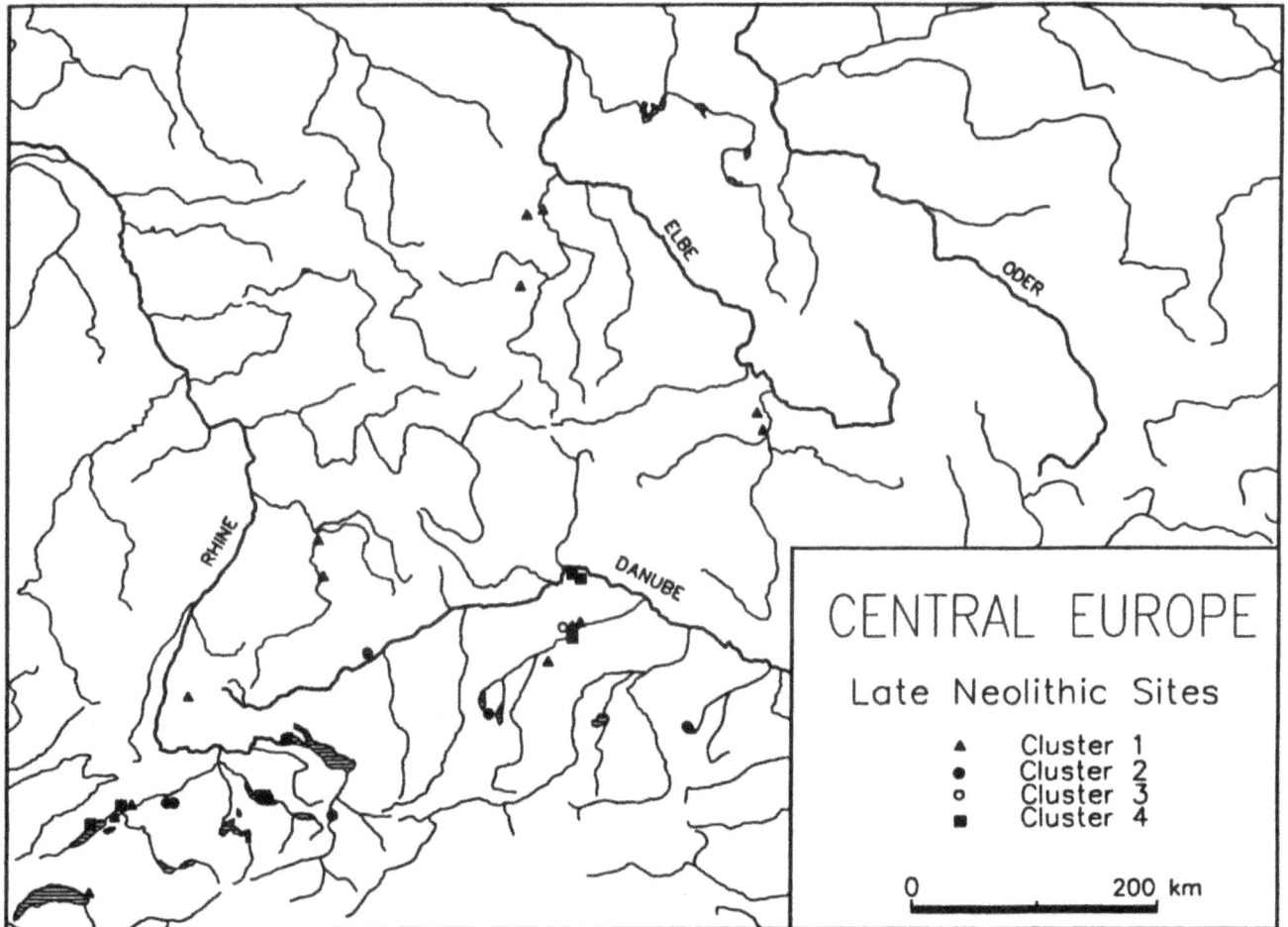

Figure 26. Geographical distribution of assemblages in each cluster for the late Neolithic.

closer to each other than they are to any of the other assemblages considered here. Hienheim seems to date to the later Bandkeramik occupation of the Danube valley near Kelheim (Modderman 1986). Regensburg-Kumpfmühl belongs to a regional variant of the Bavarian Neolithic, Oberlauterbach, which is partially contemporaneous with SBK or Rössen in neighboring areas. Oberlauterbach settlement seems to represent a continuation of the earlier Bandkeramik pattern (Bayerlein 1985), but ceramic traits show some additional influence from southeastern European groups (Petrasch 1986). Regensburg-Pürkelgut likewise contains remains from SBK and Oberlauterbach, or Bavarian Rössen (Boessneck 1958). In addition to their geographical location on the fringes of the Alpine foreland, then, these three sites also share a relatively late temporal placement within the early Neolithic (as defined here), which may be reflected in their faunal composition. It is difficult to say whether the character of these assemblages is due more to environmental, cultural or temporal factors. Additional faunal analyses from other early and middle Neolithic sites in this region must be undertaken before the economic focus of sites in this area can be discussed in any detail.

Late Neolithic

The four clusters derived from K-means analysis of the later Neolithic assemblages and the statistics related to cluster membership are given in Table 8. Three of the clusters basically represent the cattle-, red deer-, and pig-dominated assemblages identified in the taxonomic discussion. Their numbers have been expanded somewhat to include those assemblages whose membership was less obvious in the bivariate analyses presented above. A fourth group (cluster 3) comprises a single site, the Galgenberg (59), which is set apart by its unusually high frequencies of horse bones. The unique character of this assemblage is not yet fully understood, since the site has only been mentioned in brief field reports. However, a detailed comparison of the Galgenberg fauna to other late Neolithic assemblages suggests that, once the anomalous horse taxon is excluded from analysis, it most closely resembles those in cluster 3 which were grouped together by relatively high abundances of pig (Glass 1988). In effect, then, there are three main clusters based on taxonomic abundances which can be compared to cultural, temporal and regional classifications.

The most obvious place to begin is with an investigation of the geographical distributions of the various clusters. The approximate locations of late Neolithic assemblages are plotted in Figure 26. It can be seen that while sites from cluster 1 are located throughout the study area, the other groups are all restricted to the subtriangular region which extends from the Danube southward into the Alpine lake area. This points out the likelihood that some of the variability in the late Neolithic assemblages is of a

Table 9. Distribution of cluster assignments among late Neolithic archaeological cultures.

Cultures	Cluster 1	Cluster 2	Cluster 3&4	Total
Cortaillod	3	4	0	7
Michelsberg	2	0	0	2
Schussenried	2	1	0	3
Horgen	0	1	2	3
Auvernier-Lüscherz	1	0	1	2
Pfyn	2	1	0	3
Altheim	3	0	2	5
Baalberg	1	0	0	1
Mondsee	1	1	0	2
Polling	0	1	0	1
Rivnac	1	0	0	1
Bernberg	3	0	0	3
Cham	0	0	2	2
Total	19	9	7	35

regional nature, although there is still considerable overlap of taxonomic clusters within the Alpine foreland.

As pointed out at the start of this chapter, it is usually assumed that systems of animal keeping varied primarily due to cultural practices, either at the level of the archaeological culture, or at the broader scale of the cultural tradition or heritage. Table 9 provides a breakdown of the number of assemblages in each cluster for each archaeological culture. These have been grouped into eastern (Pfyn through Cham) and western (Cortaillod to Auvernier-Lüscherz) cultural spheres of influence using the interpretations of cultural affiliations presented in Chapter 3. It is apparent from this table that there is no clear association between the taxonomic clusters and the traditional cultural classifications. This illustrates the problems inherent in extrapolating an economic strategy for any archaeological culture solely from the taxonomic composition of a restricted number of assemblages.

A final explanation which has been put forward to account for variability in late Neolithic faunal assemblages pertains specifically to the assemblages associated in cluster 2 - those with high proportions of red deer and other wild fauna. The opposition of wild and domestic taxa has been identified as the major component of variability among assemblages of both periods of the Neolithic. There are really only a few sites in the later Neolithic which are dominated by wild animals. These are located along the margins of Alpine foreland, and belong to at least four archaeological cultures. It has already been mentioned that high relative abundances of this taxon have been related both to the initial colonization of new agricultural areas as well as to the need to protect crops and reduce feeding competition with domesticates. Chapter 4 suggests that such competition may not

actually be a major concern, since wild taxa like red deer tend to have less success when competing with domesticates under recent forest fodder systems.

The best explanation for the unique character of these assemblages may be the one originally put forward by Boessneck for the site of Polling (Boessneck 1956), and later phrased as a general prediction for other Neolithic contexts in Europe (Uerpmann 1977). This would relate high abundances of wild animals to the initial colonization of new areas by agricultural/stock keeping groups. Presumably an increased exploitation of wild fauna results either from higher densities of animals in these areas, or from a tendency on the part of the inhabitants to maintain only small herds of domestic animals for limited purposes. Of course a variation on this theme would be one in which these sites represented the acquisition of limited domestic stock by indigenous hunting and gathering groups in the process of shifting to an agricultural economy - the elusive phase of acculturation so often expected in the prehistory of this region, yet so difficult to detect in the archaeological record. Better chronological controls uniting sites and cultures across the Alpine foreland are required before it is possible to test any hypothesized correlations between economic variability and the sequence of occupation of this region.

Summary

In summary, the following generalizations can be made for the late Neolithic. Individual archaeological cultures in this period show a variety of local adaptations or emphases in animal exploitation. As indicated by the distribution of different taxonomic clusters on the maps presented, much of the contrast with the early Neolithic seems to be related to the occupation of new regions and environmental zones. Aspects of similarity in the taxonomic composition of early and late assemblages also emerge, especially in areas north of the Alpine foreland. The groups derived from the cluster analyses do not neatly coincide with cultural or regional specializations in animal use. Rather, a complex mosaic is created, from which more patterning would probably emerge if our understanding of temporal and spatial relationships among assemblages was better.

Some additional comments may be made relating taxonomic abundances to the process of diversification inferred for the late Neolithic. The use of numerous taxa in more even abundances has been demonstrated for the later Neolithic in general. From the discussion in Chapter 4, we can assume that attributes like a multiplicity of goals, risk minimization and the adjustment of production levels to available land and labor are characteristic of animal management strategies in all subsistence agricultural systems. Changes in taxonomic composition indicate that these goals for some reason had to be achieved differently in the early and late Neolithic, and imply some corresponding change in the land and/or labor parts of the system.

One likelihood, given the nature of the taxonomic combinations in the late Neolithic, is that there has been a general intensification of land use. This is suggested by the lower number of assemblages heavily dominated by any single species, and by a more even distribution of multiple taxa in most assemblages. It has been often noted that the carrying capacity of a given unit of land can be increased by the combination of taxa with complementary grazing behavior (Arnold and Dudzinski 1978). This could also help explain the general increase in importance of pig, which can be kept in comparatively high densities in close spatial association with humans and other animals.

Much of this assemblage variability may also be related to changes in the makeup of the basic economic unit inhabiting the particular settlements and contributing to their faunal assemblages. The greater labor expense involved in maintaining multiple domestic taxa has already been discussed. It may be that sites with high percentages of wild taxa represent those in which the local population, perhaps because of its demographic makeup, had a limited amount of labor to devote to domestic animals, and hunting may have represented a cheaper way to secure some of the animal products necessary for subsistence. Unfortunately, possible differences in the nature of the cultural or economic unit represented in each occupation at individual sites have not yet been addressed.

The investigation of variability in taxonomic composition leaves unanswered the question of any possible changes in the economic functions of specific taxa which may accompany a general process of diversification. These are addressed in the next chapter with a detailed investigation of the demographic and morphological characteristics of the major taxon in both time periods: cattle.

Chapter 8

CATTLE EXPLOITATION IN THE LATE NEOLITHIC

Cattle were unarguably the most important animal resource in the early Neolithic and, to a large extent, they retained their position as the most important domesticate in the fourth and third millennia BC. A group of late Neolithic sites have been identified in which the number of bones identified to cattle exceeds those for any other individual animal. Even in assemblages with high proportions of other taxa, notably pig and red deer, cattle are still important and often predominate if MNI and/or bone weight are used to estimate relative abundance.

The overwhelming importance of cattle in prehistory has been related to the fact that they may contribute multiple body products to a human subsistence system. The potential three-fold use of cattle for meat, milk and traction has been stressed by a number of authors (eg. Bökönyi 1974; Zeuner 1963) and is again emphasized by Sherratt in his model of the secondary products revolution (Sherratt 1981). A major hypothesis embedded in this model is that cattle were primarily important as a meat source in the early Neolithic but were exploited for specific body products in the later Neolithic. This chapter investigates the evidence which exists for the use of particular body products of cattle in the Neolithic of west central Europe.

Cattle Domestication in Neolithic Europe

Cattle are the first indigenous European domesticate of major economic importance, with the earliest examples identified in a number of sites from the southern Balkan peninsula. Cattle of the central European Neolithic cultures are generally believed to be descended from these early domestic populations, and their diffusion related to the spread of farming cultures across the continent. Wild aurochs also survived throughout the early Holocene in temperate Europe and achieved their greatest geographical distribution and highest density in the late Atlantic period (Bökönyi 1974:103). The continued presence of the wild relatives of domestic cattle in the forests of Neolithic Europe poses the question of whether these two taxa represented separate populations at all points in time, or if there was a certain amount of interbreeding or admixture between wild and domestic stock. The latter would indicate a continuation of the domestication process, presumably for the purpose of increasing the number of animals available for human use.

Perhaps the best known model hypothesizing an early intensification of cattle exploitation comes from the cultural sequence within the Carpathian basin, and also involves an intensified domestication of local aurochs. A period of "domestication fever" focusing on aurochs has been identified for Neolithic Hungary, and associated with a shift from an emphasis on ovicaprines to one on cattle (Bökönyi 1971, 1974). This episode was interpreted from rather poorly dated assemblages from sites of the Szakalhat and Tisza cultural groups. A few radiocarbon determinations and associations with adjacent cultural groups suggest their placement in the mid-fifth millennium BC (Bognar-Kutzian 1971). This increase in domestication has been integrated into a model of regional exchange in which cattle from the central and eastern Hungarian plain were possibly exported to surrounding highland areas in exchange for groundstone, obsidian and fine pottery (Sherratt 1982, 1983a). Continued domestication of aurochs fueled the supply of necessary cattle, which fulfilled a combined role as subsistence item and social commodity.

Although the full implications of this regional model remain to be tested, its value here is in the role which has been suggested for aurochs domestication. Essentially, domestication is described as important for supplementing herds which are undergoing constant depletion. In the Hungarian context, Sherratt has posited regional exchange as the immediate cause of this depletion. It is important to note that this whole scenario takes place in a context of an intensification of production, related primarily to the settlement aggregation which occurs in the Carpathian basin in the fifth millennium BC. However, this is not the only circumstance under which supplementation of domestic herds by wild aurochs may be envisioned. A similar phenomenon may be predicted if there is a primary dependence on cattle, in particular as a meat source. It has already been pointed out in Chapter 4 that taxonomic specialization in general is comparatively risky, regardless of the object of focus. Cattle, while fairly productive in terms of body yield, are also relatively expensive because of their food requirements (particularly if winter foddering is practiced) and long reproductive cycle. With a predominant meat focus, the average lifespan of an individual is shorter. This means that in order to maintain production levels, there must be either increased reproduction or supplementation of the herd by the addition of wild relatives. Means for increasing reproduction under primitive stock keeping conditions are limited. The only effective way to increase the number of animals available would be to increase the overall number of stock, which raises both labor requirements and risk. If aurochs were present in sufficient density, replacement or supplementation from local wild populations may have represented a cheaper alternative, allowing animals to be kept at an optimal herd size for

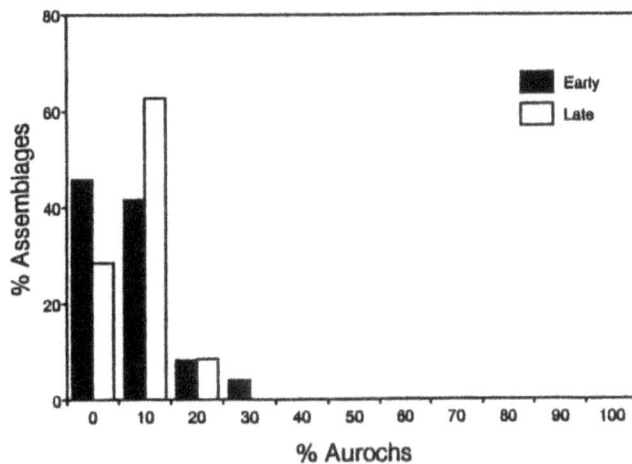

Figure 27. Histogram of percent aurochs in early and late Neolithic assemblages.

maintaining production levels. In this sense, supplementation of domestic stock by incorporating members of an indigenous wild population may be considered a herd security strategy offering two advantages: minimization of risk from fluctuations in herd size under conditions of high mortality and minimization of labor costs associated with meat production strategies.

Given the hypothesis that aurochs domestication represents a herd security strategy associated with cattle management, it is interesting to ask whether good evidence for domestication exists in the early and/or the late Neolithic. From his analysis of the Hungarian material, Bökönyi has described four criteria which may be useful in identifying local domestication (Bökönyi 1974:111): (1) Bones of wild and domestic forms are found together at the same locality; (2) Transitional forms also appear at a site; (3) Sex ratios and age profiles of the wild taxon show characteristic changes: Adults are expected to be in the majority since they must be killed in order to gain access to the young, which are caught and tamed. It is especially important to kill wild bulls, while females and young may often be incorporated into domestic herds in a casual form of husbandry; (4) Implements or buildings for capturing wild forms are present, or there is some representation of capture. Although this may be the most difficult criterion to identify archaeologically, it is worth pointing out that the enclosed ditch sites of central and northern Europe have often been interpreted as relating to cattle management (eg. Kaufmann 1982; Sherratt 1983a:23). The presence of the first three categories of evidence can be evaluated from Neolithic faunal assemblages.

Co-occurrence of Aurochs and Cattle

Figure 27 presents the relative abundance of aurochs in early and late Neolithic sites. It can be seen that aurochs occurs only in low percentages in both groups of assemblages, and it is difficult to tell whether or not there is any significant difference in the relative abundances of this taxon. Approximately 90% of both early and late

groups have 10% or fewer bones identified to aurochs. There is one early assemblage in which aurochs reaches a high of 22% NISP.

A slightly different impression of the relative importance of aurochs can be gained from a consideration of the results of the cluster analysis presented in the preceding chapter. In cluster 1 for the early Neolithic, aurochs is the most abundant wild taxon, based on mean %NISP given for the statistics defining membership for this group. In the high diversity sites from this period, which show relatively more wild taxa overall, the percentage of aurochs follows that for red deer and exceeds the other wild taxa. For the late Neolithic, the mean percentage of bones from red deer and wild pig exceed those for aurochs in every group. From these comparisons, it can be concluded that, although present in relatively small quantities in both periods, aurochs may have been slightly more important in the early Neolithic.

Ratios of Sex and Age of Aurochs

Sex and age determinations of aurochs are rare, particularly for the early Neolithic. In the early period, the central German data for all sites pooled gives a sex ratio based on horncores of four females and two males (Müller 1964:16). Burgäschisee-Süd is the only late Neolithic site with enough aurochs remains to provide both age and sex determinations. Based on mandibles, 55% of the individuals identified as aurochs were immature (infant or juvenile), compared to a similar figure of 50% for domestic cattle. Among adults, there were more cows than bulls: 85% of the bones identified to sex were from females (Stampfli 1963). Three small samples of aurochs from other late Neolithic sites also provide some information on sex of these animals. Only females were identified at Twann and Hetzenberg, while 80% males and 20% females were identified at Homolka (based on astragali). With the possible exception of this last site, sex ratios in all of these assemblages differ from observations on Neolithic assemblages from Hungary, where most aurochs killed were identified as adult bulls (Bökönyi 1974).

Presence of Transitional Forms

The appearance of animals with characteristics intermediate to those of the wild and domestic forms is most likely attributable to the presence of newly domesticated individuals at an early stage of manipulation (Bökönyi 1974:111). One major distinction between wild and domestic forms of the same taxon is a difference in body size. Individuals intermediate in size may represent early forms of domesticates.

Differences in body size are related to a number of factors, most of which have to do with a progressive diminution which is coincident with increased control of an animal by humans. Diminution occurs relatively quickly after an animal comes under human control. In the initial stages of human-animal interaction, smaller animals may be easier for humans to manage, and further decreases in body size may represent an adaptation to conditions of increased environmental stress under domestication (Herre and Röhrs 1973:88). More specifically, body sizes of domesticates seem to be related to differences in the growth cycle which stem from the human control of nutrition through restricted food intake and/or range (Higham 1969; Noddle 1983).

Differences in body size are relatively easy to observe in zooarchaeological material, and are often recognizable even in fragmentary bones. More importantly, these differences have been monitored and quantified by use of osteometric data. Two kinds of observations provide information on body size: inspection of individual series of measurements, and consideration of estimates of body size which have been derived from these measurements. While measurements of individual bones are the most immediate data, derived body size estimates are often easier to visualize, and facilitate comparison among multiple sets of data (von den Driesch and Boessneck 1974). The most common derived estimate used for such comparisons is withers height (WRH), with the result that there is a good idea of the major changes in body size this taxon has undergone throughout prehistory and history.

WRH is used here to provide estimates of body size of Neolithic cattle from as many assemblages as possible, and compare these with estimates of aurochs sizes. Because of the great amount of sexual dimorphism present in cattle, especially primitive forms, it is important to control for the sex of the animal if any meaningful comparisons of body size are to be made. For this reason, WRH has been calculated only from metapodials from mature individuals which have been reliably sexed. From the limited sex ratios presented above, it appeared likely that there would be more observations of females than males. Consequently, the following analysis compares WRH from females only within all samples. All withers heights have been calculated from the raw data presented in original reports. Factors derived by Matolcsi (Matolcsi 1970) are used, with modifications as suggested by von den Driesch and Boessneck (von den Driesch and Boessneck 1974). The greatest length of metacarpals has been multiplied by a factor of 6, metatarsals by 5.3.

Only a few observations are available for the early Neolithic. These are drawn from the LBK sites in central Germany, and comprise three measurements on female cattle, none on males and none on male or female aurochs. The lack of aurochs measurements may be especially problematic because of the possibility of a decrease in size of the wild taxon from the earliest LBK to the later Neolithic approximately two millennia later. It was originally asserted that the size of aurochs had declined since the start of the Neolithic, to a similar extent as the size decrease noted for the domestic form (eg. Lehmann 1949). It is now thought that prehistoric aurochs were more variable than previously assumed, and that what has

been observed was not a continuous phylogenetic decrease in size from the end of Pleistocene through the Neolithic to the Middle Ages, but more likely a decrease through selective hunting of larger individuals by humans especially in the later periods (Müller 1964:26). A similar argument has been put forward for red deer, with the possibility that after an initial size decrease at the beginning of the Holocene, body size of the animal remained the same and the apparent size decrease is primarily attributable to human selection in the early Middle Ages (Pietschmann 1977). Both Müller (1964) and Nobis (1954) thought it valid to compare body sizes of early Neolithic cattle with aurochs sizes determined on specimens from the later Neolithic. This practice is also followed here.

Withers height for five samples are compared in Figure 28. LBK cattle are from Müller (1964). Data labeled as

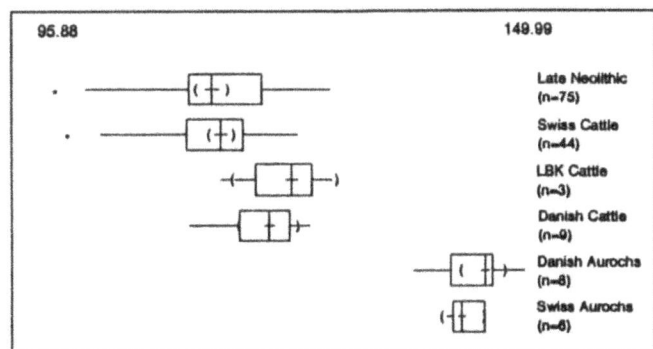

Figure 28. Comparison of withers heights of Neolithic female cattle and aurochs.

"late Neolithic" are from nine late assemblages which had three or more females per site. Two additional samples of late Neolithic domestic cattle have been abstracted from the literature. Imhof (1964) presented data from late Neolithic sites on the Bielersee, from which withers heights have been recalculated as described above. Degerbol (1970) presented a series of observations on Danish cattle from sites roughly dated by their association with Subboreal pollen deposits. Most sites from both of these samples date to the fourth and third millennia BC, although it is possible that each contain a small number of observations from slightly later contexts as well. Finally, two samples of female aurochs measurements are included: one from Burgäschisee-Süd (Stampfli 1963), the other from Denmark (Degerbol 1970).

Data presented in this box plot include the median, hinges or quartiles and standard error (indicated by ()) for each sample. This figure basically represents a graphical analysis of variance based on ranked data, with a 95% probability that samples are different if the ranges of boxes do not overlap (Wilkinson 1987). The larger size of the LBK and Danish cattle relative to the other late Neolithic sites is obvious in this plot. The failure of the LBK samples to approach those of either aurochs sample is somewhat puzzling, given the fact that domestication in the early period has been suggested by a number of researchers (Boessneck 1958, 1982; Müller 1964; Stampfli 1965). Undoubtedly the explanation lies in the small size of the sample, and the fact that withers heights based on the complete lengths of metapodials cannot always be expected to encompass the full range of variability in the sample population due to the fragmentary nature of most faunal remains. Indeed, Müller does point out that breadth measurements on fragmentary articular ends suggest a larger average size for LBK cattle than this plot would seem to indicate and that there is a continuous distribution between cattle and aurochs for several measurements (Müller 1964:35).

It is clear that little or no significant size overlap exists between cattle from the LBK and those from the later Neolithic assemblages published by Imhof or presented here, and there is even less of a possibility that the cattle size ranges overlap with those of aurochs. The relatively large size of the Subboreal Danish cattle is somewhat surprising at first, given their approximate contemporaneity with the other two late Neolithic samples. It must be remembered, however, that although these samples are chronologically late, they belong to some of the earliest Neolithic groups in northern Europe. Their greater size could be related to their derivation from the relatively large LBK stock (Higham 1968), possibly maintained by continued additions from the local aurochs population. In contrast, the smaller stature of the Swiss and southern German cattle has been cited as possible evidence for their original derivation from a different population of stock in western Europe (Clason 1967). The effects of the harsher climate of the Alpine foreland have also been suggested as a factor contributing to the greater diminution of these animals (Higham 1968).

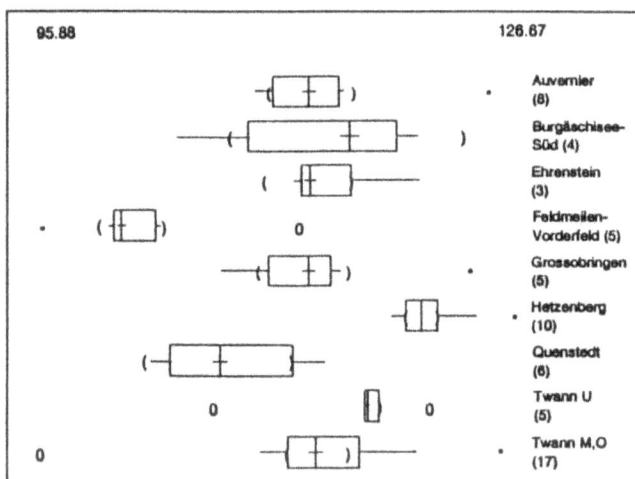

Figure 29. Comparison of withers heights for female cattle from nine late Neolithic assemblages.

Figure 29 provides a box plot of the WRH data for female cattle at nine late Neolithic sites. These can be used to address the suggestion that cattle from this region of central Europe were derived from two separate popula-

tions. A few sites in this plot are from areas with dense LBK occupation: Grossobringen, Quenstedt and Hetzenberg. These might be expected to still show higher withers heights, if derived from significantly larger stock than, for instance, the lake-side sites of further south and west. This does not seem to be the case for two of these: Grossobringen and Quenstedt show values similar to those for cattle from sites like Burgäschisee-Süd and Auvernier. Hetzenberg, however, does show exceptionally large female cattle in comparison to other assemblages.

An additional feature can be pointed out in the layers from Twann. The lowermost strata at this site were analyzed separately (identified here as Twann U) (Becker 1981), while middle and upper layers were considered together by investigators (here given as Twann MO) (Becker and Johansson 1981). The lower layer shows considerably larger females than those from the middle and upper layers, suggesting the presence of an early population of relatively large size. This would indicate either that much diminution occurred through the course of the Neolithic in the Alpine area, or that the earlier Cortaillod occupants had cattle derived from a different population than those of the later inhabitants of the site. Finally, two extremes illustrated in this plot must be mentioned. The presence of unusually small cattle is indicated in the Horgen layers at Feldmeilen-Vorderfeld, while very large animals were recovered at Hetzenberg. If differences in the body sizes of domestic animals reflect differences in management strategies in a very general sense, this suggests the presence of widely varying systems of cattle use within the later Neolithic of this area.

Cattle and Aurochs in Neolithic Sites

In conclusion, there is some suggestion from taxonomic representation and cattle withers heights that supplementation of herds with locally domesticated aurochs was part of the animal exploitation systems of the early Neolithic occupants in this area of Europe. Since many of these assemblages also show a focus on cattle as the major taxon, the combination of these two bovids may represent a herd security strategy under conditions of meat production as described at the beginning of this section. In contrast, there is no good evidence for continued domestication of local aurochs in later Neolithic sites considered here. The presence of aurochs at Burgäschisee-Süd is possibly related to the hunting focus suggested by the faunal assemblage as a whole, which was accompanied by some limited stock keeping. There is no evidence from body size to suggest the integration of wild individuals into the breeding stock of domesticates. Hetzenberg is the only assemblage in which such an integration may have taken place, resulting in the larger sizes of cattle at this site. However, neither the early Neolithic nor this single site in the later period show the degree of concentration on aurochs and cattle which was identified for the

Hungarian plain in the fifth millennium BC. The assemblages show the same scale of size decrease identified by Boessneck (1956) for early to late Neolithic, which has also been traced in other areas (Bökönyi 1974; Nobis 1954). If continued manipulation of wild populations took place, it was of a different nature than criteria abstracted from the situation in Hungary would lead us to expect.

Economic Functions of Cattle in the Neolithic

Ethnographic descriptions of domestic animal production systems have noted that the flow of animal goods in the subsistence economy is regulated through the manipulation of age and sex structures of the animal herd (eg. Dahl and Hjort 1976). In the past decade, sex ratios and age distributions have become the most frequently used data for abstracting inferences on economic roles filled by animals in prehistoric sites. Most interpretations of the meaning behind the relative abundances of specific age and sex categories have been derived from observation and modeling of Near Eastern ovicaprine exploitation, which is comparatively specialized in nature (eg. Cribb 1987; Hesse 1984; Payne 1973; Redding 1981). Still, some generalizations from these studies may apply to the manipulation of age and sex categories within other domestic animal herds as well. An analysis of the age and sex structure of cattle in Neolithic assemblages must be restricted to the later assemblages since few of the early Neolithic ones considered here contain the necessary information.

Age Data

Age determinations for cattle have been taken from the original analyses. Only information on mandibular tooth eruption and wear has been used. Observations on epiphyseal fusion are frequently not available, and would assume greater comparability in element representation and identification among all sites. In contrast, observations on teeth are more consistently recorded and reported. It was not always possible to ascertain whether minimum numbers of dentitions were reported or if the figure reported was merely NISP. In cases where both were given, MNI has been chosen. The possibility that some observations may still refer to numbers of specimens rather than individuals is probably not too critical since these data are converted to percentages for comparison. To a large extent, the usual incompatibility between numbers of bones and numbers of individuals is avoided since only one skeletal element is considered.

The raw data were recorded in the same degree of precision as originally reported, then collapsed to form three age categories. An attempt was made to relate these categories to the standard age groups used in the European faunal literature in general. Most analysts classify remains as infant, juvenile, subadult or adult, and accept the schedules given in Habermehl (1975) as valid approximations of tooth eruption and replacement in

cattle. As used here, the category of infant includes those specimens in which M1 has fully erupted and is in the early stages of wear. This tooth erupts at about five to six months of age and begins to show occlusal wear shortly thereafter, between about seven and 14 months. Juveniles include those mandibles in which M2 is present (erupts at 15 to 18 months) up to the age at which the complete permanent dentition is present and premolars and M3 exhibit slight wear. This upper stage approximates an age of three years. Subadult and adult categories are lumped in a single adult group here. As of yet there is no uniform use of crown height measurements or occlusal wear to aid discrimination between age categories for domestic cattle after the full dentition is present. Table 10 provides the number of observations made for each age category for the late Neolithic assemblages which contained adequate information of this nature.

Although it is likely that the absolute timing of tooth eruption may have been slightly different in primitive, slow-maturing breeds of cattle, the relative sequence of these events has probably remained largely the same. Two of these age categories can be further related to physiological stages which may have some meaning in economic terms. First, the percentage of the assemblage composed of adult mandibles can be taken as an indication of the proportion of the death assemblage which is composed of individuals in the breeding segment of the population. Second, the juvenile category includes animals between two and three years of age, generally considered an optimal point for butchering if an animal contributes primarily meat to the local subsistence economy (Uerpmann 1973:316).

Sex Data

In the construction of sex ratios for cattle from Neolithic sites, consideration has been restricted to those elements which express sexual dimorphism fairly clearly: horncores, metacarpals, metatarsals, pelvis, astragalus, and calcaneum. A discussion of specific criteria used for determining sex of cattle bones can be found in Grigson (1982), as well as many of the individual analyses. Horncore and pelvis sex determinations are usually based on morphological criteria combined with metric observations on the crosssection of the horncore base and length of acetabulum. An identification of sex for the other elements is normally based on analyses of individual dimensions or length/breadth ratios. Since element representation and fragmentation vary among assemblages, the use of multiple elements was necessary to obtain ratios for as many assemblages as possible. For each element, the number of bones identified by the original analyst as male, female or castrate was recorded. All sex determinations based on these elements have been used as long as the original investigator expressed sufficient confidence in their identifications. Questionable determinations have been included if a single category was identified (eg. "male?") but were not used if the tentative

Table 10. Numbers of age determinations made on cattle mandibles from late Neolithic assemblages.

No.	Assemblage	Infant	Juvenile	Adult
26*	Auvernier	(37%)	(10%)	(53%)
28	See	3	6	4
29	Hetzenberg	9	1	9
30	Makotrasy	7	1	2
31	Feldmeilen-Vorderfeld	6	4	4
32	Fischergasse	3	2	4
33	Riekofen	1	4	13
35	Feldmeilen-Vorderfeld	10	6	11
36*	Altheim	0	(50%)	(50%)
37*	Altenerding	0	(50%)	(50%)
41*	Burgäschisee-Süd	0	(50%)	(50%)
42	Twann US	21	5	11
43	Mintranching	2	0	4
44	Twann	2	6	7
45	Eschner Lutzengüetle	20	22	28
46	Eschner Lutzengüetle	10	13	19
47	Eschner Lutzengüetle	3	7	8
49	Ehrenstein	11	6	6
50	Grossobringen	0	0	15
51	Schalkenburg bei Quenstedt	0	346	48
52	Dölauer Heide	0	2	5
53	Burgäschisee-SW	9	10	30
59	Galgenberg	2	0	2

* only percentage data given in original reports

identification included multiple categories (eg. "male or castrate", "male or female"). Only sex determinations made on subadult or adult bones have been considered here as determinations made on immature bones are often questionable. Table 11 lists the late Neolithic assemblages for which sex determinations were available, along with the total number of bones identified for each sex category. Percentages of males, females and castrates were calculated from these raw data.

Assumptions About Representation of Age and Sex Classes

Due to the coarse and secondary nature of these data, no attempts have been made to reconstruct separate mortality curves or to discuss the representation of sexes for specific sites. These are, in most cases, more thoroughly and appropriately addressed in the original works. The approach taken here is to investigate patterning between age and sex categories and some of the types of assemblage variability which have been identified in the diversity and taxonomic abundance analyses. At this point it is useful to outline some basic assumptions about possible meanings behind differences in the relative abundances of certain age and sex categories for determining herding strategies.

The most basic assumption is that, since the age and sex categories are closely interrelated in different productive strategies (Cribb 1987), the presence of differential patterning of these categories indicates the pursuit of different strategies. On a more specific level, we can associate certain productive strategies with the presence of certain age and sex categories. Two particular assumptions are used here. First, within age groups, we might assume that high juvenile mortality, that is, high proportions of individuals in the herd killed between about one and three years of age, is indicative of meat use. Second, within sex categories, it has been suggested that an adult sex ratio highly skewed toward females indicates milk production, possibly combined with high infant mortality to gain access to greater quantities of milk (Payne 1973). This killoff of infants may not be necessary in the case of cattle, which may more often yield milk in excess of the immediate needs of their calves. Two proportions, percent juveniles and percent adult females, are the focus of more detailed analyses.

The relative proportions of different age and sex categories can be illustrated using triangle graphs. Considerably less analytical value is placed on these

Table 11. Numbers of cattle bones identified to sex in late Neolithic assemblages.

No.	Assemblage	Female	Male	Castrate
26	Auvernier	13	0	0
28	See	16	5	1
29	Hetzenberg	23	6	9
30	Makotrasy	16	7	0
31	Feldmeilen-Vorderfeld	36	6	2
32	Fischergasse	3	0	1
33	Riekofen	8	17	0
34	Homolka	6	6	2
35	Feldmeilen-Vorderfeld	29	4	0
36	Altheim	1	2	0
37	Altenerding	1	1	0
38	Galgenberg	3	1	0
40	Ludwigsburg	1	0	0
41	Burgäschisee-Süd	15	1	0
42	Twann US	18	6	1
43	Mintranching	6	3	0
44	Twann	13	5	0
45	Eschner Lutzengüetle	15	2	1
46	Eschner Lutzengüetle	13	5	0
47	Eschner Lutzengüetle	1	0	1
48	Hornstaad-Hörnle	1	0	0
49	Ehrenstein	22	6	0
50	Grossobringen	20	8	0
51	Schalkenburg bei Quenstedt	6	2	9
52	Dölauer Heide	2	2	0
53	Burgäschisee-SW	5	1	0
59	Galgenberg	1	2	2
Total		273	89	27

graphs than, for instance, by Greenfield (1988). Rather they are used here merely as a convenient way to summarize and present the basic data. These graphs can be read by simply viewing the apexes of the triangles as zones with high representation of the category indicated by the nearest label.

Inspection of the relative abundances of age categories (Figure 30) shows that there are a few sites with high infant mortality, and a few with high juvenile mortality. Most assemblages contain a high percentage of individuals killed as adults, combined with lower frequencies of one of the immature categories. The frequently high percentage of adult animals is somewhat puzzling, given the results of simulations of herd population dynamics carried out by Cribb (1985, 1987). He notes an obvious problem with the viability of populations showing high rates of adult mortality, and suggests such a pattern may be related to some problem of sampling, either in a behavioral context or an archaeological one. Also note the relative absence of individuals in the infant category. It is difficult to know if this reflects a real scarcity of individuals killed at this age, or if it reflects the underrepresentation of immature individuals common at many sites and attributed to preservation and identification biases.

Figure 31 presents a triangle graph of the relative percentages of bones identified as males, females or castrates for late Neolithic assemblages. It can be seen that comparatively few assemblages have elements which were thought to have come from oxen. Given the small number of bones with sex determinations at some of these sites, too much weight should probably not be placed on the presence of this sex category. The appearance of oxen in these samples could be interpreted in two ways. Castration results in an attenuation of the growth process, and increases the ability of an animal to store fat. Thus, it

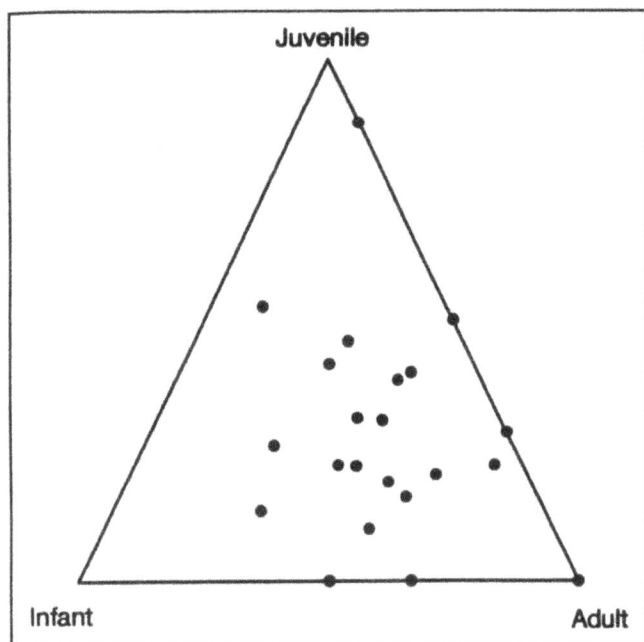

Figure 30. Triangle graph of cattle age categories.

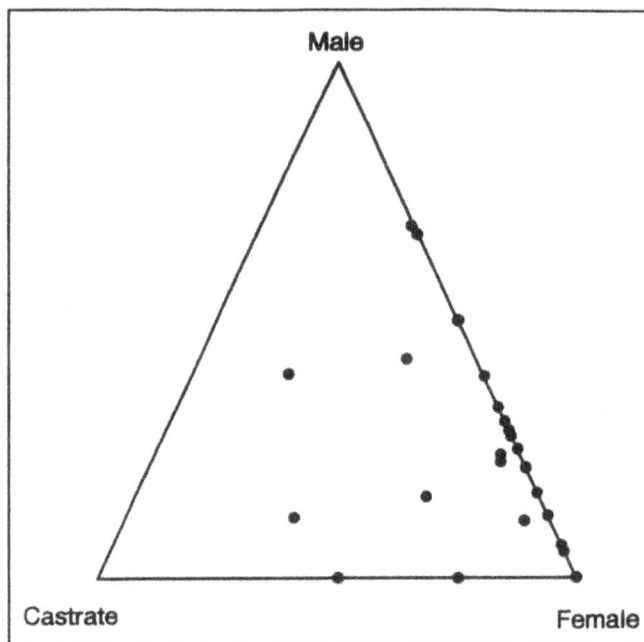

Figure 31. Triangle graph of cattle sex categories for late Neolithic assemblages.

could relate to a specialized technique for increasing the meat yield of individual animals. On the other hand, castration reduces the level of agonistic behavior in an animal, especially that related to reproduction, thereby increasing its tractability. On analogy with the training and use of oxen for plow agriculture in historic times, it is often inferred that the presence of castrates in archaeological faunal samples indicates some use of this animal for draft purposes. While interpretation is fairly straightforward in some cases (for example, in the rare case of paired oxen burials (Behrens 1964)) it is unclear how remains from general site debris should be understood. Given that the sex determinations presented here refer to mature individuals, some form of the latter interpretation appears more likely.

Figure 31 shows that most assemblages are dominated by high percentages of adult females, with the corresponding number of reproducing males often quite low. Among African cattle pastoralists, age-related mortality in males has been related to a variety of social, cultural and economic factors while the loss of females in different age categories seems more closely related to purely natural processes (Dahl and Hjort 1976:30). This could logically be expected to almost always result in an adult sex ratio highly skewed toward females, as is the case here. The percentage of males in a herd may be positively related to herd size (Dahl and Hjort 1976) or to the existence of an extensive pasturing system (Arnold and Dudzinski 1978:168) to name only a few of the many possible factors involved.

Cattle and Assemblage Diversity

Considerable variability has already been identified for these late Neolithic assemblages in terms of diversity and the domination of specific taxa. One major question

which may be addressed concerns the relationship between assemblage diversity, that is, the presence of multiple taxa, and the role of cattle, a taxon which can potentially contribute multiple body products to the subsistence economy.

Figure 32 plots the percent juvenile mortality for cattle in late Neolithic assemblages against their heterogeneity. The label numbers refer to the taxonomic groups created in the cluster analysis. Cluster 1 sites tend to have lower heterogeneity and somewhat higher percentages of juveniles than sites belonging to the other clusters. Remember that these assemblages are also characterized by relatively high percentages of cattle compared to those in the other

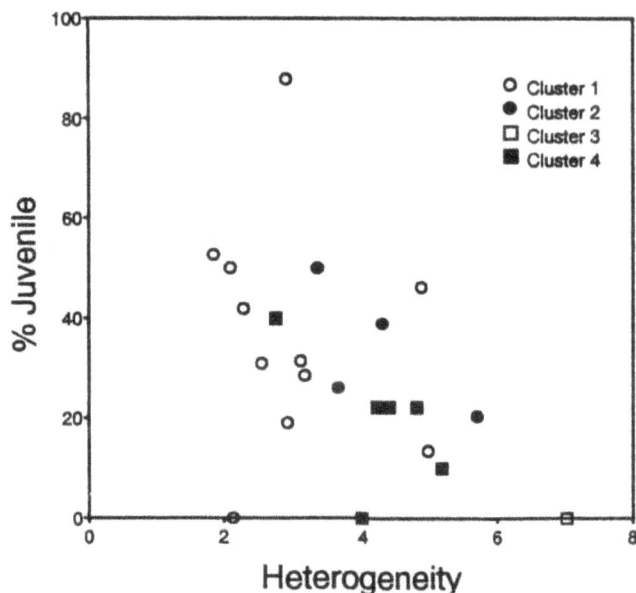

Figure 32. Plot of percent juvenile cattle and heterogeneity for late Neolithic assemblages.

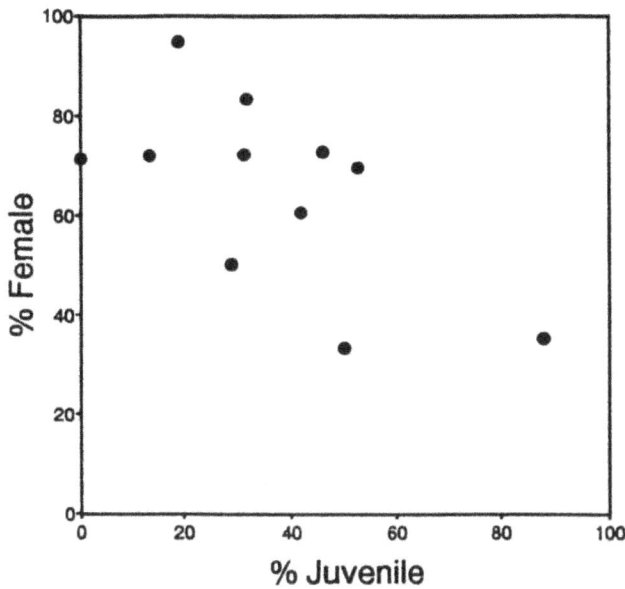

Figure 33. Plot of percent juveniles and percent females for cattle in cluster 1 sites.

groups. If the assumption about the meaning of juvenile mortality is correct, this can be interpreted as showing a greater emphasis on meat production in assemblages which are less heterogeneous and in which the dominant taxon is cattle. It is important to stress that this statement is a relative one, and does not necessarily indicate an *exclusive* focus on meat. A general implication of this graph is that cattle in less heterogeneous assemblages appear to be more important in terms of meat production than they are in assemblages with greater heterogeneity. The more heterogeneous assemblages show greater abundances of pig and/or red deer, in addition to the presence of other taxa, and it is these animals which may be hypothesized to have contributed more to the meat protein needs of the occupants. This suggests that the use of cattle may differ in a predictable fashion between the two major groups of assemblages (ie. cattle-dominated, less heterogeneous assemblages and more heterogeneous assemblages dominated by other taxa).

The possibility of such a pattern can be further investigated by closer inspection of the less heterogeneous, cattle-dominated sites. It might be predicted that if the inference of a primary focus on cattle for meat production is valid, there should be a negative relationship between percent juvenile mortality and percent adult females. Such a relationship is observed in Figure 33 ($r = .62$, $.05 > p > .01$). The presence of assemblages at both extremes of these distributions suggest a modified interpretation of a dual use of cattle for meat and milk at sites within this group as a whole, rather than a specialized focus on either type of production. This may relate to an observation by Cribb based on his simulation of ovicaprine mortality about the interrelations between economic strategies. He noted that an enhancement of the milk-producing capacity tends to improve the productivity of meat yields of flocks as well. It is important to note that he is dealing with a specialized stock breeding system in the ethnographic data from which this particular observation was derived. This may possibly be generalized to a statement that, in a specialized economy (ie. one with low heterogeneity), if the focal taxon provides multiple body products, we may expect a strategy to emerge which optimizes use of those multiple body products. That is, low taxonomic heterogeneity is positively related to the exploitation of a single major taxon for multiple goals. Conversely, we may expect that in assemblages with high taxonomic heterogeneity there may be a coincident use of animals for a more restricted range of body products. Low sample sizes in the non-cattle-dominated group of Neolithic assemblages considered here prevents the full testing of this hypothesis. Nevertheless, there is limited confirmation in a comparison of the average percentages of various taxonomic and demographic categories presented in Table 12. It can be seen that more heterogeneous assemblages have a lower percentage of cattle. At these sites, there is a lower incidence of juvenile mortality and a correspondingly higher percentage of animals are killed as adults. Among these adults, there is a higher percentage of females than males. The suggestion, then, is that cattle represent a multiple purpose animal in less heterogeneous assemblages while there is more of an emphasis on use of these animals for milk production in assemblages with high heterogeneity.

Comparison with Early Neolithic Data

This pattern shows the coexistence in the late Neolithic of different strategies of cattle management within a relatively limited area of central Europe. It is possible that some of this pattern may be extrapolated to the earlier

Table 12. Average values of cattle age and sex characteristics in late Neolithic clusters.

Characteristics	Cluster 1	Clusters 2-4
Mean % Cattle	51.94	21.99
Mean % Female	65.53	73.93
Mean % Juvenile	36.55	22.91
Mean % Adult	42.84	50.00
Mean Diversity	2.93	4.34

Table 13. Cattle abundance, age and sex data for early Neolithic assemblages.

No.	Assemblage	Heterogeneity	%Cattle	%Juvenile	%Adult	%Female
4	Kraichtal-Gochsheim 12	1.79	72.87	100.0	0.0	37.5
5	Kraichtal-Gochsheim 3	1.51	37.87			69.2
6	Bylany	2.94	81.27	22.0	78.0	
19	Regensburg-Pürkelgut	5.01	31.54			100.0
20	Regensburg-Kumpfmühl	5.16	22.22			50.0
21	Brzesc Kujawski	1.74	74.0	20.0	70.0	
7-18	(See Table 2 for site names)	2.15	52.2	27.9	72.0	51.3

period. Recall that early sites are predominantly characterized by low heterogeneity values and dominated by either ovicaprines or cattle. Thus, we might suspect that there was a corresponding use of the dominant taxa for multiple body products in the early period. In this light, the relationship between ovicaprine and cattle representation noted in the chapter on taxonomic abundance becomes more understandable. Both taxa represent alternatives with the potential for more than one body product: meat, milk, traction and products like hides and horns for cattle; and milk, meat and possibly hides for ovicaprines. Table 13 provides what little information there is available for comparison from the early Neolithic assemblages. The relationships between various categories of information follow the same pattern as described above.

The presence of a few heterogeneous assemblages in the early period remains confusing. The data available from two of these three sites (19 and 20) suggest a similar use of cattle as in the heterogeneous sites of the later period (ie. possible focus on milk production). This may be related to the slightly later dates expected for these sites, based on their cultural affiliations. Alternatively, it may indicate the presence of two large regional traditions of animal use prior to the fourth millennium BC, one north of the Danube basin and one along the margins of the Alpine area. It is especially unfortunate that there are no complementary data on other early Neolithic sites in this area. Finally, it is equally unclear how the presence of cluster 1 sites in the late Neolithic are to be interpreted: do they represent a continuation of or development from the dominant Bandkeramik pattern of animal use?

Cattle Management in Neolithic Central Europe

These analyses suggest some differences in the strategies which were used for the management of domestic cattle in the early and late Neolithic. There is some indication that there was a slightly greater use of aurochs in the early period. This could reflect a greater accessibility of aurochs in the local environments of these sites. There is also the possibility that it relates to a strategy of herd security in a context where the major economic emphasis was placed on a narrow range of domestic taxa. There is comparatively little evidence for extensive use of aurochs in the later period, with the exception of a few sites where they appear in high frequencies (eg. Burgäschisee-Süd) or where body sizes of domesticates are surprisingly high in comparison to other fourth and third millennium assemblages (eg. Hetzenberg). No other clear patterning in cattle body size could be discerned.

A surprising degree of variability has also been identified for strategies of cattle management within the late Neolithic alone. Assemblage heterogeneity seems to be a fair predictor of cattle exploitation as indicated by age and sex data. Two main patterns have been identified. In the first, less heterogeneous assemblages show age and sex ratios which are interpreted as the exploitation of cattle for both meat and milk production. The second pattern shows a more specific use of cattle as milk animals in a context in which a much greater variety of taxa are exploited. There is some suggestion that the first pattern may represent the continuation of an early Neolithic system or, perhaps more accurately, the existence of similar social or environmental constraints on land and/or labor availability in both periods. There are still major difficulties in the comparison of faunal assemblages from early Neolithic contexts, mostly related to small sample sizes. The degree of economic variability within the early Neolithic as a whole remains obscure.

Chapter 9

ANIMAL USE AND ECONOMIC CHANGE IN THE NEOLITHIC

Current and past models of Neolithic economic and social development have relied to varying degrees upon interpretations of the subsistence economy of this period. In some cases, changes in the resources and technology associated with subsistence practices have been given a degree of causal priority. In other cases, subsistence changes are treated more as epiphenomena which mirror aspects of social organization or cultural complexity. In either instance, it is necessary to trace and understand variability in subsistence data if these are to be integrated at all into models of prehistoric culture change.

This research has addressed basic questions about the animal component of the subsistence economy in Neolithic central Europe: What is the nature of the differences in the animal component of the subsistence economy between the early and late Neolithic, and what do these differences suggest about strategies of animal exploitation?

Problems in Faunal Interpretation

A number of problems have been encountered in the selection and manipulation of faunal assemblages for this study. These can be related to our incomplete understanding of the process of agricultural expansion across Europe and imprecise knowledge of chronological and spatial relations among Neolithic cultural groups.

Unequal sampling of assemblages from different Neolithic archaeological cultures poses a serious problem. Given the different hierarchical levels at which archaeological cultures have been identified, it is difficult to estimate the number of faunal samples which would be necessary to assure comparable coverage for each group. To some extent, this question of equal representation has been begged here by the creation of early and late groups of assemblages, and the comparison of specific types of variability between these groups as an alternative to the use of a traditional cultural classification. However, this approach is also not completely satisfactory, given the incomplete nature of many local occupation sequences and related problems of establishing the synchroneity of Neolithic cultures over broad areas. The reality of apparent occupational gaps in many areas needs to be addressed and the implications of settlement continuity or discontinuity fully understood. For instance, until the relationship between long-term regional settlement and the availability of wild animal resources is clarified, we cannot be sure of the meaning of heterogeneous sites in the early Neolithic or of less diverse sites in the late period.

Some of the confusion encountered in the interpretation of analyses presented here relates to regional differences in faunal preservation and the absence of fine-scaled chronological controls for most faunal collections. Undoubtedly, many inconsistencies in the trends identified above could be clarified if a true diachronic sample were available over a large area. Even having absolute dates for all assemblages concerned would be an improvement. It is also important to point out that the geographical area considered here was dictated by a concern to maximize the number of faunal assemblages considered in order to address general questions of changes in animal economy. As a result, this sample includes assemblages from areas with quite distinct cultural sequences - for example, the Alpine foreland and central Germany, southern Poland. There is no reason to believe that processes of economic intensification were exactly synchronous in these regions.

Early Neolithic Animal Production

There are still substantial problems associated with sampling of faunal material from early Neolithic contexts. Assemblages tend to have low numbers of bones, and there is a geographical bias on sites from the northern region of settlement distribution, especially central Germany. A few sites considered here as early Neolithic are from further south, in southern Germany, and do show differences in taxonomic composition. This could be due to the fact that they are from localized cultural variants that tend to be late in the early Neolithic occupational sequence, or it could indicate the existence of regional economic patterning within the late sixth - early fifth millennium BC.

A single pattern of domestic animal use has been identified for the majority of early sites considered here. This involves a primary focus on a relatively narrow range of domestic animals - cattle and ovicaprines. The selection and exploitation of these taxa probably relate to characteristics of their productivity, in particular to the fact that both taxa can potentially yield protein in the form of both meat and milk. These assemblages have comparatively low abundances of pig, the domestic taxon with the highest reproductive potential but only a single value as meat contributor. Regarding more specific use of cattle, dependence on this animal for its meat yield might be expected to lead to the development of herd security measures to cope with circumstances of relatively high mortality in a resource population with a relatively low reproductive capacity. Limited data suggests the continued incorporation of aurochs into domestic stock herds in the early Neolithic, possibly representing evidence of one herd security measure.

Late Neolithic Animal Production

Different kinds of sampling problems affect our knowledge of later Neolithic subsistence economies. Late Neolithic assemblages tend to be larger, though it is still unclear if this relates to differences in the length of occupation, number of inhabitants, or economic activities at later sites in comparison to early ones.

The greater number of taxa identified in late Neolithic contexts seems to be at least partially related to the larger sizes of individual samples relative to those from the early Neolithic. However, once sampling effects have been removed, the results of the richness and heterogeneity analyses do confirm the traditional observation of greater variability in numbers and relative abundances of both domestic and wild taxa in assemblages from the later Neolithic. At least two patterns of animal use can be identified within this sample of assemblages, differentiated on the basis of heterogeneity combined with inferred techniques of cattle management.

Assemblage Diversity and Taxonomic Dominance in the Late Neolithic

Major patterns of faunal exploitation in the late Neolithic were derived from the analysis of taxonomic representation rather than by combining individual site assemblages into groups based on archaeological cultures. Three groups and one unique assemblage were identified, which can be distinguished from each other by their heterogeneity and dominant taxa. Most less heterogeneous assemblages tend to be dominated by cattle, though not often to the degree seen in the early Neolithic. More heterogeneous assemblages are generally characterized by greater evenness in the relative abundances of major taxa. Within these more diverse sites, either red deer or pig outnumber the other taxa. One site, the Galgenberg, stands out by its abundance of horse, in combination with correspondingly lower percentages of all other major domesticates. These groups of sites do not correspond exclusively to cultural or temporal associations generally accepted for this period of the Neolithic. However, there is some geographical patterning showing the cattle-dominated sites to be both north and south of the Danube, while the more heterogeneous assemblages with their greater variety of dominant taxa lie in the Alpine lake and foreland region. Much of the variability in representation of specific taxa at individual sites undoubtedly relates to immediate circumstances of environment and cultural geography. These may be investigated when a more uniform picture of the occupational history of this portion of Europe has emerged.

Cattle Management in the Late Neolithic

Different types of cattle management appear to covary in a predictable way with assemblage heterogeneity and species dominance. Cattle in more heterogeneous assemblages not only appear in low frequencies, but suggest a pattern of primary exploitation for milk production, based on assumptions about juvenile mortality and adult sex ratios. Cattle in assemblages with low heterogeneity appear to be more oriented toward meat production. However, sex and mortality data of cattle in assemblages with less heterogeneity are also compatible with some use of these animals for milk. It has been noted that milk and meat production in domestic taxa are often complementary, and that both kinds of productivity can be optimized by maintaining certain ratios of age and sex classes within a herd (Chang and Koster 1986; Cribb 1987). Rather than hypothesizing specialized meat production at less diverse sites, it is suggested here that they represent a strategy of exploitation of cattle for multiple purposes. In contrast, the greater numbers of females and lower juvenile mortality at more heterogeneous sites supports a picture of a more specific use of cattle for milk.

Comparison of Early and Late Neolithic Production Strategies

It may be valid to extrapolate the pattern of cattle exploitation identified for the group of less diverse, cattle-dominated assemblages in the late Neolithic to the majority of early Neolithic sites, which are also less diverse and dominated by cattle or ovicaprines. The degree to which ovicaprines fit this general scheme remains to be investigated. Based on their structure alone, early Neolithic assemblages appear to represent a relatively specialized economy. A strategy of specialization in animal production is generally characterized as one of potentially high productivity, associated with higher risk but rather lower labor demands because of the possibility of greater synchronization of labor in tending a smaller variety of animals with individual needs.

In contrast, a strategy of diversification in domestic stock management may be characterized as more expensive in terms of both land and labor requirements. Diversification is most often interpreted as evidence of some desire to spread risk by the maintenance of multiple taxa. The use of taxa for specific purposes within a diversified system may reflect greater attention to scheduling decisions. The increased use of pig, with its low maintenance requirements, and greater use of wild fauna at some sites may also relate to an attempt to minimize labor associated with animal production, possibly because of conflicts with some other component of the subsistence economy.

Diversification may or may not imply a greater attention to the animal component of subsistence economy, depending on the characteristics of the social groups involved in such production strategies. One possibility is that differences in taxonomic heterogeneity between assemblages may relate to the occupation of sites by different numbers of household production units. In the case of occupation by a greater number of households, some sort of economic differentiation may be necessary to ensure the viability of individual households while coordinating use of the local environment. In this sense, the greater taxonomic heterogeneity of late Neolithic assemblages may reflect the settlement aggregation characteristic of this region in the fourth and early third millennium more than it reflects an increased emphasis on animal production per se.

The presence of assemblages of both high and low heterogeneity and the implications of each for different production strategies indicates a greater range of variability in late Neolithic subsistence economies than previously identified. Differences in heterogeneity between early and late assemblages may also represent major differences between these periods in terms of the structure of the labor resources available for animal production tasks and the integration of these tasks into a schedule compatible with other basic subsistence and social activities.

Animals and Economic Intensification

The results of this study have a number of implications for existing ideas about economic intensification in the Neolithic, especially as pertains to the secondary products model. I suggest that the whole secondary products phenomenon is best conceptualized in terms of the diversification of animal production as discussed in Chapter 4. In this way, it is more easily integrated into general models of changes in resource use associated with the long-term consequences of the shift to agriculture.

From the evidence presented in this study, it seems true that there was an increase in the number of taxa exploited from the early to the late Neolithic. This corresponds with the kind of change in resource diversity associated with the transition to agriculture and the early stages of intensification, as modeled by Christenson and others. There is also some support for the hypothesis that this increase in the number of resources was accompanied by a differentiation in the functional exploitation of domestic animal taxa. In particular, the investigation of Neolithic cattle has provided some confirmation for the idea that economic change in this period included the use of different animals for different body products. This development is not an immediately obvious implication of the generalized model, but rather relates to ideas stimulated by Sherratt.

One important observation derived from these analyses is that differences in the functional use of animals (as shown here with cattle) are related to the diversity of a faunal assemblage. As a result, some restructuring of the secondary products model may be appropriate. The major change seems to involve not a shift in domestic animal exploitation from the use of one body product (eg. meat) to another (eg. milk), but rather, a shift from a focus on limited taxa (cattle or ovicaprines) for multiple products to use of a number of animals for specific purposes.

Questions about the identification of particular animal products as "secondary" have already been raised by other authors, and the unity of the secondary products complex has been criticized a number of times (eg. Clason 1988; Renfrew 1988). If this concept is to be retained, we need to reconsider the ranking of milk production, and possibly also traction (as evidenced by presence of oxen), as "secondary". There is some suggestion that milk use became an integral part of ovicaprine exploitation systems of the Near East very soon after domestication (Cribb 1987), and there seems no good reason not to expect a similar pattern in cattle exploitation. Sherratt's model has led to the important recognition that the use of animals for different body products is an outgrowth of general economic intensification. However, its validity as a formal horizon of largely imported economic traits is questionable.

The relationship demonstrated in this study between assemblage composition and functional use of animals has not been immediately apparent from previous analyses. It has only emerged after the detailed investigation of empirical evidence. In the past, some analysts have assumed that functional differentiation within the domestic animal spectrum should be accompanied by a pattern of assemblage dominance by a narrow range of taxa (eg. Greenfield 1988). Although others have questioned this assumption (Hesse 1988), it has been more an intuitive questioning than systematic testing with data. This is symptomatic of a more general problem: The links between agricultural intensification, animal production and faunal assemblage variability remain to be fully explored.

This research has attempted to contribute to this problem from both theoretical and methodological perspectives. First, the discussion of the relationship between strategies of specialization or diversification and economic intensification has provided an initial framework within which explicit and tenable hypotheses about animal production may be phrased. This discussion has also highlighted the danger in confounding taxonomic specialization with functional specialization. The formal terminology and theoretical constructs with which we approach domestic animal production as an economic strategy are not yet developed enough to phrase these observations as parsimoniously as possible. Nevertheless, the results of this study suggest the importance of keeping such concepts separate.

Methodologically, diversity has proven to be an extremely useful descriptive tool for monitoring shifts in animal use in the Neolithic. Specifically, heterogeneity provides a relatively simple way to summarize the kinds of variability which structure faunal assemblages. It can be used as a background against which more specific assemblage or taxonomic characteristics (eg. mortality curves and sex ratios) can be assessed and is fairly easy to relate to the concept of economic diversification.

Finally, the investigation of diversity in combination with analyses of specific taxa has contributed to the general model of resource diversification in the process of agricultural intensification as it exists in the literature. A sequence may be proposed in which an initial increase in the number of resources exploited is followed by a functional differentiation among those resources. Only in later stages can we expect a further shift, combining resource specialization (focus on fewer types of resources) with functional or productive specialization. In terms of domestic animal production, I suggest that such a pattern is not seen until much later in Bronze Age Europe, when stronger interregional trade networks allowed the initial development of regional specializations which combined a focus on specific taxa with the exploitation of specific body products of animals. A classic example is the development of sheep herding after the introduction of wool sheep, and perhaps the emergence of pastoralism in a more general sense. This would lead to a situation in which faunal remains are expected to show evidence of *both* large herd sizes *and* age and sex ratios indicating the use of animals for specific functions.

These conclusions also clear the way for the integration of a major category of subsistence data, faunal remains, into more general models of change in Neolithic Europe. The shifts in animal economy demonstrated here are clearly related to economic and social change for this period of prehistory. Intensification of animal production has been shown to accompany the movement of agricultural settlements to new regions and environmental zones beginning by the fourth millennium BC. Changes in the settlement pattern data for this period should also be recalled: site aggregation has been related to a hypothesis of endemic conflict stemming at least partially from competition and pressure for land. Faunal evidence suggests that some of this pressure on land resources may be due to the increased area needed for stock keeping and associated tasks like grazing and fodder collection; it is not exclusively a matter of pressure on land available for cultivation purposes.

The differentiation of animal products also has direct implications for labor organization. The elaboration of particular strategies, for instance, milk production, suggests an increase in task specialization. Minimally, the exploitation of new combinations of animals and animal products also signals a new concern for scheduling. Given the inequities between labor demands and agricultural tasks at the household level, the reorganization of labor is expected to lead to changes at higher-order levels of social integration. The net result of such a process of changes in the mobilization of resources is the increased potential for differential accumulation of wealth and consequent increased stratification at or above the level of the individual production unit.

References Cited

Adams, S. N.
1975 Sheep and Cattle Grazing in the Forests: A Review. *Journal of Applied Ecology* 12: 143-152.

Aitchison, Stewart
1989 Neue Ergebnisse der Ausgrabung in der Altheimer Feuchtbodensiedlung von Ergolding-Fischergasse, Lkr. Landshut. In *Vorträge des 7. niederbayerischen Archäologentages*, edited by Karl Schmotz, pp. 9-16. Marie L. Leidorf, Buch am Erlbach.

Albright, J. L.
1969 Social Environment and Growth. In *Animal Growth and Nutrition*, edited by E.S.E. Hafez and I.A. Dyer, pp. 106-120. Lea and Febiger, Philadelphia.

Aldenderfer, Mark S. and Roger K. Blashfield
1984 *Cluster Analysis*. Sage Publications, Beverly Hills.

Allan, William
1965 *The African Husbandman*. Greenwood Press, Hartford, Connecticut.

Ambros, Cyril
1968 Remains of Fauna Found in the Eneolithic Settlement on Homolka (1960-1961). In *Homolka: An Eneolithic Site in Bohemia*, edited by Robert W. Ehrich and Emilie Pleslová-Stiková, pp. 440-469. American School of Prehistoric Research Bulletin 24. Peabody Museum, Cambridge.

Arnold, G. W. and M. L. Dudzinsky
1978 *Ethology of Free-Ranging Domestic Animals*. Elsevier, Amsterdam.

Bakels, Corrie C.
1982 Zum wirtschaftlichen Nutzungsraum einer bandkeramischen Siedlung. In *Siedlungen der Kultur mit Linearkeramik in Europa*, pp. 9-16. Archäologisches Institut der Slowakischen Akademie der Wissenschaften, Nitra.

Baranski, A.
1971 *Geschichte der Thierzucht und Thiermedicin im Altertum*. Georg Olms Verlag, Hildesheim.

Barker, Graeme
1985 *Prehistoric Farming in Europe*. Cambridge University Press, Cambridge.

Barlett, Peggy F.
1980 Introduction: Development Issues and Economic Anthropology. In *Agricultural Decision Making*, edited by Peggy F. Barlett, pp. 1-16. Academic Press, New York.

Barthel, Hans-Joachim
1985 *Die Tierreste aus einer "Grabenanlage" der neolithischen Bernberger Kultur*. Beiträge zur Archäozoologie III. Weimarer Monographien zur Ur- und Frühgeschichte 13. Weimar.

Barthel, Hans-Joachim and Jutta Cott
1977 Eine Sumpfschildkröte aus der neolithischen Station Erfurt-Gispersleben. *Ausgrabungen und Funde* 22(4): 170-173.

Bayerlein, P. M.
1985 *Die Gruppe Oberlauterbach in Niederbayern*. Materialhefte zur bayerischen Vorgeschichte, Reihe A, 53. Kallmünz.

Becker, B., R. Krause and B. Kromer
1989 Zur absoluten Chronologie der frühen Bronzezeit. *Germania* 67(2):421-442.

Becker, Cornelia
1981 *Tierknochenfunde, dritter Bericht*. Die neolithischen Ufersiedlungen von Twann 16. Staatlicher Lehrmittelverlag, Bern.

Becker, Cornelia and Friederike Johansson
1981 *Tierknochenfunde, zweiter Bericht: mittleres und oberes Schichtpaket der Cortaillod-Kultur*. Die neolithischen Ufersiedlungen von Twann 11. Staatlicher Lehrmittelverlag, Bern.

Behnke, Roy H., Jr.
1980 *The Herders of Cyrenaica: Ecology, Economy and Kinship Among the Bedouin of Eastern Libya*. Illinois Studies in Anthropology 12. University of Illinois Press, Urbana.

Behrens, Hermann
1964 *Die neolithisch-frühmetallzeitlichen Tierskelettfunde der Alten Welt*. Veröffentlichungen des Landesmuseums für Vorgeschichte in Halle 19. VEB Deutscher Verlag der Wissenschaften, Berlin.

1973 *Die Jungsteinzeit im Mittelelbe-Saale-Gebeit*. Veröffentlichungen des Landesmuseums für Vorgeschichte in Halle 27. VEB Deutscher Verlag der Wissenschaften, Berlin.

Beyer, Alix Irene
    1970 *Tierknochenfunde der Michelsberger Kultur vom Hetzenberg bei Heilbronn-Neckargartach und aus siener Umgebung.* Institut für Palaeoanatomie, Domestikationsforschung und Geschichte der Tiermedizin der Universität München, Munich.

Binford, Lewis R.
    1984 *Faunal Remains from Klasies River Mouth.* Academic Press, New York.

Binford, Lewis R. and Jack B. Bertram
    1977 Bone Frequencies - and Attritional Processes. In *For Theory Building in Archaeology*, edited by Lewis R. Binford, pp. 77-113. Academic Press, New York.

Blome, Wolfgang
    1968 *Tierknochenfunde aus der spätneolithischen Station Polling.* Institut für Paleoanatomie, Domestikationsforschung und Geschichte der Tiermedizin der Universität München, Munich.

Bobrowsky, Peter T. and Bruce F. Ball
    1989 The Theory and Mechanics of Ecological Diversity in Archaeology. In *Quantifying Diversity in Archaeology*, edited by R.D. Leonard and G.T. Jones, pp. 4-12. Cambridge University Press, Cambridge.

Boelicke, U., E. Koller, R. Kuper, H. Löhr, J. Lüning, W. Schwellnus, P. Stehli, M. Wolters and A. Zimmerman
    1977 Untersuchungen zur neolithischen Besiedlung der Aldenhovener Platte VII. *Bonner Jahrbücher* 177: 481-560.

Boelicke, U., D. von Brandt, J. Eckert, J. Lüning, W. Schwellnus, P. Stehli, J. Weiner, M. Wolters and A. Zimmerman
    1980 Untersuchungen zur neolithischen Besiedlung der Aldenhovener Platte X. *Bonner Jahrbücher* 180: 275-303.

Boelicke, U., D. von Brandt, J. Lüning, P. Stehli and A. Zimmermann
    1988 *Der bandkeramische Siedlungsplatz Langweiler 8, Gemeinde Aldenhoven, Kr. Düren.* Rheinische Ausgrabungen 28. Rheinisches Amt für Bodendenkmalpflege, Bonn.

Boessneck, J.
    1956 *Tierknochen aus spätneolithischen Siedlungen Bayerns.* Studien an vor- und frühgeschichtlichen Tierreste Bayerns I. Tieranatomisches Institut der Universität München, Munich.

    1958 *Zur Entwicklung vor- und frühgeschichtlicher Haus- und Wildtiere Bayerns im Rahmen der gleichzeitigen Tierwelt Mitteleuropas.* Studien an vor- und frühgeschichtlichen Tierresten Bayerns II. Tieranatomisches Institut der Universität München, Munich.

    1963 Schluss. In *Seeberg Bürgäschisee-Süd. Teil 3: Die Tierreste,* by J. Boessneck, J.-P. Jéquier and H.R. Stampfli, pp. 201-206. Acta Bernensia II. Stämpfli und Cie, Bern.

    1982 Neolithische Tierknochenfunde von Kraichtal-Gochsheim, Kreis Karlsruhe. *Fundberichte aus Baden-Württemberg* 7: 13-30.

Boessneck, Joachim and Johann Schäffer
    1985 Zooarchäologische Beurteilung neolithischer Tierknochenfunde aus dem Gebeit von Mintranching, Ldkr. Regensburg. *Bayerische Vorgeschichtsblätter* 50: 72-80.

Boessneck, J., J.-P. Jéquier and H. R. Stampfli
    1963 *Seeberg Burgäschisee-Süd, Teil 3: Die Tierreste.* Acta Bernensia II. Verlag Stämpfli & Cie, Bern.

Bognar-Kutzian, Ida
    1971 Zoology and Chronology in Prehistory. *American Anthropologist* 73: 675-679.

Bogucki, P.
    1979 Tactical and Strategic Settlements in the Early Neolithic of Lowland Poland. *Journal of Anthropological Research* 35: 238-246.

    1982 *Early Neolithic Subsistence and Settlement in the Polish Lowlands.* British Archaeological Reports International Series 150. Oxford.

    1984 Ceramic Sieves of the Linear Pottery Culture and Their Economic Implications. *Oxford Journal of Archaeology* 3(1): 15-30.

    1985 Theoretical Directions in European Archaeology. *American Antiquity* 50(4): 780-788.

    1987 The Establishment of Agrarian Communities on the North European Plain. *Current Anthropology* 28(1): 1-24.

Bökönyi, S.
    1971 The Development and History of Domestic Animals in Hungary: The Neolithic Through the Middle Ages. *American Anthropologist* 73(3): 640-674.

    1974 *History of Domestic Mammals in Central and Eastern Europe.* Akadémiai Kiadó, Budapest.

Boserup, Ester
  1965 *The Conditions of Agricultural Growth*. Allen and Unwin, London.

Brain, C. K.
  1981 *The Hunters or the Hunted? An Introduction to African Cave Taphonomy*. University of Chicago Press, Chicago.

Breunig, Peter
  1987 ^{14}C *Chronologie des vorderasiatischen, südost- und mitteleuropaischen Neolithikums*. Böhlau Verlag, Köln.

Burger, Ingrid
  1988 *Die Siedlung der Chamer Gruppe von Dobl, Gemeinde Prutting, Ldkr. Rosenheim, und ihre Stellung im Endneolithikum Mitteleuropas*. Materialhefte zur bayerischen Vorgeschichte, Reihe A, 56. Graf, Fürth.

Burkitt, M. and V. G. Childe
  1932 A Chronological Table of Prehistory. *Antiquity* 6: 185-205.

Busch, Andreas
  1985 *Tierknochenfunde aus einer endneolithischen Siedlung bei Riekofen/Ldkr. Regensburg*. Institut für Palaeoanatomie, Domestikationsforschung und Geschichte der Tiermedizin der Universität München, Munich.

Buttler, W.
  1936 Das bandkeramische Dorf von Köln-Lindenthal und seine Bedeutung für die Entwicklung des Bauerntums. *Zeitschrift für Ethnologie* 67: 68-74.

Butzer, Karl
  1971 *Environment and Archaeology: An Ecological Approach to Prehistory*. Aldine, Chicago.

Casteel, Richard W.
  1978 Faunal Assemblages and the "Wiegemethode" or Weight Method. *Journal of Field Archaeology* 5(1): 71-77.

Chaix, Louis
  1976 La faune de la station d'Yvonand III (Cortaillod récent). *Jahrbuch der schweizerische Gesellschaft für Ur- und Frühgeschichte* 59: 61-65.

Champion, Timothy, Clive Gamble, Stephen Shennan and Alasdair Whittle
  1984 *Prehistoric Europe*. Academic Press, New York.

Chang, Claudia and Harold A. Koster
  1986 Beyond Bones: Toward an Archaeology of Pastoralism. In *Advances in Archaeological Method and Theory*, Vol. 9, edited by Michael B. Schiffer, pp. 97-148. Academic Press, New York.

Chayanov, A. V.
  1966 *The Theory of Peasant Economy*. Richard D. Irwin, Homewood, Illinois.

Chibnik, Michael
  1980 The Statistical Behavior Approach. In *Agricultural Decision Making*, edited by Peggy F. Barlett, pp. 87-114. Academic Press, New York.

Childe, V. Gordon
  1929 *The Danube in Prehistory*. Oxford University Press, Oxford.

  1942 *What Happened in History*. Penguin Books, London.

  1950 *Prehistoric Migrations in Europe*. Instituttet for Sammenlignende Kulturforskning, Oslo.

  1957 *The Dawn of European Civilisation*, sixth edition. Paladin, St. Albans.

  1958 Retrospect. *Antiquity* 32: 69-74.

Chisolm, Michael
  1979 *Rural Settlement and Land Use: An Essay in Location*, third edition. Hutchinson, London.

Christenson, Andrew L.
  1980 Change in the Human Food Niche in Response to Population Growth. In *Modeling Change in Prehistoric Subsistence Economies*, edited by Timothy K. Earle and Andrew L. Christenson, pp. 31-72. Academic Press, New York.

Clark, Colin and Margaret Haswell
  1967 *The Economics of Subsistence Agriculture*. St. Martin's Press, New York.

Clark, Geoffrey and Seonbok Yi
  1983 Niche-Width Variation in Cantabrian Archaeofaunas: A Diachronic Study. In *Animals and Archaeology 1: Hunters and Their Prey*, edited by Juliet Clutton-Brock and Caroline Grigson, pp. 183-208. British Archaeological Reports International Series 163. Oxford.

Clark, J. G. D.
  1945 Farmers and Forests in Neolithic Europe. *Antiquity* 19: 57-71.

Clark, J. G. D.
1952 *Prehistoric Europe: The Economic Basis*. Stanford University Press, Stanford.

1965 Radiocarbon Dating and the Expansion of Farming from the Near East over Europe. *Proceedings of the Prehistoric Society* 21: 58-73.

Clason, A. T.
1967 *Animal and Man in Holland's Past*. J. B. Wolters, Groningen.

1970 The Animal Bones of the Bandceramik and Middle Age Settlements Near Bylany in Bohemia. *Palaeohistoria* 14: 1-18.

1973 Some Aspects of Stock-Breeding and Hunting in the Period After the Bandceramik Culture North of the Alps. In *Domestikationsforschung und Geschichte der Haustiere*, edited by J. Matolcsi, pp. 205-212. Akadémiai Kiadó, Budapest.

1977 Die Tierknochen. In *Die neolithische Besiedlung bei Hienheim, Ldkr. Kelheim*, by P. J. R. Modderman, pp. 101-120. Bayerisches Landesamt für Denkmalpflege, Munich.

1985 Animal Bones and Implements. In *Makotrasy: A TRB Site in Bohemia*, by Emilie Pleslová-Stiková, pp. 137-162. Fontes Archaeologici Pragenses 17. Museum Nationale Pragae, Prague.

1988 Comment on Greenfield's Origins of Milk and Wool Production: A Zooarchaeological Perspective. *Current Anthropology* 29(4): 588-589.

Clutton-Brock, T. H., F. E. Guinness and S. D. Albon
1982 *Red Deer: Behavior and Ecology of Two Sexes*. University of Chicago Press, Chicago.

Cohen, Mark Nathan
1977 *The Food Crisis in Prehistory: Overpopulation and the Origins of Agriculture*. Yale University Press, New Haven.

Cribb, Roger
1985 The Analysis of Ancient Herding Systems: An Application of Computer Simulation in Faunal Studies. In *Beyond Domestication in Prehistoric Europe: Investigations in Subsistence Archaeology and Social Complexity*, edited by Graeme Barker and Clive Gamble, pp. 75-106. Academic Press, London.

1987 The Logic of the Herd: A Computer Simulation of Archaeological Herd Structure. *Journal of Anthropological Archaeology* 6: 376-415.

Cunliffe, Barry
1973 Introduction. In *The Dawn of European Civilisation* by V. Gordon Childe, reprinted and revised sixth edition, pp. 15-28. Paladen, St. Alban.

Dahl, Gudrun and Anders Hjort
1976 *Having Herds: Pastoral Herd Growth and Household Economy*. Stockholm Studies in Social Anthropology 2. Stockholm.

Daniel, Glyn
1971 From Worsaae to Childe: the Models of Prehistory. *Proceedings of the Prehistoric Society* 38: 140-153.

Degerbol, Magnus
1970 Zoological Part. In *The Urus (Bos primigenius Bojanus) and Neolithic Domesticated Cattle (Bos taurus domesticus Linné) in Denmark*, by M. Degerbol and B. Fredskild, pp. 5-178. Det Kongelige Danske Videnskabernes Selskab Biologiske Skrifter 17(1). Copenhagen.

Dieckmann, B.
1987 Ein bermerkenswerter Kupferfund aus der jungsteinzeitlichen Seeufersiedlung Hornstaad-Hörnle I am westlichen Bodensee. *Archäologische Nachrichten aus Baden* 38/39: 28-37.

Dolukhanov, Paul M.
1979 *Ecology and Economy in Neolithic Eastern Europe*. Duckworth, London.

Driehaus, Jürgen
1960 *Die Altheimer Gruppe und das Jungneolithikum in Mitteleuropa*. Römisch-Germanisches Zentralmuseum, Mainz.

Driehaus, Jürgen and Hermann Behrens
1961 Stand und Aufgaben der Erforschung des Jungneolithikums in Mitteleuropa. In *L'Europe á la fin de l'âge de la pierre*, pp. 233-275. Académie tschécoslovaque des Sciences, Prague.

Dunnell, Robert C.
1989 Diversity in Archaeology: A Group of Measures in Search of Application? In *Quantifying Diversity in Archaeology*, edited by R.D. Leonard and G.T. Jones, pp. 142-149. Cambridge University Press, Cambridge.

Dyson-Hudson, N. and R. Dyson-Hudson
1970 The Food Production System of a Semi-Nomadic Society, the Karimojong, Uganda. In *African Food Production Systems, Cases and Theory*, edited by P. McLoughlin, pp. 91-123. Baltimore.

Eadie, J.
1969 Sheep Production and Pastoral Resources. In *Animal Populations in Relation to Their Food Resources*, edited by Adam Watson, pp. 7-24. British Ecological Society Symposium 10. Blackwell Scientific Publications, Oxford.

Edlin, H. L.
1960 *Wildlife of Wood and Forest*. Hutchinson, London.

Ehrich, Robert W. and Emilie Pleslova-Stikova
1968 *Homolka: An Eneolithic Site in Bohemia*. American School of Prehistoric Research Bulletin 24. Peabody Museum, Cambridge.

Eibl, Franz
1974 *Die Tierknochenfunde aus der neolithischen Station Feldmeilen-Vorderfeld am Zürichsee I. Die Nichtwiederkäuer*. Institut für Paläoanatomie, Domestikationsforschung und Geschichte der Tiermedizin der Universität München, Munich.

Farrugia, J.-P., R. Kuper, J. Lüning and P. Stehli
1973 *Der bandkeramische Siedlungsplatz Langweiler 2, Gemeinde Aldenhoven, Kr. Düren*. Rheinische Ausgrabungen 13. Rheinisches Amt für Bodendenkmalpflege, Bonn.

Fel, Edit and Tamas Hofer
1969 *Proper Peasants: Traditional Life in a Hungarian Village*. Viking Fund Publications in Anthropology 46. Wenner-Gren Foundation for Anthropological Research, Corvina Press, Budapest.

Firbas, Franz
1949 *Spät- und nacheiszeitliche Waldgeschichte Mitteleuropas nördlich der Alpen. Erster Band: Allgemeine Waldgeschichte*. Gustav Fischer Verlag, Jena.

1952 *Spät- und nacheiszeitliche Waldgeschichte Mitteleuropas nördlich der Alpen. Zweiter Band: Waldgeschichte der einzelnen Landschaften*. Gustav Fischer Verlag, Jena.

Flannery, Kent V.
1968 Archaeological Systems Theory and Early Mesoamerica. In *Anthropological Archaeology in the Americas*, edited by Betty J. Meggars, pp. 67-87. Anthropological Society of Washington, Washington, D.C.

Fleming, Andrew
1972 The Genesis of Pastoralism in European Prehistory. *World Archaeology* 4: 179-191.

1985 Land Tenure, Productivity and Field Systems. In *Beyond Domestication in Prehistoric Europe: Investigations in Subsistence Archaeology and Social Complexity*, edited by Graeme Barker and Clive Gamble, pp. 129-146. Academic Press, New York.

Förster, Wolfgang
1974 *Die Tierknochenfunde aus der neolithischen Station Feldmeilen-Vorderfeld am Zürichsee II. Die Wiederkäuer*. Institut für Palaeoanatomie, Domestikationsforschung und Geschichte der Tiermedizin der Universität München, Munich.

Fratkin, Elliot
1988 Household and Community in Ariaal Rendille, Nomadic Pastoralists of Northern Kenya. Paper presented at the 21st Chacmool conference, Calgary, Alberta.

Frenzel, B.
1976 Zur postglazialen Paläökologie der Donau und ihrer Südlichen Zuflüsse um deutchen Alpenvorland. In *Führer zur Exkursionstagung des IGCP Projektes 73/1/24*, edited by B. Frenzel, pp. 74-75.

1977 Postglaziale Klimaschwankungen im südwestlichen Mitteleuropa. In *Dendrochronologie und postglaziale Klimaschwankungen in Europa*, edited by Burkhard Frenzel, pp. 297-322. Franz Steiner Verlag, Wiesbaden.

Gallay, Margarete
1970 *Die Besiedlung der südlichen Oberrheinebene in Neolithikum und Frühbronzezeit*. Badische Fundberichte Sonderheft 12. Staatliches Amt für Ur- und Frühgeschichte, Freiburg im Breisgau.

Glass, Margaret
1988 Faunal Variability in Late Neolithic Southern Germany. *Archaeozoologia* 7:307-318.

Gradmann, Robert
1900 *Das Pflanzenleben der Schwäbischen Alb*, second edition. Verlag der Schwäbischen Albvereins, Tübingen.

Grayson, Donald K.
1978 Reconstructing Mammalian Communities: A Discussion of Shotwell's Method of Paleoecological Analysis. *Paleobiology* 4: 77-81.

1981 The Effects of Sample Size on Some Derived Measures in Vertebrate Faunal Analysis. *Journal of Archaeological Science* 8: 77-88.

Grayson, Donald K.
1984 *Quantitative Zooarchaeology*. Academic Press, New York.

Greenfield, Haskel J.
1988 The Origins of Milk and Wool Production in the Old World: A Zooarchaeological Perspective from the Central Balkans. *Current Anthropology* 29(4): 573-593.

Gregg, Susan A.
1988 *Foragers and Farmers: Population Interaction and Agricultural Expansion in Prehistoric Europe*. University of Chigaco Press, Chicago.

Grigg, D. B.
1974 *The Agricultural Systems of the World: An Evolutionary Approach*. Cambridge University Press, Cambridge.

Grigson, Caroline
1982 Porridge and Pannage: Pig Husbandry in Neolithic England. In *Archaeological Aspects of Woodland Ecology*, edited by Martin Bell and Susan Limbrey, pp. 297-314. British Archaeological Reports International Series 146. Oxford.

Groenman-van Waateringe, W.
1971 Hecken im westeuropäischen Frühneolithikum. *Berichten van de Rijksdienst voor Het Oudheidkundig Bodemonderzoek* 150(20-21): 295-299.

Grzimek, Bernhard (editor)
1972 *Grzimek's Animal Life Encyclopedia* 13(4). van Nostrand Reinhold Co., New York.

Guyan, W.-U. (editor)
1955 *Das Pfahbauproblem*. Monographien zur Ur- und Frühgeschichte der Schweiz 11.

Gwynne, D. C. and J. Morton Boyd
1969 Relationships Between Numbers of Soay Sheep and Pastures at St. Kilda. In *Animal Populations in Relation to Their Food Resources*, edited by Adam Watson, pp. 289-302. British Ecological Society Symposium 10. Blackwell Scientific Publications, Oxford.

Habermehl, Karl-Heinz
1975 *Die Altersbestimmung bei Haus- und Labortieren*, second edition. Verlag Paul Parey, Berlin.

Hafez, E. S. E.
1968 Principles of Animal Adaptation. In *Adaptation of Domestic Animals*, edited by E.S.E. Hafez, pp. 3-17. Lea and Febiger, Philadelphia.

Hafez, E. S. E., M. W. Schein and R. Ewbank
1969 The Behavior of Cattle. In *The Behavior of Domestic Animals*, edited by E.S.E. Hafez, pp. 235-295. Bailliere, Tindall and Cassell, London.

Hamond, F. W.
1981 The Colonisation of Europe: The Analysis of Settlement Processes. In *Pattern of the Past: Essays in Honour of David Clarke*, edited by Ian Hodder, Glyn Isaac and Norman Hammond, pp. 211-248. Cambridge University Press, Cambridge.

Hardesty, D.
1975 The Niche Concept: Suggestions for its Use in Human Ecology. *Human Ecology* 3: 71-85.

Hartmann-Frick, H.
1960 *Die Tierwelt des prähistorischen Siedlungsplatzes auf dem Eschner Lutzengüetle, Fürstentum Liechtenstein (Neolithikum bis La Téne)*. Jahrbuch des historischen Vereins für das Fürstentum Liechtenstein 59: 5-223.

Herre, Wolf and Manfred Röhrs
1973 *Haustiere - zoologische gesehen*. Gustav Fischer Verlag, Stuttgart.

Hescheler, Karl and Jakob Rüeger
1942 Die Reste der Haustiere aus den neolithischen Pfahlbaudörfern Egolzwil 2 (Wauwilersee, Kt. Luzern) und Seematte-Gelfingen (Baldeggersee, Kt. Luzern). *Vierteljahrsschrift der naturforschenden Gesellschaft in Zürich* 87: 383-486.

Hesse, Brian
1984 These Are Our Goats: The Origins of Herding in West Central Iran. In *Animal and Archaeology 3: Herders and Their Flocks*, edited by Juliet Clutton-Brock and Caroline Grigson, pp. 243-264. British Archaeological Reports International Series 202. Oxford.

1988 Comment on Greenfield's Origins of Milk and Wool Production: A Zooarchaeological Perspective. *Current Anthropology* 29(4): 590-591.

Higham, C. F. W.
1966 Stock Rearing in Prehistoric Europe. Unpublished PhD thesis, Cambridge University.

1968 Size Trends in Prehistoric European Domestic Fauna and the Problem of Local Domestication. *Acta zoologica fennica* 120: 3-21.

Higham, C. F. W.
1969 Die Cortaillod-Kultur - ein Beitrag zur urgeschichtlichen Wirtschaftskunde. *Zeitschrift für schweizerische Archäologie und Kunstgeschichte* 326(1): 1-7.

Hodder, Ian
1982 Sequences of Structural Change in the Dutch Neolithic. In *Symbolic and Structural Archaeology*, edited by Ian Hodder, pp. 162-177. Cambridge University Press, Cambridge.

1984 Burials, Houses, Women and Men in the European Neolithic. In *Ideology, Power and Prehistory*, edited by D. Miller and C. Tilley, pp. 51-68. Cambridge University Press, Cambridge.

Imhof, Urs
1964 Osteometrische Untersuchungen an Rinderknochen aus Pfahbauten des Bielersees. *Mitteilungen der naturforschenden Gesellschaft in Bern* 21: 138-237.

Ingold, Tim
1980 *Hunters, Pastoralists and Ranchers*. Cambridge University Press, Cambridge.

Iversen, J.
1941 Land Occupation in Denmark's Stone Age. *Danmarks Geologiske Undersogelse* 2(66): 1-68.

Jacomet, Stefanie and Jörg Schibler
1985 Die Nahrungsversorgung eines jungsteinzeitlichen Pfynerdorfes am unteren Zürichsee. *Archäologie der Schweiz* 8: 125-141.

Jahnkuhn, Herbert
1969 *Vor- und Frühgeschichte: vom Neolithikum bis zur Völkerwanderungszeit*. Deutsche Agrargeschichte 1. Verlag Eugen Ulmer, Stuttgart.

Jarman, M. R., G. N. Bailey and H. N. Jarman (editors)
1982 *Early European Agriculture: Its Foundations and Development*. Cambridge University Press, Cambridge.

Jones, George T., Donald K. Grayson and Charlotte Beck
1983 Artifact Class Richness and Sample Size in Archaeological Surface Assemblages. In *Lulu Linear Punctated: Essays in Honor of George Irving Quimby*, edited by Robert C. Dunnell and Donald K. Grayson, pp. 55-73. Anthropological Papers of the Museum of Anthropology, University of Michigan 72. Ann Arbor.

Josien, Therese
1956 Etude de la faune de gisements néolithiques (niveau de Cortaillod) du Canton de Berne (Suisse). *Archives Suisses D'Anthropologie Generale* 21: 28-62.

Kaufmann, Dieter
1982 Zu einigen Ergebnissen der Ausgrabungen im Bereich des linienbandkeramischen Erdwerks bei Eilsleben, Kreis Wanzleben. In *Siedlungen der Kultur mit Linearkeramik in Europa*, pp. 69-91. Archäologisches Institut der Slowakischen Akademie der Wissenschaften, Nitra.

Keefer, Erwin
1983 Eine Schussenrieder Siedlung bei Eberdingen-Hochdorf, Kr. Ludwigsburg. PhD Dissertation, Fakultät für Kulturwissenschaften, Institut für Vor- und Frühgeschichte, Eberhard-Karls Universität. Tübingen.

Keller, Ferdinand
1866 *The Lake Dwellings of Switzerland and Other Parts of Europe*. Longmans, Greene and Co., London.

Kim, Jae-On and Charles W. Mueller
1978 *Factor Analysis: Statistical Methods and Practical Issues*. Sage Publications, Beverly Hills.

Kintigh, Keith W.
1984 Measuring Archaeological Diversity by Comparison with Simulated Assemblages. *American Antiquity* 49(1): 44-54.

1989 Sample Size, Significance, and Measures of Diversity. In *Quantifying Diversity in Archaeology*, edited by R.D. Leonard and G.T. Jones, pp. 25-36. Cambridge University Press, Cambridge.

Klein, Richard G. and Kathryn Cruz-Uribe
1984 *The Analysis of Animal Bones from Archaeological Sites*. University of Chicago Press, Chicago.

Knörzer, Karl-Heinz
1972 Subfossile Pflanzenreste aus der bandkeramischen Siedlung Langweiler 3 und 6, Kreis Jülich, und ein urnfelderzeitliche Getreidefund innerhalb dieser Siedlung. *Bonner Jahrbücher* 172: 395-403.

Kokabi, Mostefa
1985 Vorläufiger Bericht über die Untersuchungen an Tierknochenfunden aus Hornstaad-Hörle I am westlichen Bodensee. *Materialhefte zur Vor- und Frühgeschichte in Baden-Württemberg* 7: 148-163. Stuttgart.

Kokabi, Mostefa
    1987 Die Tierknochenfunde aus den neolithischen Ufersiedlungen am Bodensee - Versuch einer Rekonstruktion der einstigen Wirtschafts- und Umweltverhältnisse mit der Untersuchungsmethode der Osteologie. *Archäologische Nachrichten aus Baden* 38/39: 61-66.

Köninger, Joachim
    1986 Moorsiedlungen des Federseerieds. *Archäologische Ausgrabungen in Baden-Württemberg* 1985: 66-70.

Kristiansen, Kristian
    1982 The Formation of Tribal Systems in Later European Prehistory: Northern Europe 4000-500 BC. In *Theory and Explanation in Archaeology*, edited by Colin Renfrew, Michael J. Rowlands and Barbara Abbot Seagraves, pp. 241-280. Academic Press, New York.

Kruk, Janusz
    1980 *The Neolithic Settlement of Southern Poland.* British Archaeological Reports International Series 93. Oxford.

Kubasiewicz, M.
    1956 O metodyce badan wykopaliskowich szczatkow kostynch zwierzecych. *Materialy Zachodnio-Pomorskie* 2: 235-244.

Kuper, R., H. Löhr, J. Lüning and P. Stehli
    1974 Untersuchungen zur neolithischen Besiedlung der Aldenhovener Platte IV. *Bonner Jahrbücher* 174: 424-508.

Kuper, R., H. Löhr, J. Lüning, P. Stehli and A. Zimmermann
    1977 *Der bandkeramische Siedlungsplatz Langweiler 9, Gemeinde Aldenhoven, Kreis Düren*. Rheinische Ausgrabungen 18. Rheinisches Amt für Bodendenkmalpflege, Bonn.

Küster, Hansjörg
    1989 Pflanzenreste in spätneolithischen Siedlungschichten von Ergolding-Fischergasse, Lkr. Landshut. In *Vorträge des 7. niederbayerischen Archäologentages*, edited by Karl Schmotz, pp. 17-28. Marie L. Leidorf, Buch am Erlbach.

Landesdenkmalamt Baden-Württemberg (editor)
    1984 *Berichte zu Ufer- und Moorsiedlungen Südwestdeutschlands 1.* Materialhefte zur Vor- und Frühgeschichte in Baden-Württemberg 4. Konrad Theiss Verlag, Stuttgart.

    1985 *Berichte zu Ufer- und Moorsiedlungen Südwestdeutschlands 2.* Materialhefte zur Vor- und Frühgeschichte in Baden-Württemberg 7. Konrad Theiss Verlag, Stuttgart.

    1990 *Siedlungsarchäologie im Alpenvorland II.* Forschungen und Berichte zur Vor- und Frühgeschichte in Baden-Württemberg 37. Konrad Theiss, Stuttgart.

Lehmann, U.
    1949 Der Ur im Diluvium Deutschlands und seine Verbreitung. *Neues Jahrbuch für Mineralogie, Geologie und Paläontologie* (B) 90: 163-266.

Liese-Kleiber, H.
    1987 Getreidepollen - ein Indikator für prähistorische Wirtschaftsformen? *Archäologische Nachrichten aus Baden* 38/39: 54-61.

Linke, Wolfgang
    1976 *Frühestes Bauerntum und geographische Umwelt.* Bochumer Geographische Arbeiten 28. Ferdinand Schöningh, Paderborn.

Long, Austin and Bruce Rippeteau
    1974 Testing Contemporaneity and Averaging Radiocarbon Dates. *American Antiquity* 39(2): 205-215.

Lowe, V. P. W.
    1960 A Discussion on the History, Present Status and Future Consideration of Red Deer (*Cervus elaphus* L.) in Scotland. In *Ecology and Management of Wild Grazing Animals in Temperate Zones*, edited by F. Bouliere, pp. 9-40. IUCN 8th Technical Meeting. Warsaw.

Lüning, J.
    1967 *Die Michelsberger Kultur. Ihre Funde in räumlicher und zeitlicher Gliederung.* Bericht der Römisch-Germanisch Kommission 48. Mainz.

    1971 Die Entwicklung der Keramik beim Übergang vom Mittel- zum Jungneolithikum im süddeutschen Raum. *Bericht der Römisch-Germanisch Kommission* 50: 1-95.

    1976 Schusssenried und Jordansmühl. In *Die Anfänge des Neolithikums vom Orient bis Nordeuropa. Teil 5b: Westliches Mitteleuropa*, edited by Jens Lüning, pp. 122-187. Böhlau Verlag, Köln.

Lüning, Jens and Jutta Meurers-Balke
    1980 Experimenteller Getreideanbau im Hambacher Forst, Gemeinde Elsdorf, Kr. Bergheim/Rheinland. *Bonner Jahrbücher* 180: 305-344.

Lyman, R. Lee
   1982 Archaeofaunas and Subsistence Studies. In *Advances in Archaeological Method and Theory*, Vol. 5, edited by Michael B. Schiffer, pp. 331-393. Academic Press, New York.

   1984 Bone Density and Differential Survivorship of Fossil Classes. *Journal of Anthropological Archaeology* 3: 259-299.

Matolcsi, Janos
   1970 Historische Erforschung der Körpergrösse des Rindes auf Grund ungarischem Knochenmaterial. *Zeitschrift für Tierzüchtung und Züchtungsbiologie* 87: 89-137.

Matuschik, Irenäus
   1985 Zur Chronologie des Spätneolithikums des bayerischen Donautals. Die Stratigraphie und Radiocarbondaten aus Oberschneiding, Ldkr. Straubing-Bogen. In *Archäologische Denkmalpflege in Niederbayern*, pp. 46-65. Bayerisches Landesamt für Denkmalpflege, Munich.

McCartney, Peter H. and Margaret F. Glass
   1990 Simulation Models and the Interpretation of Archaeological Diversity. *American Antiquity* 55(3):521-536.

Meadow, R. H.
   1980 Animal Bones: Problems for the Archaeologist Together with Some Possible Solutions. *Paleorient* 6: 65-77.

Menghin, Oswald
   1931 *Weltgeschichte der Steinzeit*. Anton Scholl, Vienna.

Milisauskas, Sarunas and Janusz Kruk
   1984 Settlement Organization and the Appearance of Low Level Hierarchical Societies During the Neolithic in the Bronocice Microregion, Southeastern Poland. *Germania* 62: 1-30.

Milojcic, Vladimir
   1949 *Chronologie der jüngeren Steinzeit Mittel- und Südosteuropas*. Archäologisches Institut, Berlin.

Modderman, Pieter J. R.
   1971 Bandkeramiker und Wandernbauertum. *Archäologisches Korrespondenzblatt* 1: 7-9.

   1975 Elsloo, a Neolithic Farming Community in the Netherlands. In *Recent Archaeological Excavations in Europe*, edited by R. Bruce-Mitford, pp. 260-286. Routledge and Kegan Paul, London.

   1982 Die Radiokarbondatierungen der Bandkeramik. In *Siedlungen der Kultur mit Linearkeramik in Europa*, pp. 177-183. Archäologisches Institut der Slowakischen Akademie der Wissenschaften, Nitra.

   1986 *Die neolithische Besiedlung bei Hienheim, Ldkr. Kelheim, II*. Materialhefte zur bayerischen Vorgeschichte, Reihe A, 57. Michael Lassleben, Kallmünz.

Moule, G. R.
   1968 Measurements of Productivity. In *Adaptation of Domestic Animals*, edited by E.S.E. Hafez, pp. 352-359. Lea and Febiger, Phildelphia.

Müller, H. H.
   1964 *Die Haustiere der mitteldeutschen Bandkeramiker*. Naturwissenschaftliche Beitrag zu Vor- und Frühgeschichte 1. Deutsche Akademie der Wissenschaften, Berlin.

   1978 Tierreste aus einer Siedlung der Bernburger Gruppe bei Halle (Saale). *Jahresschrift für mitteldeutsche Vorgeschichte* 62: 203-220.

   1985 Tierreste aus Siedlungsgruben der Bernburger Kultur von der Schalkenburg bei Quenstedt, Kr. Hettstedt. *Jahresschrift für mitteldeutsche Vorgeschichte* 68: 179-220.

Müller-Karpe, Hermann
   1961 *Die spätneolithische Siedlung von Polling*. Materialhefte zur bayerischen Vorgeschichte 17. Bayerisches Landesamt für Denkmalpflege, Michael Lassleben, Kallmünz.

Netting, Robert McC.
   1974 Agrarian Ecology. *Annual Review of Anthropology* 3: 21-56.

   1981 *Balancing on an Alp*. Cambridge University Press, Cambridge.

Neustupny, Evzen
   1968 Absolute Chronology of the Neolithic and Aeneolithic Periods in Central and Southeastern Europe. *Slovenska Archeologia* 16(1): 19-56.

   1969 Economy of the Corded Ware Cultures. *Archeologicky Rozhledy* 21(1): 43-68.

   1981 Das Äneolithikum Mitteleuropas. *Jahresschrift für mitteldeutsche Vorgeschichte* 63: 177-188.

Nobis, Günter

1954 Zur Kenntnis der ur- und frühgeschichtlichen Rinder Nord- und Mitteldeutschlands. *Zeitschrift für Tierzüchtung und Züchtungsbiologie* 63: 155-194.

1955 Die Entwicklung der Haustierwelt Nordwest- und Mitteldeutschlands in ihrer Beziehung zu landschaftlichen Gegebenheiten. *Petermanns Geographische Mitteilungen* 99: 2-7.

1977 Naturwissenschaftliche Beiträge A. Die Fauna. In *Die Schussenrieder Siedlung im "Schlosslesfeld" Markung Ludwigsburg*, edited by J. Lüning and H. Zürn, pp. 3-12. Forschungen und Berichte zu Vor- und Frühgeschichte in Baden-Württemberg 8.

1984 Die Haustiere im Neolithikum Zentraleuropas. In *Die Anfänge des Neolithikums vom Orient bis Nordeuropa. Teil IX: Der Beginn der Haustierhaltung in der "Alten Welt"*, edited by Günter Nobis, pp. 73-105. Böhlau Verlag, Köln.

Noddle, B. A.

1983 Size and Shape, Time and Place: Skeletal Variations in Cattle and Sheep. In *Integrating the Subsistence Economy*, edited by Martin Jones, pp. 211-238. British Archaeological Reports International Series 181. Oxford.

Odum, Eugene P.

1971 *Fundamentals of Ecology*, third edition. Saunders, Toronto.

Offenberger, Johann

1981 Die "Pfahlbauten" der Salzkammergutseen. In *Das Mondseeland: Geschichte und Kultur.* Ausstellung des Landes Oberösterreich 8. Mai bis 26. Oktober. Linz.

Oloff, Hans-Bernhard

1951 *Zur Biologie und Ökologie des Wildschweines.* Beiträge zur Tierkunde und Tierzucht 2. Verlag Dr. Paul Schöps, Frankfurt.

Ottaway, Barbara S.

1983 Ergolding-Fischergasse: eine Feuchtbodensiedlung der Altheimer Kultur. *Das archäologische Jahr in Bayern* 1982: 32-34.

1986 Neue Radiokarbondaten für Altheimer und Chamer Siedlungsplätze in Niederbayern. *Archäologisches Korrespondenzblatt* 16(2): 141-147.

Pape, Wolfgang

1978 *Bemerkungen zur relativen Chronologie des Endneolithikums am Beispiel Südwestdeutschlands und der Schweiz.* Tübinger Monographien zur Urgeschichte 3. Archaeologica Venatoria, Tübingen.

Patzelt, G.

1977 Der zeitliche Ablauf und das Ausmass postglazialen Klimaschwankungen in den Alpen. In *Dendrochronologie und postglaziale Klimaschwankungen in Europa*, edited by Burchard Frenzel, pp. 248-259. Franz Steiner Verlag, Wiesbaden.

Pavlu, Ivan

1982 Die Entwicklung des Siedlungsareals Bylany I. In *Siedlungen der Kultur mit Linearkeramik in Europa*, pp. 193-206. Archäologisches Institut der Slowakischen Akademie der Wissenschaften, Nitra.

Payne, Sebastian

1973 Kill-Off Patterns in Sheep and Goats: The Mandibles from Asvan Kale. *Anatolian Studies* 23: 281-303.

Perry, Tilden Wayne

1984 *Animal Life-Cycle Feeding and Nutrition.* Academic Press, New York.

Petrasch, J.

1986 Mittelneolithische Kreisgrabenanlagen in Südostbayern - die Untersuchungen im Jahre 1984. *Internationales Symposium über die Lengyel-Kultur.* Archäologisches Institut der Slowakischen Akademie der Wissenschaften in Nitra und Institut für Ur- und Frühgeschichte der Universität Wien, Nitra-Wien.

Pielou, E. C.

1975 *Ecological Diversity.* John Wiley and Sons, New York.

1977 *Mathematical Ecology.* John Wiley and Sons, New York.

Pietschmann, Werner

1977 *Zur Grösse des Rothirsches (Cervus elaphus L.) in vor- und frühgeschichtlicher Zeit.* Institut für Palaeoanatomie, Domestikationsforschung und Geschichte der Tiermedizin der Universität München, Munich.

Piggott, Stuart

1958 The Dawn: and an Epilogue. *Antiquity* 32: 75-79.

Pittioni, Richard
    1980 *Geschichte Österreichs. Band 1/2: Urzeit von etwa 80,000 bis 15 v. Chr. Geb.* Verlag der österreichen Akademie der Wissenschaften, Vienna.

Pleslova-Stikova, Emilie
    1968 Comparative Study. In *Homolka: An Eneolithic Site in Bohemia*, by Robert W. Ehrich and Emilie Pleslova-Stikova, pp. 127-224. American School of Prehistoric Research Bulletin 24. Peabody Museum, Cambridge.

    1969 Die Beziehungen zwischen Bayern und West-böhmen im Äneolithikum. *Bayerische Vorgeschichtsblätter* 34: 1-29.

    1985 *Makotrasy: A TRB Site in Bohemia.* Fontes Archaeologici Pragensis 17. Museum Mationale Pragae, Prague.

Preuss, Joachim
    1966 *Die Baalberger Gruppe in Mitteldeutschland.* Veröffentlichungen des Landesmuseums für Vorgeschichte in Halle 21. VEB Deutscher Verlag der Wissenschaften, Berlin.

Rackham, James
    1983 Faunal Sample to Subsistence Economy: Some Problems in Reconstruction. In *Integrating the Subsistence Economy*, edited by Martin Jones, pp. 251-277. British Archaeological Reports International Series 181. Oxford.

Raetzel-Fabian, Dirk
    1986 *Phasenkartierung des mitteleuropäischen Neolithikums.* British Archaeological Reports International Series 316. Oxford.

Rappaport, Roy A.
    1968 *Pigs for the Ancestors: Ritual in the Ecology of a New Guinea People.* Yale University Press, New Haven.

Redding, Richard William, Jr.
    1981 *Decision Making in Subsistence Herding of Sheep and Goats in the Middle East.* University Microfilms International, Ann Arbor.

Redding, Richard William, Jr.
    1988 A General Explanation of Subsistence Change: From Hunting and Gathering to Food Production. *Journal of Anthropological Archaeology* 7: 56-97.

Reichstein, H.
    1977 Bemerkungen zu einigen Tierknochen aus früh-neolithischen Siedlungsgruben von Rosdorf, Kr. Göttingen. *Nachrichten aus Niedersachsens Urgeschichte* 46: 1-26.

Renfrew, Colin
    1979a Introduction: Problems in European Prehistory. In *Problems in European Prehistory*, by Colin Renfrew, pp. 1-21. Edinburgh University Press, Edinburgh.

    1979b *Before Civilization: The Radiocarbon Revolution and Prehistoric Europe.* Cambridge University Press, Cambridge.

    1987 *Archaeology and Language: The Puzzle of Indo-European Origins.* Cambridge University Press, Cambridge.

    1988 "Archaeology and Language" A CA Book Review. *Current Anthropology* 29(3):437-468.

Renfrew, Colin and Stephen Shennan (editors)
    1982 *Ranking, Resource and Exchange: Aspects of the Archaeology of Early European Society.* Cambridge University Press, Cambridge.

Rösch, Manfred
    1987 Zur Umwelt und Wirtschaft des Jungne-olithikums am Bodensee - Botanische Unter-suchungen in Bodman-Blisshalde. *Archäologische Nachrichten aus Baden* 38/39: 42-53.

    1990 Vegetationsgeschichtliche Untersuchungen im Durchenbergried. In *Siedlungsarchäologie im Alpenvorland II*, edited by Landesdenkmalamt Baden-Württemberg, pp. 9-64. Forschungen und Berichte zur Vor- und Frühgeschichte in Baden-Württemberg 37. Konrad Theiss, Stuttgart.

Rowley-Conwy, P.
    1981 Slash and Burn in the Temperate European Neolithic. In *Farming Practice in British Prehistory*, edited by Roger Mercer, pp. 85-96. Edinburgh University Press, Edinburgh.

    1984 The Laziness of the Short-Distance Hunter: The Origins of Agriculture in Western Denmark. *Journal of Anthropological Archaeology* 3: 300-324.

Rulf, J.
    1979 K relativní hustote osídlení Cech v neolitu a eneolitu. *Archeologické Rozhledy* 31: 176-191.

    1986 Environment of the Earliest Agricultural Settlements of Bohemia. In *Archaeology in Bohemia 1981-1985*, pp. 19-25. Archeologicky ustav CSAV, Prague.

Ruttkay, Elisabeth
1981 Typologie und Chronologie der Mondsee-Gruppe. In *Das Mondseeland: Geschichte und Kultur*, pp. 269-294. Ausstellung des Landes Oberösterreich 8. Mai bis 26. Oktober 1981, Linz.

1987 Die Chamer Gruppe in Niederösterreich? *Annalen der Naturhistorischen Museums* 88: 163-181. Vienna.

Sakellaridis, Margaret
1979 *The Mesolithic and Neolithic of the Swiss Area*. British Archaeological Reports International Series 67. Oxford.

1981 Die wirtschaftliche Grundlage neolithischer Siedlungen am Zürichsee. *Helvetia Archaologica* 45/48: 153-160.

Sangmeister, E.
1951 Zum Character der bandkeramischen Siedlung. *Bericht der Römisch-Germanisch Kommission* 33: 89-109. Mainz.

Scheck, Klemens
1977 *Die Tierknochen aus dem jungsteinzeitlichen Dorf Ehrenstein*. Forschungen und Berichte zur Vor- und Frühgeschichte in Baden-Württemberg 9. Landesdenkmalamt Baden-Württemberg, Stuttgart.

Schier, Wolfram
1985 Zur vorrömischen Besiedlung des Donautales südöstlich von Regensburg. *Bayerische Vorgeschichtsblätter* 50: 9-80.

Schlichterle, H.
1987 Bodman-Blissenhalde - Eine neolithische Ufer-siedlung unter dem Steilhang des Bodanrücks. *Archäologische Nachrichten aus Baden* 38/39: 38-41.

Schmid, Elisabeth
1958 Die "Nebenfunde" auf dem Munzinger Berg. *Badische Fundberichte* 21: 41-55.

Scollar, Irwin
1959 Regional Groups in the Michelsberg Culture. *Proceedings of the Prehistoric Society* 25: 52-134.

Shanks, Michael and Christopher Tilley
1982 Ideology, Symbolic Power and Ritual Communication: A Reinterpretation of Neolithic Mortuary Practices. In *Symbolic and Structural Archaeology*, edited by Ian Hodder, pp. 129-154. Cambridge University Press, Cambridge.

Shennan, Stephen
1986 Central Europe in the Third Millennium BC: An Evolutionary Trajectory for the Beginning of the European Bronze Age. *Journal of Anthropological Archaeology* 5: 115-146.

1987 Trends in the Study of Later European Prehistory. *Annual Review of Anthropology* 16: 365-382.

Sherratt, A.
1980 Water, Soil and Seasonality in Early Cereal Cultivation. *World Archaeology* 11: 313-330.

1981 Plough and Pastoralism: Aspects of the Secondary Products Revolution. In *Pattern of the Past: Studies in Honour of David Clarke*, edited by Ian Hodder, Glynn Isaac and Norman Hammond, pp. 261-305. Cambridge University Press, Cambridge.

1982 Mobile Resources: Settlement and Exchange in Early Agricultural Europe. In *Ranking, Resource and Exchange: Aspects of the Archaeology of Early European Society*, edited by Colin Renfrew and Stephan Shennan, pp. 13-26. Cambridge University Press, Cambridge.

1983a Early Agrarian Settlement in the Körös Region of the Great Hungarian Plain. *Acta Archaeologica Academiae Scientiarum Hungaricae* 35: 155-169.

1983b The Secondary Exploitation of Animals in the Old World. *World Archaeology* 15(1): 90-104.

Shotwell, J. A.
1955 An Approach to the Paleoecology of Mammals. *Ecology* 39: 271-282.

Sielmann, Burchard
1971a Der Einfluss der Umwelt auf die neolithische Besiedlung Südwestdeutschlands unter besonderer Berücksichtigung der Verhältnisse am nördlichen Oberrhein. *Acta Praehistorica et Archaeologica* 2: 65-197.

1971b Zum Verhältnis von Ackerbau und Viehzucht im Neolithikum Südwestdeutschlands. *Archäologisches Korrespondenzblatt* 1: 65-68.

Sklenar, Karl
1983 *Archaeology in Central Europe: The First 500 Years*. Leicester University Press, Leicester.

Slicher van Bath, B. H.
1963 *The Agrarian History of Western Europe AD 500-1850*. Translated by Olive Ordish. Edward Arnold Publishers, London.

Soudsky, Bohumil
1973 Higher Level Archaeological Entities: Models and Reality. In *Explanation of Culture Change: Models in Prehistory*, edited by Colin Renfrew, pp. 195-207. Duckworth, London.

Soudsky, Bohumil and Ivan Palvu
1972 The Linear Pottery Culture Settlement Patterns in Central Europe. In *Man, Settlement and Urbanism*, edited by P. J. Ucko, R. E. Tringham and G. W. Dimbleby, pp. 317-328. Duckworth, London.

Spenneman, Dirk R.
1984 *Burgerroth: Eine spätneolithische Höhensiedlung in Unterfranken.* British Archaeological Reports International Series 219. Oxford.

Stampfli, H. R.
1963 Wisent, *Bison bonasus* (Linne, 1758), Ur, *Bos primigenius* Bojanus, 1827, und Hausrind, *Bos taurus* Linne, 1758. In *Seeberg Burgäschisee-Süd. Teil 3: Die Tierreste*, by J. Boessneck, J.-P. Jéquier and H.R. Stampfli, pp. 117-195. Acta Bernensia II. Stämpfli and Cie, Bern.

1964 Vergleichende Betrachtungen an Tierresten aus zwei neolithischen Siedlungen am Burgäschisee. *Mitteilungen der naturforschenden Gesellschaft in Bern* 21: 113-136.

1965 Tierreste der Grabung Müddersheim, Kr. Düren. In *Müddersheim: Eine Ansiedlung der jüngeren Bandkeramik im Rheinland*, by Kurt Schietzal, pp. 115-126. Böhlau Verlag, Köln.

1976a Die Tierknochen von Egolzwil 5: osteoarchäologische Untersuchungen. In *Das jungsteinzeitliche Jäger-Bauerndorf von Egolzwil 5 im Wauwilermoos*, by R. Wyss, pp. 125-140. Archäologische Forschungen 134.

1976b *Osteo-archäologische Untersuchung des Tierknochenmaterials der spätneolithischen Ufersiedlung Auvernier La Saunerie.* Stampfli, Solothurn.

1980 Tierknochenfunde. In *Die Siedlungsreste der Horgener Kultur*, edited by Alex R. Furger, pp. 141-177. Die neolithischen Ufersiedlungen von Twann 7. Staatlicher Lehrmittelverlag, Bern.

Starling, N.
1983 Neolithic Settlement Patterns in Central Germany. *Oxford Journal of Archaeology* 2(1): 1-11.

Stehli, Petar
1989 Merzbachtal - Umwelt und Geschichte einer bandkeramischen Siedlungskammer. *Germania* 67(1):51-76.

Strahm, C.
1987 Zur Einführung. Das Forschungsvorhaben: "Siedlungsarchäologische Untersuchungen im Alpenvorland". *Archäologische Nachrichten aus Baden* 38/39: 4-9.

Stuiver, M. and R. S. Kra (editors)
1986 Radiocarbon Calibration Issue: Proceedings of the Twelfth International Radiocarbon Conference, June 24-28, 1985, Trondheim, Norway. *Radiocarbon* 28.

Sukachev, V. and N. Dylis
1968 *Fundamentals of Forest Biogeocoenology.* Translated by Dr. J.M. Maclennan. Oliver and Boyd, Edinburgh.

Suter, Peter J.
1985 Neue absolut datierte Fundkomplexe aus dem Raume Zürich. *Archäologisches Korrespondenzblatt* 15: 431-443.

Tauber, H.
1965 Differential Pollen Dispersion and the Interpretation of Pollen Diagrams. *Danmarks Geologiske Undersogelse* 89: 1-69.

Teichert, Manfred
1969 Osteometrische Untersuchungen zur Berechnung der Widderristhöhe bei vor- und frühgeschichtlichen Schweinen. *Kühn-Archiv* 83: 237-292.

Tempir, Z.
1985 Agricultural Plants and Weeds. In *Makotrasy: A TRB Site in Bohemia*, by Emilie Pleslova-Stikova, pp. 178-180. Fontes Archaeologici Pragenses 17. Museum Nationale Pragae, Prague.

Tringham, Ruth
1971 *Hunters, Fishers and Farmers of Eastern Europe: 6000-3000 BC.* Hutchinson University Library, London.

Troels-Smith, J.
1984 Stall-Feeding and Field Manuring in Switzerland about 6000 Years Ago. *Tools and Tillage* 5(1): 13-25.

Uerpmann, Hans-Peter
1973 Animal Bone Finds and Economic Archaeology: A Critical Study of the "Osteo-archaeological" Method. *World Archaeology* 4: 307-322.

Uerpmann, Hans-Peter
 1977 Betrachtungen zur Wirtschaftsformen neolithischer Gruppen in Südwestdeutschland. *Fundberichte aus Baden-Württemberg* 3: 144-161.

 1988 Bemerkungen zu den Tierknochenfunden aus Dobl. In *Die Siedlung der Chamer Gruppe von Dobl, Gemeinde Prutting, Ldkr. Rosenheim, und ihre Stellung im Endneolithikum Mitteleuropas*, by Ingrid Burger, pp. 279-181. Materialhefte zur bayerischen Vorgeschichte, Reihe A, 56. Graf, Fürth.

von den Driesch, Angela and J. Boessneck
 1974 Kritische Anmerkungen zur Widerristhöhenberechnung aus Längenmassen vor- und frühgeschichtlicher Tierknochen. *Säugetierkundliche Mitteilungen* 22: 325-348.

von Thünen, J. H.
 1910 *Der Isolierte Staat in Beziehung auf Landwirtschaft und Nationalökonomie*. Gustav Fischer Verlag, Jena.

Vouga, P.
 1929 Classification du néolithique lacustre suisse. *Anzeiger für schweizerische Altertumskunde* 31: 81-91, 161-180.

Waterbolk, H. T.
 1962 The Lower Rhine Basin. In *Courses Toward Urban Life*, edited by R. J. Braidwood and G. R. Willey, pp. 227-253. Aldine, Chicago.

Watson, J. P. N.
 1979 The Estimation of Relative Frequencies of Mammalian Species: Khirokitia 1972. *Journal of Archaeological Science* 6: 127-137.

Welten, M.
 1955 Pollenanalytische Untersuchungen über die neolithischen Siedlungsverhältnisse am Burgäschisee. In *Das Pfahlbauproblem*, edited by W. V. Guyan, pp. 59-88. Basel.

Whittle, Alasdair
 1985 *Neolithic Europe: A Survey*. Cambridge University Press, Cambridge.

Wilkinson, Leland
 1987 *SYSTAT: The System for Statistics*. SYSTAT, Inc., Evanston, Illinois.

Willerding, Ulrich
 1986 *Zur Geschichte der Unkräuter Mitteleuropas*. Schriften zur Vor- und Frühgeschichte 22. Karl Wachholz Verlag, Neumünster.

Winiger, J.
 1971 *Das Fundmaterial von Thayngen-Weier im Rahmen der Pfyner Kultur*. Monographien zur Ur- und Frühgeschichte der Schweiz 18. Basel.

 1981 *Das Neolithikum der Schweiz*. Seminar für Ur- und Frühgeschichte, Basel.

Wolff, Petra
 1977 *Die Jagd- und Hausfauna der spätneolithischen Pfahlbauten des Mondsees*. Jahrbuch des oberösterreichischen Musealvereines 122(1): 269-347. Linz.

Wyss, Rene
 1970 *Die Pfyner Kultur*. Verlag Paul Haupt, Bern.

Zapotocka, M. and M. Zapotocky
 1986 The Aeneolithic Hillfort Above the "Dänemark" Mill by Kutná-Hora. *Archaeology in Bohemia 1981-1985*: 57-64. Archaeological Institute of the Czechoslovak Academy of Sciences, Prague.

Zeuner, Frederick E.
 1963 *A History of Domesticated Animals*. Harper and Row, New York.

Appendix 1. Numbers of identified specimens for Neolithic faunal assemblages analyzed in this study. See Table 2 for site names.

Taxon	1	2	3	4	5	6	7	8	9	10	11	12	13	14	15
Bos taurus	76	120	55	137	382	460	156	52	307	151	97	317	539	42	229
Ovis/Capra	10	19	15	12	205	29	164	145	32	86	39	98	69	110	38
Sus domesticus	16	32	26	26	405	57	25	7	18	66	16	65	130	16	13
Canis familiaris	0	1	1	0	0	1	0	0	0	0	0	1	0	0	0
Equus sp.	0	4	0	0	1	0	1	1	1	0	0	0	0	0	6
Bos primigenius	2	33	0	0	0	10	1	1	3	0	0	0	3	2	1
Cervus elaphus	0	2	29	8	9	4	3	1	0	1	0	7	6	0	3
Sus scrofa	2	3	5	5	8	4	7	0	1	5	0	31	12	1	3
Capreolus capreolus	0	2	7	0	7	1	11	5	2	1	0	1	4	0	4
Small Rodent, indet.	1	1	0	0	0	4	0	0	0	0	0	0	0	0	0
Lepus europaeus	0	0	0	0	1	1	0	0	0	0	0	0	1	0	0
Meles meles	0	0	0	0	0	0	0	0	0	0	0	0	0	0	0
Ursus arctos	0	0	1	1	0	0	1	0	0	0	0	0	0	0	0
Castor fiber	0	0	4	0	0	0	0	0	0	0	0	1	1	0	0
Alces alces	0	0	3	0	0	0	0	0	0	0	0	0	0	0	0
Lynx lynx	0	0	0	0	0	0	0	0	0	0	0	0	0	0	0
Vulpes vulpes	0	0	0	0	0	0	0	10	0	0	0	1	0	0	0
Bison bonasus	0	0	0	0	0	0	3	0	0	0	0	0	0	0	0
Canis lupus	0	0	0	0	0	0	0	0	0	0	0	1	0	0	0
Felis sylvestris	0	0	0	0	0	0	0	0	0	0	0	0	0	0	0
Putorius putorius	0	0	0	0	0	0	0	0	0	0	0	0	0	0	0
Martes sp.	0	0	0	0	0	0	0	0	0	0	0	0	0	0	0
Erinaceus europaeus	0	0	0	0	0	0	0	0	0	0	0	0	0	0	0
Sciurus vulgaris	0	0	1	0	1	0	0	0	0	0	0	0	0	0	0
Lutra lutra	0	0	0	0	0	0	0	0	0	0	0	0	0	0	0
Rupicapra rupicapra	0	0	0	0	0	0	0	0	0	0	0	0	0	0	0
Insectivore, indet.	0	0	0	0	0	0	0	0	0	0	0	0	0	0	0
Capra ibex	0	0	0	0	0	0	0	0	0	0	0	0	0	0	0
TOTAL	107	217	147	188	1019	571	372	221	364	310	152	523	768	171	297

93

Appendix 1 (continued).

Taxon	16	17	18	19	20	21	22	23	24	25	26	27	28	29	30
Bos taurus	98	24	188	141	26	484	921	440	71	99	1902	154	641	1618	1699
Ovis/Capra	68	80	89	26	10	97	497	95	6	3	1937	3	376	1500	181
Sus domesticus	9	9	64	54	22	15	35	61	0	76	4183	8	135	189	376
Canis familiaris	0	0	0	6	0	2	0	0	0	0	293	0	65	2	50
Equus sp.	0	0	2	0	1	2	0	1	3	1	19	0	0	0	14
Bos primigenius	0	0	0	100	13	0	31	17	0	8	63	2	7	10	5
Cervus elaphus	0	0	3	88	34	21	7	4	6	1954	409	296	354	15	30
Sus scrofa	2	0	0	24	7	0	0	0	0	702	130	12	21	7	10
Capreolus capreolus	3	0	2	8	4	26	11	1	2	35	613	1	34	2	3
Small Rodent, indet.	3	0	0	0	0	0	0	0	0	0	0	0	0	0	0
Lepus europaeus	1	0	0	1	0	3	0	0	0	0	11	0	4	0	7
Meles meles	0	0	0	0	0	0	0	0	0	0	10	2	0	0	0
Ursus arctos	0	0	0	1	0	0	0	0	0	27	55	8	12	0	2
Castor fiber	0	0	8	10	0	3	0	0	0	20	251	0	4	1	2
Alces alces	0	0	0	0	0	0	0	0	0	32	611	0	1	0	0
Lynx lynx	0	0	0	0	0	0	0	0	0	0	13	1	0	0	0
Vulpes vulpes	3	0	1	0	0	0	0	1	0	0	568	0	3	0	0
Bison bonasus	0	0	0	0	0	0	0	0	0	0	0	0	2	0	0
Canis lupus	0	0	0	0	0	0	0	0	0	1	302	0	1	0	3
Felis sylvestris	0	0	0	0	0	0	0	0	0	0	7	0	0	0	0
Putorius putorius	0	0	0	0	0	0	0	0	0	0	1	0	0	0	0
Martes sp.	0	0	0	0	0	0	0	0	0	0	310	0	9	0	0
Erinaceus europaeus	0	0	0	0	0	0	0	0	0	0	12	0	0	0	0
Sciurus vulgaris	0	0	0	0	0	0	1	0	0	0	1	0	1	0	0
Lutra lutra	0	0	0	0	0	0	0	0	0	0	10	0	2	0	0
Rupicapra rupicapra	0	0	0	0	0	0	0	0	0	0	0	35	282	0	0
Insectivore, indet.	0	0	0	0	0	0	0	0	0	0	0	0	0	0	1
Capra ibex	0	0	0	0	0	0	0	0	0	0	0	0	0	0	0
TOTAL	187	113	357	459	117	653	1503	620	88	2958	11711	522	1954	3344	2383

Appendix 1 (continued).

Taxon	31	32	33	34	35	36	37	38	39	40	41	42	43	44	45
Bos taurus	2238	255	1991	729	1054	219	343	147	302	315	357	3825	83	736	903
Ovis/Capra	273	194	1277	184	188	36	20	134	51	92	222	3867	119	261	364
Sus domesticus	977	250	3628	266	1556	68	98	111	184	244	941	1069	101	1560	319
Canis familiaris	33	36	79	16	692	3	1	6	11	3	198	332	9	5	27
Equus sp.	0	3	312	2	0	0	69	0	0	0	0	0	2	0	4
Bos primigenius	0	0	44	40	2	0	0	0	7	0	1908	0	0	5	0
Cervus elaphus	556	69	1695	109	997	1	28	0	0	1	8849	2641	31	223	122
Sus scrofa	71	9	842	12	56	7	21	0	0	4	1835	1076	1	38	41
Capreolus capreolus	6	15	303	9	22	1	3	2	1	1	1612	387	7	8	8
Small Rodent, indet.	0	3	0	0	0	0	0	0	0	0	0	0	0	0	0
Lepus europaeus	0	4	5	0	0	0	0	0	0	4	1	62	0	1	0
Meles meles	0	0	2	2	2	1	0	0	1	0	235	128	0	6	0
Ursus arctos	1	0	65	5	23	0	2	0	2	0	72	110	1	30	10
Castor fiber	85	8	97	5	34	0	0	0	0	0	593	5	5	20	18
Alces alces	4	0	9	0	0	0	0	0	0	0	0	30	0	0	0
Lynx lynx	0	0	0	0	0	0	0	0	0	0	0	5	0	0	0
Vulpes vulpes	10	3	12	1	1	0	0	0	0	0	131	213	0	22	0
Bison bonasus	0	0	0	0	0	0	0	0	0	0	109	0	0	0	1
Canis lupus	0	1	2	0	0	0	0	0	0	0	61	0	0	0	1
Felis sylvestris	1	0	17	1	2	0	0	0	0	0	42	109	0	0	0
Putorius putorius	0	0	0	0	0	0	0	0	0	0	21	2	0	0	0
Martes sp.	36	1	18	0	0	0	0	0	0	0	43	53	0	2	0
Erinaceus europaeus	1	0	1	0	11	0	0	0	0	0	13	16	0	0	0
Sciurus vulgaris	0	0	24	0	0	0	0	0	0	0	8	19	0	1	0
Lutra lutra	0	0	0	0	0	0	0	0	0	0	38	6	0	0	0
Rupicapra rupicapra	8	0	0	0	36	0	0	0	0	0	0	24	0	0	0
Insectivore, indet.	0	0	0	0	0	0	0	0	0	0	0	0	0	0	0
Capra ibex	3	0	0	0	42	0	0	0	0	0	0	0	0	0	4
TOTAL	4303	851	10423	1381	4718	336	585	400	559	664	17289	13979	359	2918	1822

Appendix 1 (continued).

Taxon	46	47	48	49	50	51	52	53	54	55	56	57	58	59
Bos taurus	650	183	176	1683	3064	1568	106	1335	89	523	1292	2551	717	214
Ovis/Capra	225	78	1	372	570	793	44	207	49	122	412	545	517	122
Sus domesticus	209	113	15	2858	364	405	35	464	51	59	421	866	178	325
Canis familiaris	5	8	1	22	163	105	2	83	0	0	158	794	540	305
Equus sp.	1	2	0	100	127	26	22	0	0	0	0	23	1	436
Bos primigenius	0	2	56	121	1	12	1	420	3	144	11	181	34	13
Cervus elaphus	24	247	252	4182	262	38	2	1136	26	136	479	6760	1105	285
Sus scrofa	29	21	11	357	6	27	3	478	0	16	114	1194	296	271
Capreolus capreolus	0	5	3	408	31	66	1	368	6	24	21	233	43	57
Small Rodent, indet.	0	0	0	0	0	0	0	0	0	0	0	0	1	7
Lepus europaeus	0	0	0	3	0	1	0	0	1	0	1	11	7	1
Meles meles	0	0	0	10	1	4	1	33	0	0	8	136	26	5
Ursus arctos	2	11	0	26	13	2	0	50	0	2	27	240	45	9
Castor fiber	2	14	5	85	6	1	0	66	0	4	0	44	12	14
Alces alces	0	1	0	0	1	0	0	17	0	0	2	116	105	0
Lynx lynx	0	0	0	1	1	0	0	0	0	0	0	0	0	0
Vulpes vulpes	0	1	0	4	2	9	0	2	0	1	3	24	20	4
Bison bonasus	0	0	0	0	0	4	0	39	0	0	0	0	0	0
Canis lupus	0	0	0	22	0	3	0	7	0	0	1	43	2	0
Felis sylvestris	0	0	0	15	0	4	0	0	0	0	1	5	1	0
Putorius putorius	0	0	0	0	0	0	0	0	0	0	0	5	0	0
Martes sp.	0	2	0	0	0	7	0	3	0	0	0	1	1	1
Erinaceus europaeus	0	0	1	0	0	0	0	0	0	0	3	19	11	0
Sciurus vulgaris	0	0	0	0	0	0	0	0	0	0	3	7	2	1
Lutra lutra	0	0	0	3	0	0	0	0	0	0	0	3	1	0
Rupicapra rupicapra	0	5	0	0	0	0	0	0	0	0	0	0	0	0
Insectivore, indet.	0	0	0	0	0	0	0	0	0	0	0	8	0	0
Capra ibex	1	8	0	0	0	0	0	0	0	4	0	0	0	0
TOTAL	1148	701	521	10321	4662	3126	269	4761	279	1035	2957	13809	3665	2070

www.ingramcontent.com/pod-product-compliance
Lightning Source LLC
Chambersburg PA
CBHW061300270326
41932CB00029B/3421